B.O.L.L.O.C.K.S TO THAT

I CHOOSE TO SHINE

A COLLECTION OF EXTRAORDINARY TRUE-LIFE STORIES ABOUT FINDING LIGHT IN A WORLD OF UNCERTAINTY

Dear Suzie,

Thank you for helping me uncover my courage to put my journey into words to help others.

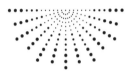

Jen ♡

Dec 2019.

CONTENTS

INTRODUCTION

B.O.L.L.O.C.K.S to that – I choose to shine!

A collection of extraordinary true-life stories about finding light in a world of uncertainty

"This book shines a light on the everyday pressures of modern living. Life can suck, things can go to sh*t, but there is always a way back. And these inspiring stories light you up inside with how these ordinary people went about it."

STEVE PARKINSON – Managing Director Magic and KISS Radio

WHAT PEOPLE ARE ALREADY SAYING ABOUT THIS BOOK

This book makes a standout statement – In a busy 21st century world it's really difficult being a human being. Whether fighting anxiety or depression, whether it was bullying or burn out, addiction or abuse, these ordinary people tell extraordinary stories.

It helps to know there are others out there that have lived through challenging, often harrowing, periods of their lives. And how they have come through the other side. Happier and grateful. Sharing their light bulb moment, or rather light up moment, as they take back control, is both inspiring and uplifting.

STEVE PARKINSON – Managing Director, Magic and KISS Radio

I was very touched to be asked to review this book, and what a deeply moving experience reading the manuscript was! These are stories told from the heart. Not always perfectly written, but truly authentic and, at times, emotionally challenging because they speak of our own insecurities and fallibilities. What's extraordinary is that regardless of the diverse adversities, even tragic events, faced by the contributors, they have each rediscovered their awesome inner worth and a path to a better place through their journey with Light Up.

SALLY GRINDLEY - multi-award-winning children's author of more than 150 published books

Sometimes, in our hectic lives we can forget to say "Bollocks - I CHOOSE to shine instead". This must be your new mantra! It will be your best guide. That's why saying "Bollocks To That" should be a new religion and why this book is so important. Now more than ever.

SAFFRON BENTLEY - blogger/writer and mum to a superhero

www.facebook.com/babywipesandwine and on Insta@realbadmomma

I found these real life stories of real people, going through real life challenges, collected in this inspiring book, a celebration of our precious shared common humanity. A victory of the human spirit. A proof that even after years of suffering, it is always possible to reconnect with our own intrinsic value, our own self-worth as human beings.

MAX DELLI GUANTI - hypnotherapist, trainer and managing director of The Peiffer Foundation International, Academy of Applied Positive Philosophy.

People often say that they have read a book that was 'life-changing'. Maybe you read the same book too but it had little impact on your life. You will find something in this book that will inspire you. This book demonstrates life-changing experiences for many souls. If life is all about making great decisions, then make the decision to read this book. I guarantee that you will make some kind of a change.

GINA MACKIE - radio presenter, writer and events host

This book is a life changer on every level. Not only does it enable a sense of connection by exploring people's journeys through this often crazy life, furthermore it gives practical solutions for overcoming even the most abhorrent experiences. This work can facilitate healing from children to the aged and the magic I have seen when offered to trafficked women is beyond all measure. From victim to warrior in only a few hours. The power to heal is within us all and this remarkable offering allows us to recognise our true potential. No matter the depth of the darkness we can always reconnect to our own light.

EMMA CREWS – feminist actor, in support of women escaping forced prostitution

http://www.lafl.fr www.teteacorps.com

Knowledge is power and the knowledge and accounts within this book will rock your world in the most uplifting way. If you're feeling unfulfilled in your life in any way, now is your time. Say Bollocks to that, and choose to shine. It helps. It works. I promise!

LAURA BOUCHET – radio executive producer, Australia

I have struggled for years with my mind, forever putting on a face when deep inside everything is black, anxious and paranoid. DNA Light Up takes me out of this place, it helps me find happiness and light every day and be the person I know my soul wants me to be. I can be happy, successful, powerful, fun and I GLOW!

JO PARKERSON - Entertainment & Lifestyle Content Director, Bauer Media

What struck me straight away was the strength that shines through all these stories. It is a reconnection to their true self, their real self, the part that was pushed into the shadows. It was hidden for a while and yet it could not be extinguished.

Many people look for tools in order to grow, to find what is missing in their lives. It is easy to see through these stories that the strength, the beauty and the light was always there. It is powerful and inspirational.

ANIKA GRIMM - yoga therapist

If like me you have been searching your entire life up until this point for answers, for reasons why you feel so empty, vulnerable, frightened and a slave to your emotions, then this is the book that will complete your search.

Having spent much of my life feeling like I didn't fit in anywhere and that I was just too emotional, (not a good look for a man in the business of creating "Leaders of Tomorrow") and too soft to take control of difficult situations. I now know this is all a load of old "B.O.L.L.O.C.K.S" and I choose to shine.

PAUL BURTON – Director, Ignite Business Development

An amazing collection of raw and real stories that demonstrate the power of positivity and healing. Heart-warming and encouraging to hear how people have changed their lives, achieving balance and joy though complete adversity. How wonderful that the proceeds of the book go towards supporting other people to achieve this.

GILLIAN JONES-WILLIAMS - Managing Director, Emerge Leadership Training

I was seriously touched by the openness and honesty of the lovely people who have chosen to share. As with many books of this nature the stories shared tend to be women, so it is a delight to have heartfelt male input. I feel these are inspirational, honest and thought provoking shining example of what amazing human beings we all are. CONGRATULATIONS one and all.

KATHRYN CHAPMAN – Reiki master

The search to reconnect with our inner selves and find our way past the traumas that often create dark places within us lead us to different 'solutions', be they years of therapy, medication, counselling, substance abuse or other external sources of answers and comfort.

We are born powerful with all of the answers that we'll ever need to be our best selves. Our most enlightened, strong and beautiful selves are waiting to shine. BOLLOCKS to anything that keeps you from reading this amazing and important book and recommending it to everyone that you know. Let your light shine for all to see.

GEORGE MARCOU – Director SALT Business Growth

ACKNOWLEDGMENTS

THANK YOU SHARON

I don't have enough words to thank my beautiful friend, the incredible Sharon Bott. From the very moment she turned up in my life (I really don't know whether it was it a couple of years or a number of lifetimes ago) she has absolutely rocked my world – in a wonderful way.

Together with her wonderful family, she's taught me the meaning of true love and friendship. She holds me when I'm wobbling, laughs with me until my sides hurt, reflects back to me when I'm being an idiot, and has been my absolute rock from the very first moment we met – or reconnected, which is far more the truth.

And, OK, yes my name may be on this book as author. And OK, DNA Light Up was originally born through me as well. And... if it wasn't for the limitless kindness, love and dedication that Sharon brings every single day, neither the work nor this book would be here as they are today. Actually, neither would I...

As our friendship and business partnership has continued to develop, we've been referred to in many ways – from Patsy and Edina to Morcambe and Wise and more recently Laurel and Hardy (yep we do a great impression!). So our talents are clearly multifaceted! Whatever people call us, it's always the name of a strong team. A great partnership. A meeting of souls, who together create something magical that brings joy to others. And these fabulous nicknames make us both giggle and smile in recognition! So... I am both grateful and proud in equal measures.

Sharon, I love you. Along with all the wonderful work that is ahead of us, here's to many more years of shenanigans and joy. Do you know how much...? ;-) Yes my dear friend, I'd absolutely walk in to that fire with you many times over.

This time around? Let's buckle up and enjoy this wonderfully bonkers and beautiful ride that calls to us every moment of every day!

PROLOGUE

Why B.O.L.L.O.C.K.S and what does it mean?

It is said that in order to train an elephant, it is tethered by the leg to a very tall tree while it is still very small. Of course the elephant is not used to being tied up and spends a long time tugging at the rope to get free. Elephants are naturally very strong, and this is why a very strong rope and a very tall tree are necessary for this part of their education. No matter how hard it pulls, how many times, and in whatever direction, the baby elephant is unable to break free. Eventually it simply gives in and stops trying.

As the elephant grows, thinner cord and smaller posts replace the thick rope and tall tree that were first used to keep the baby in check. This balance continues to shift, until eventually the adult elephant will remain tethered by a piece of twine attached to a small peg in the ground. Why? Simply because it had learned to believe it couldn't escape.

By this time, of course (and in actual fact, for a long time before) the elephant could have broken break free from the chains with just the smallest of tugs! Yet it doesn't. It remains a prisoner, unaware that it holds the key to freedom any time it chooses to use it.

As human beings we are conditioned in much the same way. For a variety of reasons and through an endless array of methods – family, education, work, friends, society, media… you name it. We learn to shut ourselves down and dance to different tunes in order to fit in, be accepted, find love or be good enough. In many cases we do it just to survive.

Eventually, when we realise that despite our best efforts life isn't turning out the way we planned, we can start to notice what it is that has kept us stuck. Questions like "how did I get here?" and "is this all there is to life?" become more frequent, and a sense of unrest starts niggling away.

This is what we here at DNA Light Up fondly refer to as BOLLOCKS. Far from giving us all an excuse for gratuitous swearing (not only is it a word for male genitalia, Google Dictionary describes it as "nonsense: rubbish, used to express contempt or disagreement, or as an exclamation of annoyance" with the Urban Dictionary boasting thirteen different interpretations of the word!) it is actually a robust and trademarked acronym with a powerful message:

Beliefs

Often

Limit

Life's

Opportunities

Constantly

Killing

Success ®

It's also deliberately playful. It's wonderful to see and hear people of all ages and all walks of life, shouting out 'Bollocks!' as they see how and where they've been conditioned to believe they are powerless – and reclaim their freedom with a determined and smiling flourish!

This book is a collection of stories from everyday people who have done just that. The Bollocks that each of our authors have faced and dealt with, are as beautifully unique as the voices that tell these stories. The themes are ones that are prevalent in today's society. Anxiety, depression, low self-esteem, addiction are all words that can just trip off the tongue, not because the seriousness of these conditions are in any doubt, rather because they are so common in today's society that everyone at some point will either know someone who has suffered from one of these illnesses or has been affected themselves.

The purpose of this book is to raise awareness of this modern-day epidemic, and to offer hope that there are solutions. DNA Light Up came to life through my own personal despair. Exhausted by life and with no more fight left, something happened that changed my life and caused me to reconsider the things I'd believed about myself and about life for over forty years.

This is not a sales pitch for the work. This is a spark of light for humanity. The book alone is intended to boost you, our reader, simply by reading and identifying with the stories inside. All profits from the sale of each book go to fund our pro-bono work so we can take our work to people and places who otherwise would have no way to access something that can change their lives for the better. If you feel inspired by the book, come on over and take a look at our website (www.dnalight-up.net) where you'll find more stirring stories and can learn more about who we are, what we do, and meet our growing team of Activators and Ambassadors.

Thank you for buying this book. Thank you for identifying with our authors. Thank you for being here and making a difference.

You can find more information and contact details for our contributors on the website www.dnalightup.net. We'd all love to hear from you!

With love and gratitude

Mel and the team

FOREWORD

I would challenge anyone not to empathise if not identify with at least one of the brave stories in this book. Although some are hard to read they all contain hope and are up-lifting. We may not have times in our lives that have been as atrocious however we are all a product of our struggles and although they can strengthen us they often hold us back and we miss opportunities. I know I did.

I have been through the DNA Light Up process and have found that it has not only been a game changer in my personal life it has completely altered my approach in my professional life. This has enabled me as a GP to get so much more out of my patient consultations. What makes me sad is that in this day and age we are too quick to medicate people's lives. What I hope is that one day the NHS would embrace the DNA Light Up programme. It would be financially a no brainer as people would no longer be dependent on antidepressants, and it would bring more lights into the world.

Dr FENELLA POWELL, MBBS MRCGP

BOLLOCKS TO RESILIENCE AND POSITIVE THINKING

I STEPPED OUT OF THE MENTAL TRAP AND INTO FREEDOM

Decades training myself to be strong in the face of adversity, to control emotions so I could stand tall and carry on, all drained away in that instant. Suddenly I was wide-eyed and naked. Life would never be the same again.

Mel's Story

The birth of DNA Light Up

It was just another nameless, faceless day, somewhere around the beginning of autumn 2009. Nondescript, apart from the fact it was the afternoon when I finally hit rock bottom and knew beyond question that I just couldn't go on any more.

It had been only a few short months since the day I'd discovered the truth about my husband, and his subsequent disappearance. The struggle was relentless. On a daily basis I resigned myself to labouring through the endless quagmire of debts, deceit and debris that had continued to surface since I started uncovering his treachery.

On this particular day, the disparaging tone of a sharply spoken man at the mortgage company, who queried how it could possibly be that I hadn't realised the mortgage had been left unpaid for so many months, had already had me squirming and flushing with shame. Then my divorce solicitors informed me that I was unable to continue down the route they had advised me to take, because my husband consistently refused to respond to their letters. I was now faced with the prospect of a long-haul battle through the courts.

Despite the oily reassurances of the locum solicitor that '*I can assure you, we will have the full force of the law behind us*', by this time I knew his promises were hollow. If they'd already failed to get answers themselves, what difference would a lengthy court case make – apart from dragging everything out for a minimum of three years, and racking up a legal bill of tens of thousands.

I had neither the time nor the money - finding enough to buy food was a daily struggle at that time, and unopened bills continued to pile up on the shelf. Right now I didn't have any more willpower to continue fighting. I hung up the phone and felt the world spinning around me.

Until that moment, I was a firm believer in the power of the mind. I truly thought I'd nailed all this positive thinking stuff – after all, I was living proof of how it all works! Orphaned as a child, emotionally abused by my guardian, fighting for justice and resolutely battling on regardless, I had spent decades training myself how to survive and stay strong in the face of challenges (oh yes, I referred to my experiences as *challenges* – heaven forbid I actually label them as 'traumas' because that wouldn't fit in the world of diminishing emotion in the place of positive results!). In the process, I had trained and qualified in all manner of personal and professional development techniques, and loved the work that came as a result!

For the previous ten years, I'd been running a very successful training company (together with my husband) coaching leaders and their teams to break through limiting beliefs and be the very best they could be – as individuals and as teams. I absolutely loved my work and was constantly blown away by the amazing results we continued to achieve! Resilience and positivity was what I was all about, and I was thrilled to be able to share all my hard earned techniques with others. I was a professional coach, a proven 'expert' in my field, with a fantastic reputation for the work I was delivering. So yes. In a nutshell, I absolutely knew my stuff. Or so I thought ...

Now my life was in tatters and, even though I didn't realise it, everything (yes everything) was about to change forever.

Here I stood, barely holding on. And in that moment, I felt it all bleeding out from me: the battle, the fight, the get-up-and-go, the determination. All the things that had kept me going – through the past few months, as well as through the traumas of my childhood. I'd learned well, I'd been a top grade student for goodness sakes! I knew exactly how to pull myself up by my bootstraps. How to carry on regardless. To stand up against injustice. To tell myself 'I can do it'. To be strong for others. To keep those emotions at bay. To paint on a smile. To maintain a positive mental attitude at all costs ... It was the only way I knew how to be. And after decades of training, I was darned good at it.

Until now. Now I was nobody. Now I was empty. Now there was nothing left.

Standing in my kitchen, wide eyed and blinking, I leaned heavily against the huge black oven that was the heart of my home. Holding on to the heavy chrome handle that ran along the front of the oven, I felt disassociated (yes, that's how I'd learned to label this experience) and yet curiously somehow deeply present (a less familiar sensation) as I felt the blood draining from my head, my heart, and my legs and into the ground below. Time stood still. I felt myself teetering over the edge of a bottomless void.

Shivering despite the warm weather, struggling to focus even on my surroundings let alone anything else, survival mode kicked in and I searched desperately through my memory banks for anything that could help me. Techniques, mantras, thoughts, boosters, anything.

And here it came. A few little words that were to change my life forever, although I didn't realise it at the time. I decided to tell myself that 'all I *need is already within me',* and to repeat it to myself over and over again in order to drown out the screaming opposition.

'Oh seriously? Yeah, right. Get a bloody grip will you? What a load of old mumbo-jumbo tosh that is! Have you actually looked around and noticed the mess you're in right now Melanie? It's massive! And it's real! Nothing that any amount of your positive thinking bollocks can change!' scolded the voices in my head.

'I'm scared, I'm really scared! Could it be possible....? Could it really be...? No, really...? It would be lovely to believe, but, well... you know... things can't just happen like that... I'm scared... I want to hide...' mumbled the fluttering feelings in my heart.

'Oooooh yes. At last! Now we're on the right path... Now move... keep going!' nudged a kindly, deep, smiling and steady whisper from somewhere deep within me. A voice I knew seemed familiar, and yet I had never heard before.

A deep breath and gritted teeth snapped me back into the here and now – well, at least some of my resilience techniques came in handy! And with that I marched out of my kitchen, into the courtyard, through the gate and into the unknown. Taking a deep breath and blinking away the tears, I turned left towards the top of the village I loved so deeply, and began walking. You could say blindly. You could say in desperation. You could say what you like, because I really couldn't have told you. All I knew in that moment was that I was to keep on moving. And to keep on reminding myself that everything was already within me. So I did.

It's a short walk around the village, less than two kilometres. Lots of fields. A beautiful twelfth century church. Stone houses. The river. And more fields. By the time I reached the church, I was already beginning to swing my arms in rhythm to my focused internal chanting *'All I need is within me, all I need is within me'* and as I started on the downhill section that leads towards the river, I realised that it wasn't just internal anymore.

With a hint of embarrassment, I heard my voice saying the mantra out loud. Shaking out the embarrassment and laughing at what must have been flushing cheeks, I upped the volume and walked a little taller and faster. Momentum continued to build as I started on the home straight, alongside the river. Flushing with energy (shame now long gone) and wide-eyed with wonder, I stomped, shimmied, arm-waved and shouted my way to the front gate and back into my kitchen.

Stopping in front of the oven, the place I started from, I was again wide-eyed. This time with wonder and surprise. Something had happened. The unusual quietness in my head allowed me to hear my heart - pumping confirmation that everything had changed. Because it had. Looking around the space I knew so well, I sensed that I'd stepped into a whole new world. Nothing externally had actually changed, I knew that. Of course I knew that. And yet... something I simply couldn't put my finger on was decidedly different. I noticed my hands clasped gently on my belly. And felt that same nudge from deep within. *Yes, this is real... and... you've got this'* came the same steady chocolatey whisper. Rippling goosebumps and smiling waves of recognition flooded across my face and through my body. I was home

----

Although I had no idea at the time, this was the birth of what is now known as DNA Light Up, which in turn is how this book has been born! Because from that moment on, things just seemed to change for the better. I felt better. I knew I could get through – not with the self-protecting, fighting, resilience tools I'd loved, trained and leaned on for so long. No, now it was something different. Something deep within me that was ultimately challenging me to review my entire belief system and the way I had learned to lived my life.

I'd love to say that I created DNA Light Up to serve others and change lives (because it does). I'd love also to say that I deliberately set out to develop a system that is so simple, so profound and so long-lasting that it works for everybody, every single time (because it does). And I'd be absolutely cock-a-hoop to say that I designed this to help encourage humanity to reconnect, to re-engage, and ultimately to find peace (because it does). And if I were to say that, it would be a lie.

Firstly, because I didn't create this work myself. It came through me. Secondly, because when it came through me, it wasn't because I was filled with some love-driven notion to support humanity. No; it came through at a time when I was desperate and broken. All hope had been lost, and everything I'd ever relied on had either fallen away or wasn't working any more. It was in that darkest moment of despair and surrender that it happened.

It wasn't a bolt of lightning. There was no thunder clap or choir of angels – which, looking back, is I suppose why I didn't really pay much attention to it all at the time! It was simply a shift. So subtle and yet so profound that I didn't even notice the enormity of what had happened to me until much later on.

Until I eventually heeded the nudge to go searching and find out whether other people had something similar within them as well.

It was a couple of years later and life was once again in balance. Since my own Light Up experience (although of course it didn't have a name or even an identity at that time) and despite all predictions to the contrary, I'd somehow managed to pull both myself and my son out of the gaping financial and emotional hole that had been left in the after-math of my husband's betrayals. The divorce was finalised. I had written and published my autobiography "I'm Still Standing" and been contacted by countless others who'd identified with my experiences. I had defied well-intentioned yet relentless opinions from others to *"let the house go, give up the fight, cut your losses and start again"* and was now steadily rebuilding my business as an executive coach.

So this one day, out of the blue, it happened. I'd been working for a few weeks with a leadership team within the I.T. division of an international insurance company in London. I was there, suited and booted, completing my scheduled one-to-one coaching sessions as usual. On this particular day though, something in the air felt different. I'd had butterflies in my tummy since I'd first woken up, and the unmistakable nudge came the moment my first client sat down in front of me.

'Go on,' came the smiling, steady voice I'd begun to know and trust. 'Go on.... just have a go... go on.... I bet they've got it too. Go on... take a look inside... find out for yourself!' Feeling teased (and also ashamed!) I straightened my skirt and shook my head to brush it away. I pushed it down. Did my best to ignore it and carry on the coaching as normal. Nope, the nudging continued building until I could no longer ignore it. Reluctantly I hissed my internal agreement. "All right! All right! I bloody hear you! Now just bloody shut up for a minute, let me compose myself!" (Hoping and praying that this inner-chat hadn't leaked out and external signs!)

I remember taking a deep breath, pulling myself up as tall as I could in my chair and preparing to take the plunge. So without giving any kind of overview, I gently changed the coaching conversation to deliberately search for what I knew I'd found within myself. And after the first client left, I went on and did the same with every person who came for coaching that day. The best way to describe what happened is that every single one of them simply 'popped' before my eyes. It was extraordinary. Their faces lit up, and each one left the session telling me they'd never felt that good before.

That was when it hit me. I remember taking the lift down and walking out of the building in a daze of wonderment – my whole being equally split between elation and fear. I knew then that whatever it was that had happened back in my kitchen was the key. And, without any idea of the plan, the structure, or how it was even going to start sharing this work, I knew in that moment that my mission was to share what had been given to me with the world. It was utterly bonkers – and yet it was true. I knew it. And the prospect of bringing it to life frightened the living daylights out of me.

I fully admit that as it dawned on me just how big the responsibility of birthing, shaping and sharing this was going to be, I did everything within my power to run away. And I assure you, there have been many times since then when I've been sorely tempted to do just that!

At the beginning I did my very best to ignore what I knew to be true by simply carrying on as normal. Until I started noticing that one by one, bit by bit, the normal coaching contracts I'd been determined to deliver kept dissolving away at the last minute – sometimes under the most extraordinary of circumstances. And inside, the nudge continued getting stronger and the voice became louder. Until one evening (after a couple of glasses of wine and countless tears of frustration) I found myself standing in the garden, raging fists punching the skies in exhaustion and fury, yelling out to whoever or whatever was listening.

"Alright! Alright! I'll do it then. I'm in! Quickly, before I change my mind!"

Immediately after that came my first conscious experience of what I now refer to as 'the silence', when time and space melt into nothingness. When there's nothing more to be done or said, and when things seem to be set free to take their natural course.

Rather naively, I believed that once I'd finally caved in and agreed to the deal, bringing such incredibly life-changing work to the world would somehow be supported at every level. After all, despite my initial cynicism, I knew by that stage that I had the big man, the goddess, the Universe, energy, source, flow (or whatever you like to call that force that connects every living being) on my side and pushing me forward. I knew I was in service to something much bigger than me.

I had no idea that the challenges had only just begun.

Because what I hadn't appreciated was that, whilst willingly walking forward with a smile, I was actually stepping naked and unarmed into the arena. A place where, if I was to survive and if this work was to flourish, I would be pushed to live my life more exposed, more engaged, more alive, raw, real and more 'upside down and back to front' than I'd ever been throughout my previous decades.

I'd already acknowledged (and tried to run away from) the enormity of the work ahead of me. As I was soon to discover, that enormity was equally matched by the ways in which I would be required to shift and grow as a person as well. It continues to this day – a relentless surge of continued growth and deeper feeling. Sometimes it's easy, other times excruciatingly painful. Every time though, I emerge brighter and even freer than before.

Until I started to develop what I now know as DNA Light Up, life as I knew it had been all about surviving. So therefore I'd amassed an impressive cache of weapons to conquer adversity. I'd mastered all the tools of resilience. I'd perfected the art of detachment and strategy – how to carry on regardless and keep my emotions in check. I knew how to create a business and build a team, and was fully conversant with goal setting, positive thinking and affirmations. More to the point, I'd already overcome so much using all those hard earned tools and techniques that I was convinced I would be pretty well equipped for the job that lay ahead. I was confident that this, finally, was exactly the reason I'd spent a lifetime perfecting all these skills. I was wrong.

Bringing DNA Light Up to life has been (and still is) also very much about bringing myself back to life. It's been about shedding the armour. Becoming naked. Embracing curiosity. Revelling in vulnerability. And it's a ruthlessly constant and wonderfully rewarding journey

For me, it's about removing any mask of positivity or pretence of 'sucking it up' and 'stiff upper-lipping'. Giving up any sense of fighting (either for or against) and recognising that the single real struggle is in un-learning the nonsense I had so willingly accepted as the only way to be.

Today I am more at peace with myself and the world around me than I've ever been before. Today I'm filled with a constant sense of excitement and curiosity. I find I can move through difficulties (oh yes, there are still difficulties – some of them breathtakingly painful) more quickly and easily than ever before. There's a magic to life and a sense of wonderment, safety and belonging. I am alive to my feelings, whatever they may be at any moment in time. The good, bad and ugly all have their place.

Most importantly, the fight has gone. There's nothing now for me to survive. There are no battles to win. And no requirement for any of my outworn tools of positivity and putting on a brave face that I'd depended on for so long.

I am boosted and lifted every day by ongoing examples of how our growing team is spreading this work.

- The little boy with 'behavioural problems' who moved from wishing he could simply fade away to embracing life with excitement in just a matter of hours. And who to this day is thriving at school and at home.
- The beautiful soul who had been trafficked from her African home and imprisoned as a sex slave. She arrived broken and apparently beyond help. She left embracing her power, recognising her beauty, and reclaiming her innocence. Today, two years on, she continues to shine with the beauty and power of a true warrior goddess.
- The ex-police officer diagnosed with PTSD due to the horrors he'd faced over his long career in the force. Now he sleeps at night, his family life is peaceful and supportive, and he's able to enjoy life in a way he hadn't believed could be possible.
- The highly successful executive who 'had it all' yet suffered from impostor syndrome, a deep fear of failing and being found out. Three sessions later, she is excited and determined to shine as a spokesperson for change in her male-dominated industry.

And, of course, all the beautiful true-life stories that are gathered here in this book.

And this is just the beginning. The list goes on – and continues to build as we develop and spread our work.

Today, as I'm writing this piece, I look back to where it all began that afternoon nearly ten years ago. And I am filled with gratitude. For everything.

MELANIE PLEDGER

Melanie Pledger Founder of DNA Light Up

My passion is to continue nurturing ruthless curiosity to achieve peaceful connection in our world. And not some fluffy airy-fairy or wafty-bollocks sort of peace. No. I'm talking about the laser-sharp, light fuelled peace that sees shadows for what they are and blazes through to the truth that is within all of us. I'm passionate about speaking out, calling the bollocks, and taking consistent action. Moment by moment.

There are things I know now that may have helped me when I was younger:

That being different does *not* make me wrong

That it's ok to shine bright

That I don't need fixing, because I was never broken.

Then again, had I known those things, my path may have been very different and this work may not have been born. And speaking of birth, I am dedicating my chapter to my son, Dylan Pledger. Because he was the first human being to truly light up my life.

Professionally? I've been an executive leadership development coach for over twenty years and have been lucky enough to work with some extraordinary human beings over that time. I've learned a remarkable amount from each company I've partnered with, and each person I've accompanied along their career development path. I am deeply grateful to each and every one of them.

I'm also grateful for the bad times and unkind people who've punctuated my life since early childhood. For it's through them that perhaps (willingly or not) experienced my greatest breakthroughs.

And today? For me, every day is an opportunity for continued growth. It's both exhilarating and exhausting (sometimes growth happens at such a pace that it knocks me off my feet and face down into the dirt!) and I love every moment of it. Why? Because I'm alive. Fully. Vulnerably. Colourfully. Unashamedly. And I'm grateful. Because every day I see the same thing happening with the men, women and children who find their way to Light Up through our growing team of Activators.

As I said. We've only just begun. As of April 2019, the latest count suggests there are 7.7 billion of us on this planet. Many facing similar bollocks to the ones overcome by the people in this book. We have a lot of work ahead of us. We're intent on making a difference, one person at a time.

2

BOLLOCKS TO SUICIDE

I'M BUILDING A NEW LIFE WITH TRUE FRIENDS AND FEELING CONFIDENT, STRONG AND CERTAIN.

I *can't put my finger on one particular episode that tipped me over the edge. It just all continued building up, while I gradually broke down.*

Mike's Story

That cold, dark, still winter's night in France is burned in my memory forever. Apart from my cats, I was all alone in the house. Everything was ready. I was prepared.

All was silent until my neighbours both came bursting through the patio door – David first, swiftly followed by Brenda. It was just after two in the morning. The explosion of their entrance and the shocked look on their faces stopped me dead in my tracks. You see everything had been organised. Notes written. Texts sent. Animals fed. I'd made sure I'd covered all important bases. My decision had been made. There was no going back. Until this noisy interruption. My neighbours had responded to a worried call they'd received from my mother in Wales a couple of minutes earlier. Their swift and selfless action that evening quite literally saved my life.

How had it all come to this? My lifelong friends would describe me as full of energy, successful and enjoying life to the full. I've worked all over the world and always done well in my career. I love racing cars and motorbikes and was a champion in my younger years. I'm one of those people who always seems to get up and bounce back after setbacks and, like all of us, I've experienced quite a few over the fifty-plus years I've walked this earth. So how had it got so bad that the unthinkable seemed preferable to living?

Looking back, I remember the first time my world was rocked. A young man in love and engaged to be married, I discovered my fiancée cheating on me. Her betrayal ripped my heart into pieces. My typically male response was to bottle it up and instead express it through anger and fighting. I moved away to start a new life and a few years later met my wife. We had a wonderful relationship during the most part of the eighteen years we were together. Even through her battle with cancer, which of course created a major strain on everything. She was strong, and I found I could remain strong for her as well.

It was not to be. The cancer returned. This time she told me she wanted to face it on her own. She no longer wanted to be in the beautiful home we'd built together, and instead wanted to move away to the country and out of our marriage. To this day, I still cannot get my head around exactly what caused her to do this. I simply sucked it up and went along with her wishes because I loved her.

After her death I read a letter she'd written to me, explaining in the best way she could that she couldn't bear to see me suffer again and wanted to give me freedom. The irony was that this was the last thing I wanted. I wanted to be with her. But I loved her and, while I couldn't understand what was driving her decision to end our relationship, I respected her wishes and went along with it. We remained on good terms and I continued visiting her there and also at the hospice. I am grateful and glad that we remained friendly right to the very end.

During that time, I became mesmerised by a lady I'd already met from a distance on the racing circuit. She was attractive, vivacious, and made a beeline for me. I was flattered. I was also vulnerable. Her attention made me feel better about myself and the situation I was dealing with. She would come to mine some weekends, when she'd cook for me and lavish me with attention. She had an important job, drove a top of the range car and at the beginning had no hesitation splashing the cash on expensive treats. She lightened the heavy load I'd been carrying. I went from feeling low and not going out, to feeling cared for – she got me going again. I was happy to be under her wing and our relationship went from there.

Six years later we bought a house in France. We'd spent a lot of time and had lots of holidays together, so it seemed like a great idea to invest in something together. In hindsight, the warning signs were already evident. Then again, many of us say that with hindsight we could all be wiser, happier and richer! Quite honestly, I didn't like the house and wasn't happy.

It was way too big for what I believed we wanted, and it needed an absolute fortune spending on it. But it was her dream, she had her heart set on it, and persuaded me it was a good move. I was blinded by love at that time and also used to going along with things for the sake of the other person, so I pushed down my reservations and went along with the plan, agreeing we'd pay half each for her dream property.

When the time came to put our cash into the project, it turned out that she didn't have any money. Instead she had huge credit card debts and was unable to secure a loan. I saw it as a small hurdle to overcome. It didn't matter to me, and I willingly arranged a loan for her part myself, with her promising to pay me back. I was happy. Because for me, caring for each other and building as a team is how couples work together. I was in it for the long term, and I was happy to be able to support my partner so we could build our dreams together.

Three years after buying the property, we made the permanent move over to France and moved in together. That was when the real cracks started to show. I suppose we can never really know another person, not at the core level. Living together though certainly shows up a lot more than just seeing each other regularly – even if the relationship has been going on for several years.

It happened so slowly I didn't even notice it. Little by little. Bit by bit. Drip by drip and day by day. I lost myself.

She went away to the UK a lot of the time when we first made the move over to France, leaving me alone to work on the house and the business, which upset me greatly. I explained that we'd agreed our life was here, together, and asked her to be with me more often. In return I agreed to cut down my work load so I could give her the attention she said she craved.

I ignored the ways she consistently did the opposite to things that were important to me (small things, like becoming increasingly messy when I like things to be tidy) and always took her side when friends and neighbours started falling away, brushing aside my concerns and once again pushing down my growing feelings of isolation. I even agreed to separate bedrooms so we could both sleep better at night.

She'd go to her room early saying she was tired and would then spend the next few hours on her ipad. No matter how hard I tried to make things better, nothing was ever good enough. I wasn't good enough. So I put my head down and got on with it, working hard to support us and the renovations we were doing on the house, while she became more and more distant and dismissive.

Despite my growing unease, I kept on keeping on, believing that every relationship goes through difficulties and that fundamentally we had many good times. On Valentine's day I asked her to marry me. She agreed. We held an engagement party in the summer to coincide with my birthday. So far as I was concerned we were on track and heading in the right direction. The party was filled with smiles and merriment. It was much later I found out that, during that same evening, she was already telling people how unbearable it had become living with me, and that she was planning to escape.

Roll forward a few months to October. She told me we were finished. That was that. She wanted half the house and was moving on. No discussion. She began dressing up to the nines and disappearing for days at a time. It was as if she was rubbing it all in my face. I begged and pleaded her to explain, to give us a chance, asking her if there was anyone else involved. Swearing on her child's life that there was no such nonsense going on, I again fell into shame at the idea of even imagining such a terrible thing of the person I had intended to marry. I found myself gradually closing in and shutting down. I couldn't bear to see or talk to anyone and I couldn't leave the house.

Little by little, I discovered that she was not the person I had believed her to be – not anywhere near. The lies were legendary and the chaos of twists and turns as the truth steadily unfolded were worthy of a science fiction novel. If I was to write a book about it all, people would say it was a fantasy that defies all logic and simply couldn't be true!

Looking back now, that was how it all happened. I can't put my finger on one particular episode that tipped me over the edge. It just all continued building up, while I broke down.

It was a few days after my neighbours' intervention that I had a conversation with the lady who was to take me through Light Up. It was one of those bizarre and timely coincidences. We'd briefly met some weeks earlier at a race meeting, and I knew a little bit about the work she was doing. I'd been wondering whether to make contact, and there out of the blue was a message from her asking if I was okay as she'd seen a post I'd put on Facebook.

Working with her I very quickly came to understand what had happened to me and (more to the point) how to make sense of it all. How to move through it, how to stay strong in the face of dealing with the fall out during an incredibly difficult separation, and how to continue rebuilding my life. I'm not saying it's been easy. There have been days when I've been side swiped by another blow to my spirit. Of course there have. And yet somehow, now I know beyond any question who I really am and how strong I am, it takes very little to remind myself and to get back on track.

Today, some months later, things are on the up. I am able to do what I want, I'm enjoying my work, and for the first time in months (maybe years) I'm finally sleeping well. I've found that friends and neighbours who had gradually disappeared off the scene while I was with the ex are all returning. Gradually more truths are coming out, and her craziness and anger have continued to intensify. Now they don't bother me. I can brush them off and feel good that I'm once again my own boss and standing on my own two feet.

It's cost me thousands to finalise the separation. It could have cost me my life. Instead I'm now building a new one, with true friends around me, where I can once again feel confident, strong and certain. Yes, things have most definitely turned a corner. That's for sure. And I'm never looking backwards again.

MIKE R

I've been a self-employed engineer for twenty years, passionate about motorcycles since birth (I was born into a family of racers!) I've raced successfully myself for many years.

Three things I wish I'd learned earlier are:

1. Take more time to enjoy family

2. Don't be so trusting that we lose ourselves

3. Live for the moment, because we might be dead tomorrow

I'm sharing my story because although it's been difficult, I know I'm not alone. On the face of things I was a happy-go-lucky man. Successful, cheerful, and a good provider - that's who I'd learned to be. Underneath I was desperately unhappy. Going along as usual and doing my best to please the wishes of others rather than attend to my own. I know now that if people carry on living that way, eventually there will be a big crash. In my case it was very nearly fatal.

Mine had been building for a while. The final crash came once my partner decided I was no use any more, after draining the life and finances out of me to the point where I nearly lost both my home and my business. I found myself alone in the middle of France, unable to speak the language, with no one to talk to except a couple of friends on the internet and my mother. Then I remembered Mel, who I'd met briefly a few weeks before. I was contemplating contacting her when she messaged me. The rest is in the chapter.

I have learned how to deal with issues and realised that I have a life to be enjoyed, which I never thought possible a few short months before. It's not always easy to reach out, and most of us do our best to live up to an image that's expected, so we feel accepted.

I shall be forever grateful for seeing the Bollocks for what they are, and what the Light Up experience did for me.

3

BOLLOCKS TO DOMESTIC ABUSE

I'M NOW ON A MISSION TO HELP ONE BILLION WOMEN TO SURVIVE AND BE STRONGER THAN THEY EVER IMAGIN

'*G*emma, we believe that you're a victim of one of the worst cases of domestic abuse we've seen for a long time'.

Gemma's Story

I don't know what time it was, but I remember being woken up by my mam shaking me, asking me to come into the living room, she needed my help. Sleepily I followed her.

I woke up instantly. My dad was lying there. Was he asleep? What was he doing? I couldn't tell. His eyes kept rolling into the back of his head and he was mumbling words I couldn't make sense of. I looked to my mam for guidance, reassurance, anything.

'I've got Gemma out of bed', she was saying to him. 'Tell him how much you love him, give him a cuddle,' she was telling me. I was scared so I asked her what was wrong with him. 'He's taken lots of tablets with too much alcohol; he's tried to kill himself by overdosing.' The words rang around my young brain: kill himself, tablets, alcohol, overdose?

My mam was just as scared as I was. She was crying and didn't know what to do. We didn't have a landline to call an ambulance, so we sat up with him. I was praying that he wouldn't die in front of us, wondering what had got so bad that he needed to do this.

It had been a normal day, or so I'd thought. What had caused him to do this? He was my dad! He should be protecting me! He'd always been a man's man, brought up to understand that men didn't cry, men didn't show their emotions. What was going on? I was confused, scared and trying to make sense of it all. I would have to look after him from now on: him, my mam, my sister and my brother, I thought in my young mind.

It was 1992. I was ten years old and this was my first experience of my father trying to take his own life. It wouldn't be my last.

My dad was a manic depressive. No matter how much we loved him, he pushed us away. No matter how good we were, he shouted at us. No matter how hard we worked, whether it be housework, or in our family business, it was never good enough. He even spent about six weeks in a mental hospital once as it was feared he was a danger to himself. My mam told family and friends that he was away on business. She always told me the truth, and I would always 'step up' to look after her and my little sister and brother.

He had good days, days where we would catch him laughing or smiling and we could pretend to be a 'normal' family. But then the bad days would hit and he would take to his bed for days on end. I didn't understand what mental illness was; I just thought he was moody, that he had no time for us. It wasn't until seven years later that I began to understand the true meaning of mental illness and the effects it could have on a person, the effects it had on a family, the effects it had on me.

November 20th 2000: I was off work and my sister was off school ill. It was about 1.30 pm. There was a knock at the door and two policemen stood there. We'd been notified earlier that my dad had unexpectedly left work and no one had any idea where he'd gone. Neither did we.

The previous couple of weeks had been really hard. My dad had left our family home and disappeared for two days. I had been the last person to speak to him. He'd told me on that call that he couldn't cope with life anymore. He said goodbye and that he was sorry. Then he hung up. We called and called his mobile but it was switched off, so we informed the police and they filed a missing person's report. We called every friend we could think of but it came to nothing. I remember sitting by the phone waiting for it to ring, dialling his number only to be met with the Orange answerphone message.

Then, out of the blue, he answered. He wasn't dead. After that he stayed with his brother, so at least we knew where he was. Until this morning, when we were told he'd disappeared from work.

The doorbell rang. I accompanied my mam to the front door and the policemen asked if my dad owned a blue golf. 'Yes,' mam said. They asked if they could come in and if it was okay to have a word with my mam in private. I left the room and stood in the hallway; the sound of her screaming confirmed my worst fear. I ran back in to find her a heap on the floor. I didn't need to ask what the policemen had told her, in my heart I already knew.

A stranger had been walking his dog and noticed the parked car. Dad had connected a pipe to his exhaust and put it thought the side window, blocking the gap with clothes he had in the car. After so many attempts, he'd finally done it. He had committed suicide.

I told my sister and held her as she cried. My mam was being comforted by her mam.

My brother! He was still at school, I needed to get to him. The police gave me a lift. It didn't seem real; it had only been eighteen months before that I'd left school myself. My grandma came with me and we were shown to the headmaster's office.

I remember looking around as we waited - I'd never been in the headmaster's office before. My thoughts were interrupted by the door opening. I could see the look of confusion on my baby brother's little face. Holding my hand out I guided him to sit down on my knee, put my arms around him and stroked his hair. Then I did the hardest thing I've ever had to do in my life - I broke his heart. I told him that his dad was gone forever. The man he looked up to, the man who was his idol, his role model and mentor ... gone. That feeling will live with me until the day I die.

The next few weeks passed in a blur and I don't remember much. I helped with the funeral planning, the insurance policies, and all the things a family must deal with when a loved one passes. I do remember this though: the bond I created with my brother became unbreakable. And it still is.

I went through the motions of grieving and in true 'Gemma-style' I made sure that everyone else was okay, often neglecting my own feelings. I became so angry with my dad: how could he leave us? We were his children! He didn't even leave us a note. A parent always puts their children first, right? It wasn't until I held my firstborn on my chest for the first time nearly eight years later, that I truly understood how bad my dad's illness must have been.

I remember looking down at this beautiful baby boy and I instantly hated myself for hating my dad for leaving us. For years I'd blamed him, and now I realised that it was an illness, and no matter how hard he tried to fight it, it wouldn't go away. I remember our family priest talking to us and likening depression and mental illness to cancer; he said that sometimes, no matter how hard we try to fight it, or how much medication we take, it doesn't work and the illness wins. I'd never thought about depression in this way before.

When my second baby was born twenty-one months later, as I held him for the first time, I again apologised to my dad for not understanding his reasons for leaving us.

Life with two small babies was hard. My husband worked away and I often survived on coffee alone, but it was so rewarding and I had support from his parents. I loved every minute of it. Life was good. My health visitor kept a close eye on me as she knew about my dad from my medical history. 'I know what to look out for,' I told her. 'Post-natal depression won't happen to me, I know the signs.'

Four weeks later, on a Sunday afternoon, my mobile rang. 'Hello?' I answered. As the person on the other end spoke, my world stopped. I battled to make sense of what they were saying.

My brother. Car crash. Critical. Theatre. Might not survive. Hand badly hurt.

I was with my uncle and I passed the phone to him. He took the message, then came off the phone and told me that my brother had been in a serious car accident and was currently in the Royal Victoria Infirmary in Newcastle. He was being taken down to theatre at that minute and they couldn't tell us anymore. My mam had rushed to be with him.

We waited for what felt like forever. Hours passed, then finally a phone call. It was my mam's husband who was with her at the hospital. They'd saved my brother's life but he was in a bad way. They hadn't been able to save his right arm and it had been amputated at the elbow. I dropped the phone and sank to the floor. My baby brother. I had done so much to protect him since my dad died. How could this have happened?

'Snap out of it Gemma!' a voice inside my head told me. 'This isn't about you, it's about him'. He had recently married, had a young baby of his own and a very good career as an electrician. So, I put all my energy into him and everyone else. When the hospital made an appointment for a counsellor to see him a few days later, he asked my mam and I to be there too. The counsellor spoke first with my brother, and then his wife and my mam took it in turn to ask questions. All I remember doing was holding back my screams.

That night in bed I couldn't get my head around the fact that he was still here but his arm was gone. I was grieving … and he was still alive. I sobbed myself to sleep and was woken by the sound of my baby crying next to me in his Moses basket. It was morning, and no matter how much I wanted to stay in bed and cry, I had two little boys who needed me.

The next few weeks passed in a blur of nappies and feeds, and it wasn't until my aunty visited that she made me realise there was something wrong with me. I hadn't washed my face or brushed my teeth or hair in days; my curtains were closed and the house was silent apart from the kids' crying or gurgling. I wasn't even sure when I'd last eaten. She called my mam and my husband's mother and they took me to see the local doctor.

His words might as well have been put in an envelope and posted to the other side of the world: I'd no idea what he was saying! I couldn't concentrate, my head was full. But full of what? It didn't make sense, I didn't even know how to talk; my words just wouldn't come out.

I later understood that I'd suffered a mental breakdown. I was so embarrassed. How could this be happening to me? After everything I'd been through with my dad, I should have seen it creeping up on me, I should have done more to keep it at bay.

Soon after I asked my husband to leave our home. He'd done nothing wrong, I'd just fallen out of love with him. They say in life you either grow together or you grow apart, and we had grown apart. Nothing much changed for me and life carried on as normal as I set about being a single mother.

We'd been separated for nearly eight months when I got talking to someone on social media, a local man who'd moved back to our village after separating from his wife. We had mutual friends and he seemed a nice, genuine guy. When he asked me out on a date I felt I had nothing to lose.

He invited me to his home for a cup of coffee. It was a beautiful summer's day and we sat in his garden and chatted. He only lived half a mile from my house, next door to one of my old school friends, so I felt safe. I noticed that he was extremely interested in my life and my friends. He commented that I was liked by everyone in my local pub, which was now his local too. I did find it odd that he made these remarks, but never once thought they were anything other than friendly 'chit chat'. My ex-husband had worked away and never really paid me much attention, so I was a bit flattered if I'm honest.

He walked me home and I remember feeling those little butterflies in my stomach as he kissed me goodbye. That night I went to bed with a warm fuzzy feeling inside. We texted back and forth over the next few day and seemed to have a lot in common. I was due to go on a night out with my friends and said I'd text or call him the next day. Looking at my phone half way through the night, I realised I had more than six texts from him. 'Bless him,' I thought as I messaged him back.

Things moved quite quickly after that: I was showered with love and attention. He would turn up to my house after he'd been on a night out or would invite me back to his. On one occasion he commented that he just wanted to see how I was dressed. Once again, I found it flattering as it wasn't something my ex-husband would have noticed.

It was about six months later when I first realised that something wasn't quite right. I was handing my car keys back to the finance company and suddenly it hit me. Every time I had to speak to my ex-husband about the house or our joint debts, it would cause an argument. Apparently, I was spending all my time talking to him. Maybe I am, I thought to myself. I wouldn't like it if the shoe was on the other foot, so I need to be more considerate.

I declared myself bankrupt to minimise contact with my ex and handed the house back to him. I had a roof over my head with my boyfriend and he was providing for me, so why did I need a house with my ex-husband? Next my car went. I reduced the hours I worked in my spray tanning business as this 'ate into OUR time'. Eventually my business, which seemed to cause arguments too, folded. In the end I even re-homed my two adored little dogs to please him. I no longer recognised the person I had become.

And so I started to argue back.

One night, one thing led to another and I tried to leave. He dragged me from the back door to the bottom of the stairs. I fought back as he tried to carry me up but, too sore and tired, I eventually gave up. He pushed me onto the bed and pulled at my dress to make sure I got into bed and stayed there. I resisted and managed to flee the house.

I turned up at my brother's house. I didn't even need to say what had happened; they just took me in, made me a cup of tea and gave me a bed. I didn't sleep much that night. My head was spinning. What had just happened? How had it happened?

My phone never stopped pinging with messages telling me he was sorry and that if I hadn't tried to leave it wouldn't have happened. Once again I doubted myself and wondered if it was in fact all my fault.

The next day I got a lift to his house to collect some things for me and my two boys, who'd been at their dad's the night before. As I opened the door I was shocked to see his mother standing there.' You've given my son a black eye!' she told me. I couldn't speak so I lifted my dress to show her the black and blue bruises down my left-hand side, starting from the top of my ribs and ending half way down the top of my leg. I also pointed out the ripped bra I was still wearing, a result of him trying to rip it off me to force me to stay in the house.

'These things never happened with his wife!' she told me. I left feeling confused. Had this all been my fault?

My family and friends told me how much they'd been worried about me, and how much I had changed as a person. I'd had no idea. He'd only raised his hand to me once. I'd always felt I could handle him.

With the help of my brother and grandma, I rented a house. I had nothing at all and my grandma (God rest her soul) gave me three knives, three forks and three spoons. I used to walk round to the local shop every morning and buy fresh ice and milk. I didn't have a fridge, you see, and it was the middle of summer, so I'd pour the ice into the centre of the sink to keep the milk fresh for the kids' cereal every morning. I'd walk them both to school and call in at my grandma's on the way home so I could use her washing machine. My friend had given me a corner sofa and I slept on that. The only room in the house that was decorated was the boys' room.

Around the same time a friend texted me to say that the company her mother worked for was recruiting for Area Managers. She wanted to put my name forward. I agreed and four days later I went for an interview. Next day I received the call to say I had the job. I was able to start immediately and they arranged for my company car to be delivered the following week. I honestly couldn't believe it! With my first wage I bought a fridge-freezer , washing machine and treated myself to a night out with the girls.

I was still getting text messages and phone calls all day and all night, begging me to take him back. I was exhausted, but I knew a night out would do me good. Half way through the evening I looked up and there he was, standing across the dance floor staring at me. I froze.

We moved pubs but he followed us to the next two. I was pleased when it was time to go home and tried to ignore the constant phone calls I was receiving from him. My friends dropped me off and I got into bed. I remembered a conversation I'd had with his sister a month before as we walked our dogs: she'd told me that when they'd argued in the past, he'd phone her and threaten to kill himself. I decided to turn my phone off.

The next morning I woke up and immediately turned my phone back on to check if my boys were okay and what time they would be home. As it was loading up I could see there were over fifty missed calls, numerous text messages and a video message. I clicked on the video and my heart stopped. He was sat on the floor of his living room slitting his wrists! There was blood everywhere: up the walls, in pools on the floor and all over him. He was telling me I had caused him to do it as I'd ended our relationship and was making a new life without him.

Jumping up, I called an ambulance and then his parents. By the time I got to his house, the paramedics and police had already arrived and were treating him. The police officer was awful to me and said some horrible things, she told me to leave. I walked away with the voice in my head telling me that it *was* my fault. If I'd just given him a second chance, he might not have hurt himself so badly. I couldn't save my dad from his mental illness but maybe I could save this man.

He called me the next day from his hospital bed and I agreed that I would give him a second chance.

Over the next seven months things went from bad to worse and I realised that I'd made a mistake taking him back. I walked on eggshells. Every time I said or did anything he didn't like, he threatened suicide. I became a person I didn't recognise again, lashing out and doing what I could to survive.

On December 27th 2013, after he'd been drinking all day, he tried to strangle me. The police were called and he told them we'd just had an argument. They pointed to the marks around my neck and the officer told him that it didn't look like 'just an argument'! He was arrested and given bail, his phone confiscated. I was put on first response by the police and had a panic alarm fitted.

I was visited by an organisation for victims of domestic abuse, and they explained to me that this was the type of relationship I'd been in. I'd no idea what they were talking about and explained that it was only the second time he'd raised his hand to me.

On New Year's Eve I got the call to say that he'd tried to kill himself again by driving his car off the road, and he was back in hospital. I booked an appointment with the police and asked them to drop the charges. I believed he needed medical help for a mental disorder and prison wouldn't help him. What I was told in response hit me like a ton of bricks.

'On the night of December 27th we received a call out and my officers got to your address in rapid time. They had no idea, because of the screams that could be heard through the control panel, what they would be met with, and for that reason the CPS has decided to go ahead with the charges, with or without your blessing. Gemma, we believe that you're a victim of one of the worst cases of domestic abuse we've seen for a long time'.

I left the police station in a daze.

Nothing much changed. He'd turn up at my house during the night, cold and dirty, saying he was sleeping in his car as he couldn't stand to be at his parents. I had no idea if it was true or not but I couldn't bear to see him in this state. I was trying to protect him and too blind to see what it was doing to me in the process.

We went out for a couple of drinks for Valentine's, while my boys were staying at their gran and grandad's. I did everything I could to try to keep things from kicking off or escalating, but when we returned home late that evening, things turned very nasty. I don't remember how I got there, but I was pinned on the kitchen floor, him sitting on top of me with a knife to my throat. I tried to move it away and it cut into my hand. He was spitting at me, hitting me on the head with the knife. I tried to fight back but it was no use, he was too strong. He was shouting that it was my fault, he was going to kill me and my boys would grow up without a mother.

I have no idea where I got the strength from but I kicked him off me and made for the living-room to get my panic alarm. It was gone! The box that controlled it was under my bed and I knew I had to get there. I ran upstairs, tripping on my way. It was as if things were moving in slow motion. I got under the bed and pressed the button. I could hear him coming and my life flashed before me.

I remembered the words of the policeman about not knowing what they were coming to. This time, I thought to myself, they're coming to the scene of a murder. As he reached my bedroom door the dialling tone on the alarm sounded. I knew help was on its way.

He heard the sound too. He picked up my phone and fled. Then he texted all of his family, pretending to be me. The police arrived, searched my house and put me into protection for the night.

'You bitch! They'll lock me away for this!' he said to me as he fled. They were the last words I ever heard him say. The next day I was advised that he had taken his own life.

The last five years have been hard. I have had to mentally, physically, emotionally and spiritually repair myself. I've often felt like giving up. But then I remember the pain that my dad caused when he gave up. I will never put my children through that pain.

I am now an ambassador for domestic violence, a motivational speaker and I help women learn about self-love. I teach them how to fall madly in love with themselves through my Warrior Women Academy and my Women Who Can mentorship.

DNA Light Up has been the final piece of the puzzle for me. I knew about most of the things involved, but I had never practised them in this way before. It has given me exactly what it promised: 'LIGHT'.

I am now a DNA Light Activator myself and I believe that with the help of DNA Light Up I can fulfil my mission of helping one billion women to see their own Light, to survive and to be stronger than they ever imagined

GEMMA EVANS

Gemma Evans Professional Activator

I'm a Self-love and Confidence Coach, a Health and Wellness Mentor and a motivational speaker. My passion in life is to teach females worldwide that self-love is the most important love of all.

After my dad committed suicide, after suffering from a nervous breakdown myself and after breaking free from a domestically abusive relationship, rebuilding myself mentally, physically and emotionally was my only option. Now I teach women how to do the same and take back their power.

Sharing my story is so important to help other women realise that they can take their power back after abuse of any kind and it all starts with self-love.

My Warrior Women Academy is a safe environment for Women globally and my Women Who Can mentorship teaches you how to take back your confidence and improve your health & wellness.

I dedicate this chapter to Women worldwide fighting for a better life 🤍

#IfICanYouCanToo. Connect with me.

4

BOLLOCKS TO ANXIETY AND LOW SELF-ESTEEM

SUDDENLY I CAN SEE WHAT'S HAPPENING AROUND ME AND I ACCEPT MYSELF COMPLETELY.

*A*t *ten years old, I sat alone on my bunk bed holding a photograph of my family. My brother, the one being I had left in the world, had died that morning.*

Sonia's Story

At ten years old, I sat alone on my bunk bed holding a photograph of my family. Really I was holding close to me my brother and my old dog. My brother, the one being I had left in the world, had died that morning. My dog had been rehomed a year before. I was alone now, except for my imaginary friend, the Griffin.

I remember that loneliness. I sometimes still feel it, but much less now, and I used to carry that loneliness with me everywhere.

I saw it then as a mangled mess. Now I see it as a life of pass-the-parcel with all the chaos and wrapping paper thrown all over the place, and a little gift under each layer IF I look hard enough.

I didn't look, not right away. I just kept passing the parcel and unwrapping in a dazed frenzy.

I just kept pulling at that paper, tearing it off, searching for the prize that would make me happy. What could ease this loneliness? What would fill my heart? What could stop these thoughts? I kept unwrapping and searching, in the same way a child does during the game and then passing my gifts on round the circle to each and every other child, letting my wrappers get frayed and ripped before I took myself back to unwrap another layer again. The prize is a moment's happiness and it's not long lasting. I didn't see the gift in each experience of unwrapping, I just felt the loss. I wasn't looking properly.

Does any of this make sense?

I was seeking ways to make myself feel better, and looking in all the wrong places. I didn't know. All the things I tried just led me to a feeling of increasing guilt and more loneliness. I hated myself even more.

It's like when we're on a 'diet' (I don't do those anymore.) We have a piece of cake when feeling emotional and for a few minutes, whilst we have the taste of chocolate and cream in our mouth, we feel amazing. Once we've eaten it, the feelings of guilt and shame kick in - right? We wish we hadn't done it. And then because we've unlocked those feelings, we crave something else and think 'oh well, I already ate that so I may as well have something else and eat more junk'. We're in this vicious cycle.

That was very much what life for me was about from the age of twelve until my mid thirties. It was a car crash state.

I feel very fortunate to be alive, and indeed to be in good mental health as far as I can see, (though perhaps some would disagree!).

I started my personal development journey at the age of thirty-three. I began working alongside a company founded in the United States. The first convention I went to I was confused - what the hell is this?! Everyone was smiling and happy and no alcohol or drugs were to be found. It freaked me out. My anxiety was high but so was my excitement.

It took a few years for me to settle in this environment. During that time I was still drinking in the evenings to numb my emptiness. My marriage was failing and I was self-harming when the pain was too much.

I started to change my diet, taking some supplements that a friend told me would help my skin and my weight. They did, so I was happy. Over time I noticed that my moods had started to stabilise. I didn't understand how this could be as my marriage was really troubled at this point. I had the feeling that I was totally out of control and yet my mood was becoming balanced for the first time in seventeen years.

I started doing some research and recognised the possibility that my gut health was being helped as my nutrition was being supported. This, combined with the positively crazy colleagues who gave me tools and tips to work on my mind set, helped me start to feel calmer. I came off meds more than eight years ago and haven't gone back to them, even though I'd been told I'd be on them for life.

GPs and psychiatrists are not happy that I'm no longer on the antidepressants and anti- anxiety meds. My own family panic when I have a down day and suggest I go pop a pill! I explain that it's life - we all have ups and downs and I'm just having a rough day or a difficult period. Of course they worry. They trust the pharmaceutical trade. I, however, do not.

Back then I still allowed myself to trust others more than I trusted myself and, as a result, found myself going through an extremely challenging time with someone whom I thought was accepting of me and who loved me. During this time I ended up in hospital for four months where I nearly died and almost lost my daughter, baby number six.

During my stay I was using all the mind-set tools I'd been taught and the positive self talk I'd learned from my new good friends; so I was surprised to find myself having flashbacks, nightmares and panic attacks once I returned home. I seriously thought I may need medicinal intervention again at this time as I felt I was losing my mind.

I understood that I'd been through trauma and as humans we have to process this and allow our bodies and brains to heal from it. So I was patient and nourished myself and worked hard on self-improvement. But sometimes those intrusive thoughts would come so fast that I couldn't stop them. I would wake up in total panic, fear flooding through my blood, heart pounding. I couldn't go on like this, feeling exhausted, snappy, tearful, in a constant fight or flight situation.

I had a chat with a colleague who suggested DNA Light Up. It was another year before I reached out and asked her to tell me more. A whole year spent with this rabbit in the headlights feeling. I was so frozen that I wasn't able either to stop and think or take a different step.

I was also scared that I'd have to talk about the event that threatened my life; I just couldn't face it. All other therapies that I was aware of would have made me open up that trauma and I felt that might make things worse. I used to tell the counsellors and nurses this but they said if I didn't talk about it, I would feel like this forever and they kept pushing me to open up.

DNA Light Up did nothing of the sort. I still don't know to this day how the heck the chat we had has managed to change my life so profoundly. I barely mentioned any hurt, I didn't cry, I just spoke a little about me. From this I was given a few simple tools to use. And yes, these tools and the hours I spent with my Activator were incredible. It was like she was giving me the spectacles from the Spiderwick Chronicles (great movie, watch it!).

Suddenly I could see it. Suddenly, I could see what was happening around me, I was in tune with myself, I *knew* myself and I accepted myself. I found what was causing me this panic and this anxiety. And it was not my hospital stay. That was just a part of the picture.

I am currently making changes to this trigger, using the tools Light Up gave me. I'm able to accept, not only my mistakes but also the mistakes of others, in a healthy way. I feel comfortable saying no to people, confident in my own decision making. Light Up has opened my eyes to my own intuition.

This has been, without a doubt, the fastest, simplest course/therapy (which is it?!) and it's had a bigger impact than anything I ever experienced in all those years of counselling. I now see the little gifts in each of my life's lessons, in each of my traumas, in each loss, in each cry for help. I see the little gifts in each layer of the the parcel. I'm able to take the gift and leave the wrapper now. I am grateful for the person that I am and for the life I have lived. Because had I not experienced it, I would not be me. And I, my shining lights, I am bright.

I have now decided to reach out and show others how to shine, so my next step of the journey is training as an Activator myself. I can't wait to see the brightness in the dark through other people.

Alhumdulillah, I am so grateful for being shown my path, the path that led me to meet the amazing people who are doing this work.

SONIA KEATS

Sonia Keats Professional Activator

I'm a mum of six, a rebel with a cause, the Littlest Hobo (down the road is where I'll always be) and a Find your Freedom coach : I help women to find their freedom both financially and emotionally.

I'm passionate about helping others see they can make change - change in their own lives and yes change in the world. Sometimes life seems so overwhelming and it feels like we can't do enough. And we can. When we each take one step, when we each dare to make an effort, when we each make little changes, when we each light up just a little, we are sharing and showing others that they too can do the same. When others then dare to do the same, big things start to happen. Nothing can dampen the spirits or dim the light when we unite.

It's important for me to share my chapter here with you as I KNOW, absolutely know, that if I can change, if I can get over loss, pain, depression, anxiety, overwhelm, shame, guilt, then anyone can - anyone. I just wish everyone could see what I now see. I'm spreading the word that it's possible, so if you don't believe in you just yet then allow me to believe in you until you do.

I'm dedicating my chapter to my brother Graham Julian Keats and my Nana, Ivy Rose Dronsfield. I never,ever heard either of them moan or complain or say anything negative in their lives - not once. My brother in his wheelchair and a life full of pain, my nana who worked hard in business and raised six kids. Lights in my life. Lights in the world.

5

BOLLOCKS TO CANCER

I'VE REDISCOVERED MY INNER SELF, I'M CALMER, MORE CONNECTED AND I CONTINUE TO BLOSSOM.

T*he lump was a malignant sarcoma.*

Sue's Story

It was flipping freezing on the day my friend Sue and I started out on our journey to Cuba for a well-deserved break. It was January 2013 and snow was lying thick on the ground.

All the way down to Gatwick we discussed the past year and our hopes for a better future. Sue had recently been made redundant and had started up her own catering business, but for the last few months she'd suffered recurring chest infections. Me? I was just exhausted. For the past few years my job had been extremely demanding and I'd spent over forty of the last fifty-two weeks working away from home, which had a detrimental effect on my relationships with friends and family. We agreed that two weeks in the Cuban sunshine was the pick-me-up we both needed.

It was a beautiful sunny afternoon as we landed in Cuba. Everything was colourful and bright, the Cuban people were friendly and full of smiles, the hotel was stunning with a gorgeous white sandy beach and it was warm. We had found paradise! Overnight there was a huge thunderstorm and rain flooded many of the paths around the hotel and still filled the skies as we went for breakfast.

We were ambling along happily chatting when whoosh! Suddenly my feet went out from under me and I crashed to the ground with a scream of pain. My right ankle and knee were excruciating. Lots of people rushed to my aid, helping me to stand, but I couldn't put any weight on my leg. It was just too painful. Someone fetched a wheelchair and I was taken to the hotel's medical centre. It turned out that the night before someone had spilled a tray of food and it hadn't been properly cleaned up. The Doctor said I had a severely sprained ankle and knee. I was handed painkillers and crutches and sent on my way.

My injury severely curtailed our activities, but our room was right next to the pool and we made the best of it. By now Sue had developed a really bad cough and was having trouble breathing. She too ended up at the medical centre and was told she had pneumonia. So much for a revitalising winter holiday! After two weeks we flew back to the UK, me in a wheelchair and Sue using a nebuliser.

On the ten hour flight back my leg became really swollen and painful, so I went straight to A and E on my return home where an x-ray revealed I'd been walking around on a broken leg for two weeks. Soon I was in a plaster cast almost to my hip. It seemed as if fate had decided I *really* needed a break from work!

Sue, too, ended up with vast quantities of antibiotics and a multitude of doctor's appointments, but they couldn't find what was causing all these chest infections.

Six weeks later I went to have my cast removed. My knee and hip were still very painful and x-rays showed calcium crystals in both joints. Because my bone break hadn't been immobilised at the beginning, my body had been producing extra calcium in a bid to repair the bone.

The Doctors were very reassuring and I went home with a new set of crutches and the required medication. I took the first dose as prescribed and next thing I knew, I was back in A and E with a massive allergic reaction to the medication. A series of steroid injections and keyhole surgeries began which were, unfortunately, only temporarily effective. Eventually it was decided that my best option was a total hip replacement.

Luckily I was still able to drive and I carried on working while on the waiting list for surgery, with two crutches to get around. The huge numbers of painkillers left me constantly lethargic and exhausted, falling asleep anywhere in the blink of an eye. A whole battery of tests showed I didn't have thyroid issues or diabetes, and some strange liver function results were put down as a side effect of all the painkillers.

Sue was finally referred to a lung specialist and diagnosed with a very aggressive small cell lung cancer. She was sixty years old. Her prognosis wasn't good and was further complicated by a family history of lung fibrosis. Her Dad, sister and cousin had all died from lung disease at the age of sixty-one and Sue was petrified the same would happen to her.

The one bright spot on the horizon was that she'd just found out she was to be a Grandma. One of her sons lived in Australia and he and his girlfriend had announced the happy event. It gave her something to focus on, and she was determined to go to Australia to see her grand-child once he or she was born.

Five days after beginning a really rigorous regime of chemotherapy, her hair started falling out, and within ten days she was bald. Sue's hair had always been her pride and joy and she was devastated to lose it. She bought numerous glamorous wigs and fought every step of the way, taking the decision to only tell close family and friends about her illness. Her mantra was 'No matter how bad you feel, Get Up, Dress Up, Show Up and Never Give Up'. I watched in amazement as she'd do her hair, put on lipstick and go out for an hour or two, then go home and collapse from the effort for the next few days.

After chemo came radiotherapy. The doctors decided against using radiotherapy on her lungs as it was likely to do more harm than good, but went ahead with radiotherapy on her brain as a precautionary measure (the most common place small cell lung cancer spreads is to the brain). I've never seen anyone look so ill and still keep going. Finally, there was good news - Sue was declared cancer free.

Around this time I was feeling really out of sorts. The lethargy and tiredness were getting to me. I noticed a small pea-sized lump had appeared out of the blue on my left foot. It wasn't painful but I mentioned it to my doctor who pronounced it a ganglion cyst, probably the result of me walking oddly due to the issues with my right leg. I was told not to worry as chances were it would just disappear on its own. In years gone by apparently the prescribed treatment was to hit them hard with a family bible!

My hip replacement surgery was finally agreed for mid May. I was nervous, but couldn't wait for the prospect of being pain free and able to walk around without the fuzzy state the painkillers induced. The only cloud on the landscape was the fatigue and the growing lump in my foot. After several unsuccessful attempts to have it aspirated, surgery was recommended. I half-jokingly asked my hip surgeon if he'd remove the lump when he did my hip but foot surgery requires at least two weeks without weight bearing and with hip surgery the aim is to get the patient up and walking again as soon as possible. The best option was to wait for six months.

The hip surgery went well and I felt remarkably good. For the first time in months I was pain free and the world seemed a much brighter place. Next morning I was out of bed and walking without pain too. With the aid of the physio I did twelve steps with crutches and and felt like I'd won the lottery. Sue came to see me, looking amazing and excited to have finally booked her flight to Australia in January, a couple of months after the birth of her new grandson. Things were finally looking up for us both.

My recovery was swift and I was soon back at work. My new hip was amazing and in September I went on a yachting holiday in the Greek Islands, dealing with rolling decks and gangplanks with ease. September was also my fifty-ninth birthday and Sue was sixty-one a few days later.

I wanted to mark my sixtieth year with several special events: a Mediterranean cruise and trips to visit friends and family in Scotland, Germany and Holland.

My plan was to do something significant every month; I was done with ill health and poor mobility and I was starting to feel 'normal' again. I also decided on a huge party to celebrate and set about booking rooms. Sue would do the catering and friends would supply the band and DJ. I was really going to push the boat out, 2015 was going to be a year to remember.

In November I mentioned to the doctor how lethargic and exhausted I felt. Another set of blood tests again came back with negative results. My diet and lifestyle were checked - how much was I drinking, did I smoke? A course of antidepressants was suggested. I refused the offer. I was tired, not depressed.

Christmas and New Year came and went in a blur of family celebrations and Sue jetted off to Australia to see her new grandson. Work was manic as ever and I was heavily involved with a new programme covering staff shortages and last minute changes. It was so busy that I agreed to work from home during the two weeks I would be resting my foot after the surgery to remove the lump.

Looking back I can't believe what a people pleaser I was, always putting everyone else's needs before my own. I think it stems from being the eldest of six children, the responsible one. As I was growing up I was constantly admonished to look after my younger siblings, to let them have what they wanted.

The surgery went smoothly under local anaesthetic, though I drew the line at watching it and opted to listen to disco and soul music through headphones. The surgeon was pleased, though he did remark that the tissue he'd removed 'didn't look like a ganglion cyst', more like inflamed tissue. I went home with a huge dressing and instructions to keep my foot raised for the next two weeks.

Sue drove me to the podiatry department to have my stitches removed.

She was glowing with happiness, just back from her Australian trip and full of stories of her new grandson, with hundreds of photos to show me. I left her in the waiting room, busily consulting her iPad looking for flights to go back to Australia later in the year. If it wasn't for the fact her youngest son was getting married in the UK that summer I suspect she'd have gone back straight away!

The surgeon and nurse were bright and chatty as they removed my stitches. I told them about the various plans to celebrate my upcoming sixtieth. I asked if my pathology results were back yet.

'I have to tell you, in twenty odd years as a podiatric surgeon, I have never come across this situation before. We got the results back last Friday. The lump was a malignant sarcoma.'

I'd never heard of sarcoma before but I understand what malignant means. The rest of the conversation was surreal. I listened to what they said, responded to their questions, and it all seemed as if they were talking to someone else over my right shoulder. I was in total shock. I went out into the waiting room where Sue was still busy surfing the internet for the best deals to Australia. 'I have cancer,' I told her bluntly.

She was amazing. From her own experience, she understood that I was reeling with the news and at the same time wondering how to tell my family, friends and workmates. She didn't want to leave me on my own so we ended up going for breakfast. I remember looking at my watch as we sat down; it was just before 9 am. This day had certainly started with a bang!

The next few days were a total blur. The diagnosis explained why I'd been feeling so tired - lethargy is one of the main symptoms of sarcoma. I was told that I might get away without further surgery if the initial operation had removed all the cancerous tissue. I was warned that sarcoma was rare, very tricky, and prone to spreading and late recurrence. I would need to be monitored for at least ten years. A battery of tests, x-rays, scans and MRIs were arranged and I was to return four weeks later for the results.

I started to get used to 'that look' people give when you tell them you have cancer. I found that there was another even more stricken look when I told them I had sarcoma. It was weird, I constantly felt this was happening to that mythical person behind my right shoulder and I was just observing it all.

The results of the tests weren't good - there was an area of suspicious tissue in my left foot, right up against the bone. The consensus was that I should have a below the knee amputation as a matter of urgency. I went into meltdown. How on earth would I cope? I live on my own in a house and garden with lots of stairs, I was still recovering from a hip operation in the other leg. What about chemotherapy or radiotherapy? Surely amputation wasn't my only option? I'd already been on crutches for the best part of eighteen months, I couldn't face the thought of years more in the same state. I was utterly devastated.

It was patiently explained that sarcoma was so rare that the average family doctor would never see a single case in their whole career; consequently there were no specific chemotherapy treatments for it, only broad brush treatments that they couldn't guarantee would be effective. Radiotherapy was deemed to be a poor second treatment choice. I was given three weeks to decide what I was going to do and surgery to amputate my leg was pencilled in.

Everyone was helpful and understanding, but the outlook was bleak. The orthopaedic surgeon was the one person who gave me a ray of hope. He agreed to try limb salvage surgery and only amputate half my foot, removing the fourth and fifth metatarsals up to the ankle and heel, leaving me with a functional ankle. It would mean my left foot would be like walking on an ice skating blade instead of the normal tripod of big toe, little toe and heel. He made sure I understood that I might still have to have a below knee amputation if he couldn't achieve clean margins with non cancerous tissue, and that recovery was likely to be long and arduous. The final thing he said really resonated with me: 'Always choose life over limb.'

I was advised to get rid of all my old shoes. Anything with a heel was out; court shoes, sandals and flip flops would be useless to me. In future I would always need a flat shoe with an ankle strap or laces that would stay on my foot, with inserts and special insoles to fill in the gap. For someone with a shoe collection resembling that of Imelda Marcos it was a bitter blow. I realised I'd also have to change my choice of clothes; I couldn't see myself wearing a posh frock with trainers or brogues, however fashionable they were. I was heartbroken as I sold off my designer heels on eBay and donated huge piles of shoes to the local charity shop.

Next to go was my pride and joy, my lovely Audi A3. My left foot would not cope with the pressure on it when pressing the clutch pedal and I would have to drive an automatic in future. My life was rapidly changing and I felt totally out of control. I went through my house, removing possible hazards, getting rid of prized possessions to make sure I had room to manoeuvre a walking frame or a wheelchair.

It felt like I was grieving not only for my soon to be amputated toes, but for my way of life and everything that I knew to be 'normal'. I cancelled my travel plans, the much anticipated cruise, trips to visit family, my friend's wedding. Life would never be the same but I was determined my birthday celebrations would go ahead in September.

The day of the operation came around swiftly, almost exactly a year after my hip replacement. I was back in the same hospital, on a trolley outside the same operating theatre. How on earth I didn't leg it down the corridor with my theatre gown flapping in the breeze I will never know!

It turned out I was something of a celebrity. Not only did I have a really rare cancer; they were carrying out a surgery that wasn't often performed. In the interests of medical science I'd agreed they could film my operation and use tissue and blood samples for medical research. Even so I was unprepared for the legion of medical staff in the operating theatre and the number of cameras involved.

As the anaesthetic took effect I remember wondering if I'd wake up with half a foot or half a leg. Coming round on the ward, it took me several minutes to screw up the courage to see if I still had a left foot. I did! It was covered with a huge dressing and bandaged up to the knee but it was still there. The relief was indescribable.

I drifted back off to sleep and when I woke up I wondered why there was a bus queue by my bed. I was surrounded by a group of medical students all anxious to hear about my surgery from my consultant. So began my two month stay in hospital.

I was in a ward with three other ladies. Two of them also had rare cancers, both were terminal, and the fourth bed was an overflow bed used for emergencies, so the occupant changed almost daily. Over the coming days I got to know the other ladies really well. There was Muriel: Irish, irrepressible, huge fun and with a cracking sense of humour. She'd tell anyone who would listen that she was going home that day, even though, like me, she was there for the long haul.

Linda was quieter with a dry wit. You'd expect such a ward to be full of gloom but it was actually full of fun. We shared hopes and fears, dreams and plans and talked late into the night. Humour was our safety valve, our way of coping. We were even told off by the night nurse for being worse than a group of teenage girls on a sleepover.

The first week in hospital, Sue came to see me. She'd just been told her lung cancer was back and had spread to her lymph nodes. The only treatment they could give was radiotherapy to her lungs as she'd already had the full amount of chemotherapy. There was a real risk it could cause fibrosis in her lungs. Her nightmare of dying aged sixty-one, like other members of her family, was very real.

Her treatment started immediately with daily radiotherapy sessions. She would call into see me, sometimes for just a few minutes, before going for her treatment. It was heartbreaking to see her deteriorate day by day, though the doctors were hopeful that the treatment was working.

Days blended into each other. My stitches were removed, though I was still not allowed to bear weight on my left foot. I couldn't return home as I lived on my own and it was beginning to look as if I'd have to sell my house and move into a bungalow. I was worried about my dog Archie, already into his fourth week in kennels. I was beginning to feel lost and alone.

The shock of my situation was wearing off and the grim reality starting to bite deep. My physical recovery was progressing but mentally I was struggling, not only with my own situation but also watching Sue, Muriel and Linda all deteriorate around me. They had helped me so much and not being able to help them was upsetting.

To aid my recovery I was moved to a rehabilitation hospital with a non-weight bearing bed and extensive physio facilities. Family and friends had to do at least a fifty mile round trip to visit me. My ward was full of elderly ladies recovering from falls, often with dementia and other issues. I was twenty-five years younger than most of them and thankful to be moved to a side ward on my own; at least I could have my light on to read after eight pm at night.

Sue and I phoned each other every couple of days. She was obviously struggling, and really upset because two good friends had been caught up in a terrorist incident in Tunisia and one of them shot dead. It was a tough time all round, although Sue was eagerly looking forward to her youngest son's wedding at the end of June. Always very stylish, she was out to make an impression in a new outfit and wig. Looking at the photos, you'd never have realised how ill she was.

After eight weeks in hospital, a major milestone - I was allowed to go home. I wept solidly for two days - I'd bottled up so much and at last was able to let it go. Three days later Sue was admitted to hospital, struggling to breathe.

I still had to have my foot dressed daily, but I talked my sister into taking me to see Sue in hospital. She was on oxygen and showing everyone she could the photos of her son's wedding, particularly proud of one of her with her sons and grandson, three generations of family together. Less than two weeks later she passed away from radiation induced fibrosis. She was sixty-one.

Her death hit me hard. It was a blow I found difficult to deal with.

It was becoming obvious I wouldn't be able to return to my old job. I no longer had the stamina to continue nor could I carry around all the equipment I needed. I knew I didn't want an office based job as it would have meant moving to London.

I was referred for counselling for six months to help me cope with my change in circumstances. It really helped to put into perspective my situation and my constant fear of the cancer returning. It allowed me to identify practical steps I could take: updating my will, identifying and appointing my powers of attorney, having a major clear out at home, making sure all my affairs were up to date.

Each step I took gave me peace of mind, but I felt further and further away from being me, from being normal. It felt like I was on some sort of manic merry go round and I wanted to get off!

Physically I was healing and getting better, though still on mega amounts of painkillers to cope with phantom limb pain. I kept having severe reactions to the medication and my doctor was running out of new drugs to prescribe. I was also getting really bad digestive issues. All in all I was a mess.

Monthly blood tests revealed that I had a rare autoimmune condition where my body was attacking my bile ducts. The recommended treatment was a liver transplant. What was it about my genes that meant I'd developed not one but two rare diseases?! The diagnosis marked my lowest point. It coincided with the day of Sue's funeral.

The day of my sixtieth birthday dawned. I'd invited almost two hundred people to my seventies themed party, asking everyone to don fancy dress and bring their dancing shoes. It was a fantastic day and I was totally amazed at the lengths some of my guests went to. I even managed a couple of visits to the dance floor with my crutches. Looking back I feel the party was a major milestone, the start of my recovery and the first normal happy event in my life for quite some time.

I took early retirement from my job, expecting to feel a huge sense of freedom. Instead I felt rudderless. I'd lost my purpose and sense of identity. I hadn't realised just how much I'd allowed my job to define me. Out of necessity I'd become a career woman and suddenly all I had were memories.

I'd kept in touch with Linda and Muriel after I left hospital. Sadly Linda died in December and Muriel the following February. I felt lost and alone, numb, unable even to cry. Nothing seemed to help the disconnect I felt within. Would I ever feel normal again?

I'd decided it was time to try something different and a friend introduced me to Forever Living's range of aloe vera products. Amazingly they seemed to make a difference, particularly with the phantom limb pain and my digestive issues. The natural remedy helped where conventional medicine hadn't. Slowly I began to wean myself off the painkillers and other medication.

I decided to get more involved with Forever, becoming a business owner, attending events and training sessions. It was at one of these sessions, chatting during a coffee break, that I first heard about DNA Light Up and became intrigued. Not only did it sound really interesting, I began to wonder if it could help me. Coffee break over we went back to the training and it slipped from my mind. However over the next few days I started mulling it around and resolved to find out more.

I discovered that the woman I'd been talking to was a DNA Activator, trained to take others through the Light Up process. I explained my situation to her, how I felt disconnected from myself and was searching to find the real me inside, my new normal. I remember her smile as she said she thought I was a perfect candidate for Light Up.

So we arranged to meet in June 2017, and she took me through the process. I talked and she listened, intently. We laughed and cried together. She shared simple tools with me and with each discovery I began to feel calmer, less anxious and more connected to myself.

I began to realise as I rediscovered my inner self that I was very much the person I had always been, the person I'd buried under layers of repressed emotion as a way of coping. I also began to realise I needed to experience all these emotions, to feel them in order to grow and become myself and find my 'normal' again.

I discovered 'Pink Squidgy' deep inside of me, my mental picture of my soul, my inner self. I drew it, painted it, covered it with glitter and discovered it also radiated bright multi coloured flashes of light. As we progressed I discovered that inside Pink Squidgy was a beautiful lotus flower that opened up to reveal a sapphire blue spinning jewel which emitted the flashing lights.

Since that time I have gradually blossomed. I've started a part time job, begun travelling again, and even started a new relationship. Life is good, life is ... normal. My Normal.

SUE MUTCH

After many years working for the Police and the Civil Service, I took early retirement due to my Sarcoma Cancer diagnosis.

I dedicate this chapter to the selfless Doctors, Nurses and Physio's who work in the NHS Sarcoma Units around the UK and bring hope to those affected by this awful disease, and especially to my family and friends without whom I would never have got through the last four years.

Having a serious illness, like most traumas, makes us re-examine our lives. It made me fully realise the importance of family, and how all those things I'd worked for, the nice home, the new car, are actually far less important than I believed.

I remember coming back from the hospital at one point, looking around my home and realising that nothing I owned, nothing I'd worked for could help me in any way.

So take the holiday, use the good crockery, wear the sexy undies, light the fancy candles and live each day to the full, as we never know how long we have.

6

BOLLOCKS TO NOT FITTING IN

I AM MY OWN SOUL-MATE AND WILL
NEVER FEEL LONELY AGAIN.

E*very day during those two years I would dream of ending it all as the emotional pain was too intense.*

- Beth's Story

For as long as I can remember, I have felt that I was different. Different from how other people looked, how they behaved, how they felt. I didn't fit into the mould of 'average person'.

Sometimes I was happy with that. I enjoyed my uniqueness and would fight fiercely to defend it. Often it left me with a bizarre jarring feeling inside that I didn't understand. If I believed that I didn't want to be like everyone else, why did it feel so uncomfortable, so like I didn't belong, as if I was not connected to anything or anybody?

I had a relatively unremarkable childhood and believed at the time that it was a happy one, although looking back, I don't remember much love or laughter. I had two parents and a sister and generally speaking we all rubbed along fairly well together. As I grew into a teenager, things started to change as I became aware more of who I was within the family dynamic. It was apparent that I very much took after the paternal side of the family, and my feelings were often and a lot of what I was feeling was dismissed as be as over-emotional nonsense, or me simply being 'moody like your father'.

This added to the feeling of being different, and started to manifest itself as feeling 'wrong'. There was surely something wrong with me for feeling things deeply, for expressing emotions, and for a very long time I truly believed that it was an irritation for everyone else to have to deal with me being like that.

At school I was teased for being overweight, and it took a massive toll on me. Again I felt that there was something wrong with me, that not being thin and fitting into the normal mould was obviously my fault. I subsequently spent thirty-five years of my life believing that the shape of my body was the most important factor when it came to how people saw me.

For the majority of my life, everything revolved around my weight; if somebody paid me a compliment, I would add the words 'for a fat girl' onto the sentence in my head. For a few years, I cycled into work and I remember one day a car pulling out to pass me, very considerately giving me lots of space, and me believing that it was because I was so fat that the car had to give me extra room to pass.

I felt that I was constantly and continuously being judged, that everyone else believed me to be fat, unattractive and unlovable, even when I had friendships and relationships. The sad irony is that I was actually right. The person that I was being harshly judged by was the most important person in my life – me.

Over the course of those thirty-five years, I tried countless diets, exercise plans and eating regimes. I believed that if only I could be slim, then I'd be happy. In fact the only time in my entire life that I've felt that I was 'normally slim' is when my marriage broke up.

It was one of the most stressful and unhappy times I've lived through. I remember loving the way that I looked when I was slim - it felt like an out of body experience. I could get to be someone else and live a more carefree life for a while. I'd constantly look at myself in any reflective surface I could find, as if I couldn't quite believe that it was me and needed to double-check all the time. It was such a contrast to how desperate and miserable I was feeling on the inside.

Now I know that, if ever there were a situation where I were forced to choose between being slim and miserable or curvy and happy, I'd go with the latter every single time.

After finishing my O and A levels at school, I went to university. I don't recall this being a conscious decision, something that I chose to do, more that it was just what everyone did. My first year at Oxford Polytechnic, as it was called back then, was an interesting one. I met a lot of new people and was able to start exploring who I really was. I lived in halls of residence and met some really great people and had a lot of fun.

The feeling of being different was still there and because I was meeting people from a huge variety of backgrounds, it felt like we were all being different together. I really benefited from that. I was finally getting external validation that it was actually great to be different.

I started to experiment with dressing and thinking in a different way, and for a while all was well. The nagging doubts about feeling unattractive and unlovable were still there, I just ignored them for a while as I was too busy with this new life. I had a new community of people, those who I lived with in my halls of residence and those on my course, and I felt safe. I felt like I belonged.

Everything changed in my second year when I moved out into a shared house. A lot of the friends from my first year were spending time in work placements or abroad, and those that I ended up living with were not necessarily the ones that I felt to be 'my people'. I lived in a room at the very top of the house and aside from the tiny kitchen, there was no communal living space.

I found myself feeling very isolated and would spend large amounts of time alone in my room. I was confused and bewildered and couldn't understand how everything had changed so quickly. The university life that I'd experienced in my first year seemed to have completely disappeared and I felt very low and miserable.

Again I wondered what was wrong with me. I started to feel that I had let everyone down, that I had yet again reverted to being an irritation, and I felt desperately unhappy. Shortly after starting my second term, I knew that I couldn't carry on living like this, feeling so lonely and miserable, and I made the decision to leave and return home to live with my parents. This experience was the first of many dark episodes in my life that led me to believe, many years later, that I suffered from depression.

Having left university, I spent a few years working in Paris, which was an incredible experience, and then moved to London in my mid-twenties. Living abroad, I'd felt comfortable with my 'difference'. Most people found the English girl to be quirky and charming, and I enjoyed that.

Moving back to London, I slipped back into the old habits from adolescence of feeling out of place with myself and questioning my role in the world. I started to become a people pleaser. I was introduced to a guy and we began dating. We quickly moved in together and became engaged.

From this point on I felt my own identify slipping away, little by little. I don't blame him for this – he was a lovable force of nature and it became easier for me to identify myself through him than to try to work out and understand who I was. When our relationship ended, my primary emotion was one of relief. It probably would have been a great time for me to begin to learn about myself and come to terms with who I was.

And Life had other ideas.

In August 1997, my beloved father died. It was the same month that Princess Diana died, and two months after I discovered that the guy who had been my first love had also died. I didn't cope very well, and slipped into a depressive episode that lasted around two years.

Every day during those two years I would dream of ending it all as the emotional pain was too intense. I didn't feel that I had the courage to actually take my own life and I knew that what I wanted more than anything was for something to come along and take this decision out of my hands. The ideal scenario that played out in my head was being involved in a fatal coach crash.

Whilst I recognised at the time that I was suffering from depression, I felt that it was my duty to bring myself through this, not to turn to medication, and that this somehow proved my strength. I believe now that I would have got through that episode a lot quicker and with far fewer lasting consequences had I sought help.

In the years that followed, I was completely lost. I didn't know who I was, what I wanted out of life, how to get it, how to be happy. I became very good at hiding all of these feelings. Outside of my depressive episodes, I've always been outgoing and seemingly confident. Those traits were not simply a disguise. I always felt like a complete dichotomy – I was confident, independent and successful, and I also felt miserable, lonely and a failure. My brain was unable to compute how all those feelings could co-exist, which only added to my confusion and misery. I felt a complete freak of nature.

During those years, I started to change my appearance on a regular basis. It felt important to me at that time to show the world that I wasn't the fat, boring, irritating person I felt on the inside. My 'thing' became to experiment with different hair colours, and it was during this time, when my hair was pillar box red, that I wrote the following poem.

> *The girl with the red hair*
> *Stands out in a crowd*
> *You may think she's brash*
> *And confident and loud*

The girl with the red hair
Leads an interesting life
She fills it with colour
Looks vibrantly alive

The girl with the red hair
Seems bubbly and fun
She will make you laugh
And feel the warmth of the sun

The girl with the red hair
Is honest and kind
She'll always be truthful
Believes she knows her own mind

The girl with the red hair
Lives life to the full
Tries everything she can
To ensure her world is not dull

The girl with the red hair
Surrounds herself with friends
Gives herself to her loved ones
On whom she depends

But the girl with the red hair
When she's on her own
Often feels pale, insignificant
Frightened and alone

Friends who I speak to now about the feelings that I had during that time are amazed. I obviously did a great job at hiding them. I wasn't aware of consciously wanting to deceive people and hide the real me, it was more that I felt that my emotions were wrong, too introspective, too dramatic and would simply be irritating to others. The other side of me that was jolly and confident and successful was the bit that people seemed to like and as I'd become a people pleaser, it seemed natural and easy for this to be the me that I showed to everyone.

Of course, there were times when I couldn't hide the misery and looking back now, I imagine that people might have been confused as these unhappy episodes seemed to come out of nowhere. People were certainly surprised when my marriage broke up. Including my husband unfortunately.

I was finally diagnosed with depression at the age of forty-two when, a year or so after my marriage had ended, my amazing best friend Geninne could see the state I was in and very firmly convinced me to see my doctor. I clearly remember being in the consultation and I couldn't stop crying. The doctor said to me, 'How would you feel if I told you that tomorrow you were going to win the lottery'. I snuffled and said that it wouldn't make any difference at all. He then announced that in his opinion I was depressed and he put me on a course of antidepressants.

Those little pills made an enormous difference to me at the time. They gave me relief from over-thinking my misery and allowed me to see more clearly. I will remain eternally grateful to Geninne for getting me to the doctor that day.

Clearer thinking didn't actually give me any answers. It took the hard edges off the pain, which was a blessing in itself. The feelings of inadequacy and not belonging remained. I was still 'wrong' and I still couldn't work out how to make myself right.

I always described myself as being the black sheep of the family, even though in traditional terms, I was the most successful one, and the only one to go to university (albeit briefly). I had a good job and a relatively good income. Again: that juxtaposition, that dichotomy that I couldn't understand. Scared to go back to the pain, I stayed on the anti-depressants for a few years.

By 2017 I felt like I was on the edge of some precipice. I knew that I couldn't for much longer continue feeling the way that I had for years. Although I didn't know what the change was going to be or how I was going to achieve it, I knew that a change was absolutely vital and that it *was* going to come. I'd started to feel resentment towards cherished friends. My people-pleasing had reached the point where I was giving so much of myself and, without noticing it, was expecting the same in return ... and being disappointed. I was deeply unhappy in my job. Nothing was giving me any pleasure. I'd also started to go through menopause and was not having a great time with it. Life was pretty miserable and I was fed up with feeling fed up.

It was at this point that, serendipitously, through an old friend of mine Mandy, I met an amazingly strong warrior woman called Roni. Roni had been through some tough times and been helped by a process called Light Up. It had completely shifted her world and changed her life in ways that she couldn't ever have imagined. I was curious and keen to learn more.

In August 2017, Roni and her partner Alexis held a house-warming party at their new home, where I met Melanie Pledger. Mel and I connected instantly and I felt, and knew, that Mel was going to be an important person in my life. By the end of the evening, I'd made the decision to go through Light Up with Mel at her house in France.

Going through the two sessions, held on consecutive days, was for me a series of massive revelations, of rediscoveries.

The first was that *I* am my own soulmate and I would never feel lonely again as I always had me. Each step along the way helped me to see that I was different because we are *all* beautifully unique, and that I also belonged - to a wonderful, magnificent, amazing group of people who had been on this journey too. I could now see things in a different way, and could accept, enjoy and celebrate the dichotomy that had troubled me all my life. It was such a relief and a delight.

I remember lying on the bed after having completed the two sessions (for that is amazingly all that it takes), experiencing the feelings of being in love. I was, still am, completely in love with me and with life.

The revelations that I uncovered during those sessions enabled me to make some - for me - pretty incredible life choices. I quit my job, set up as a freelance project management consultant, stopped taking my anti-depressants and, most importantly of all, decided to train as an Activator. I knew this work was very special and felt that it was part of my future to take this work out and introduce it to as many people as I possibly could. There is so much pain, anger, fear, confusion and misery in the world, and it is obvious to me that I have a part to play in dispelling that.

Since then, everything has changed, and I am more me than I have ever been. The feelings of inadequacy are gone. I am enough, I am me and I am glorious.

I see you, I love you

For all that you are

I am with you, to hold you

No matter how far

I hear you, I know you

Understand who you are

This wonderful brilliance

This bright shining star

I feel you, I trust you

You've got this, my friend

I am here to guide you

Till this journey's end

I see you, I love you

I hear you and know

I feel you, I trust you

Together we glow

BETH FLITTON

Beth Flitton Professional Activator

I am currently a Project Management Consultant and DNA Light Up Activator, living in Woking, Surrey with my gorgeous fur baby Coco.

I am very passionate about my friends and family (which includes the aforementioned cat!), my Am Dram hobby and, most importantly, spreading the work of Light Up. I became a Light Up Activator in 2018, having gone through the Light Up programme at the end of 2017, and life has changed beyond measure since, for me and those around me.

I was asked which 3 things I wish I'd known earlier in life and I can honestly say that I am perfectly happy that I have learned the things in the order in which I learned them. Life has not always been easy, and I would not be here, in the place that I am right now, if I hadn't had experienced the difficulties. I definitely know now to embrace my beautiful uniqueness and that I love me, and that is the most important thing.

I was delighted to be able to share my message in this book, to reach out to anyone who has felt different in their life and not understood why, for those who have felt like they are not enough, and to let you know that you are absolutely enough, you are beautiful and unique and glorious. I dedicate my chapter to all of those people and look forward to meeting you on your journey at some point.

7

BOLLOCKS TO ANXIETY

NOW I'M DOING WHAT I LOVE AND LIVING MY DREAM.

Stepping out of the only world I'd known for over twenty years was terrifying. How would I look after my family, pay the bills, secure my future? The initial joy and relief at freeing myself from the toxic people who had drained my soul on a daily basis was soon replaced with paralysing fear.

Owen's Story

My journey started in a small room in Leeds, West Yorkshire, in 1999, with the words 'Please can you fix me?'

A vigorous nod, tears and a huge bear-hug followed. That single moment opened the door to a new way of thinking, communicating, feeling, seeing and ultimately living - and lessons were learnt that have stayed with me every day since.

Fast forward fourteen years. Another door was about to be opened, this time via a Skype call between Sheffield and a small village in France. In just under twenty four hours I was heading into the most important interview of my life. I knew my stuff, I had the right credentials and my experience was comparable to anyone else who would challenge me for the role.

BUT - I had a secret.

I suffered from anxiety. After years of working myself into periods of ill-health, all for the benefit of large 'enough is never enough' corporations around the world, I'd neglected my mental health and allowed myself to burn out. Now anxiety consumed my mind. A racing heart-rate, moments of disassociation, a dry mouth and words falling out in a jumbled mess were all regular and unwelcome guests in my life. How the hell was I going to get through this interview?

They say that when the student is ready the teacher appears. And so it happened for me. A chance Facebook connection, and before I knew it I was again facing the effervescent grin of my spiritual mentor Mel on my computer screen. She had something new to share with me. It seemed it could answer my prayers and, best of all, the solution was 'already within me'.

Looking back, I feel privileged to have been one of the first guinea pigs of what would become DNA Light Up. My memory of how it unfolded is a bit foggy now. I recall feeling a surging energy as I engaged with my light and met 'Frank' for the first time. I know that for the next week I walked taller than a giant and smashed every challenge into oblivion. I aced the interview, secured the job and celebrated my new found strength, courage and light. Anxiety be damned!

Then the challenges of the job and daily routine took over. In a month or so, I'd lost touch with 'Frank' and forgotten how it felt to be so powerful. I was ashamed. How had I let such a gift erode away? Had I taken it for granted? Been lazy in not keeping it up?

Whatever the cause, I soon returned to 'managing' my anxiety, fighting my way through the challenges I faced in an unforgiving role, working for an unhealthy company. Occasionally Frank would enter my mind and I would attempt to reconnect, with mixed results. Some days I could feel his power within. On others, the gaping hole he'd left felt bottomless. So I dug in and kept on going.

Fast forward a few years and my life changed again. I became a dad for the first time. My own father passed in a matter of weeks from his initial diagnosis. And the business I'd devoted my life to decided they needed a 'new direction'.

For years I'd compromised my values and ignored the unease gnawing at my gut, as dedicated people were overlooked and large director bonuses manifested sports cars and holiday homes. On a number of occasions, I was even told I was too honest for my own good, that we should only ever tell The Board what *we* want them to know. *Never the truth.*

It was time to walk away.

Stepping out of the only world I'd known for over twenty years was terrifying. How would I look after my family, pay the bills, secure my future? The initial joy and relief at freeing myself from the toxic people who had drained my soul on a daily basis was soon replaced with worry of what lay ahead. I was, after all, a 'worrier.'

I talked to my dad a lot, visiting almost daily the site where we'd spread his ashes, my young son strapped to my back. 'What am I going to do dad?' 'Where do I go from here?' 'I'm scared dad. How can I protect my family without work? Please help me.'

Cue the universe, and another innocuous social media post reconnected me with Mel and started my journey back to the light. Mel had been such a pivotal force in my life. We talked for hours, reminiscing about the journey we'd shared for almost two decades and shedding tears of sadness and joy.

I was desperate to experience the now fully-formed process of Light Up. Having heard the amazing results that were unfolding across the UK and France I wanted to believe that Light Up had the power to change lives forever, not fade away like 'Frank'.

I wanted in, but I also wanted to push myself. If I was going to experience the full power of Light Up, it had to be with someone other than Mel. I'd walked across fire and glass with Mel. I'd jumped off bridges despite a crippling fear of heights. I'd bent steel rods on my neck in her garden. I could do anything with Mel in my corner. Now it was time to experience Light Up. *Without her? F***!* Could it work with someone else? Would it stick? Could I enjoy the benefits for life?

Enter the wonderful human being, part of the Light Up team, who is now my friend and activator for life.

Exploring the principles and process of Light Up with the benefit of structure helped me to find 'Hummer': my enormous, floating, golden cylinder that spins and hums as it slowly turns, protecting me from all sides and radiating energy, joy, light and love. He is me and I am him.

There are days when I forget to connect to him and those days always remind me of his absolute power.

In my first 'Button Up' session my activator asked me if I'd noticed much difference since Light Up. I replied with the fact it had been subtle and nothing extraordinary - but I'd adopted the change in focus and was turning worrying thoughts into positive energy. After months of worrying about money and feeling incredibly frustrated by the lack of commercial success that my debut novel had enjoyed on Amazon, I'd given in and put my faith in the universe.

And I was able to share the news I'd been offered a publishing deal, unsolicited and completely out of the blue. A publisher had found me on Amazon, read my story and was offering me a multi-book deal. *'So nothing much has happened in the last two weeks then?'* she asked me with a wry smile.

And so it continues. Tuning into my true self, 'Hummer' has allowed me to find gratitude in all of life's events, realising that each has something to help guide me on my journey, good and bad.

Recently I stood up to talk about my business in a public arena and was overwhelmed by anxiety for the first time in over five years. I was babbling and speaking incoherently as I disassociated from the words leaving my mouth - as if hearing someone else speaking close by.

Kicking into survival mode, my plan was to use one of the many coping mechanisms I'd conjured up over the years.

As I stood contemplating which excuse to share with the room, I found myself in the moment choosing to finally tell the truth. No more tricks, no more lies, no more shame.

But I couldn't do that surely?

Yes I could and *YES I bloody well did!*

I explained to all those eyes staring back at me, wondering what the hell was going on, that I'd just had a panic attack. I took a moment to let it settle in the room and for my heart rate to drop, and then carried on. As I finished and sat down, despite my new found freedom, I fell straight into an old habit, rushing to judge myself and my perceived weakness - as had been the case each time this had happened before.

I immediately began writing down all the things *I'd done wrong* that could have caused the attack. It had to be my fault. And it was a very bad thing that *shouldn't* have happened. And *why* did I tell the truth? Why not cover it up like before? *Idiot!*

Then something amazing happened: after the event had concluded, people began approaching me to share their own experiences of the same thing.

Driving home, I contemplated why this had happened. A few days of beating myself up ensued. I didn't realise it at the time, but I was stuck in the old habit of thinking about the attack and reliving it over and over, as opposed to tuning into 'Hummer' to understand its true nature.

As the memory of the moment and the shame that came with it finally began to fade, a sense of pride appeared in its place. I had finally spoken out, finally admitted to mental health issues - issues that had never actually stopped me delivering outstanding results in any of my roles. So why had I been so worried about sharing my challenges with people in the past?

I realised for the first time that I'd finally dropped the mask I'd worn for years and I was once again being true to myself. It was so clear to me in that moment: *'This is what I'm supposed to be doing with my business - helping people with the same challenges in life'.* By facing it head on, the fear had no power over me anymore.

As I continue on my journey forward, I know I'm on the right path. I'm doing what I love and living my dream life, a gift I'm grateful for every day. It's a challenging path without the security of a monthly pay-packet - *and I wouldn't change it for the world.* I'm working with people whose lives I can really benefit and enrich, I'm writing my second novel with a third out later in the year, and I'm home to bath my boy - every single night! No corporate salary can ever match that.

I trust in Hummer because he is my true self and I trust in the process because it's led me to my true path. No more lying to myself. No more values in conflict. No more gnawing at my gut. No more toxic influences in my life.

My journey has just begun and there will no doubt be bumps in the road. And I will always remember my activator's words: *"See the challenges as confirmation you're on the right path. It's better to be green and growing - than ripe and rotting!"*

OWEN RYAN

For twenty years I worked in radio and entertainment across the UK and Australia, collaborating with household names, celebrities and music icons, accumulating a host of international writing and radio awards.

After reaching the top in my field, with all the trappings that come with corporate success, I still felt unfulfilled. Living my life on planes and trains, rarely home for bath-time and exhausted by the time the weekend came, the gnawing feeling in my gut continued to grow.

Finally, when I could ignore it no longer, I took a moment to stop and listen to my my true self, and in the summer of 2018, decided it was time to make my goals a reality:

- Be a loving, present husband and dad to my wife Kim, and son Vaughan.
- Become a full-time, published author.
- Help others find their true potential.

Focusing on what really matters helped me unleash my own power and in less than a year, I secured a publishing deal with my debut thriller 'Deadly Secrets', released this summer under my pen name OMJ Ryan, and the follow up due out later in the year. And I've set up my own coaching business in my beloved North East, unlocking the potential of business leaders and individuals, to help them enjoy more balanced, successful and fulfilling lives.

Most importantly of all, I now choose how much I work and with whom, to ensure I'm there for my family every day, living my dream life.

8

BOLLOCKS TO WALKING ON EGGSHELLS

I'M NOW A BIGGER AND BETTER ME THAN I'VE EVER BEEN.

I've travelled to the ends of the earth, quite literally, to get away from me and to hide from myself.

Sarah's Story

I'm finally beginning to believe that I am enough.

My childhood was quite unremarkable. I was bullied a couple of times - who wasn't, eh? I developed my people pleasing tendencies young. I was the bright one, the one who would do well at school. Except I didn't.

My sister was the star of the show and I was the one who never quite lived up to expectations. We moved around a lot and being the one who got very little of the attention at home, I found there was no reason to excel. It wasn't worth the effort and it felt like no one actually cared anyway. I made friends, and none of the friendships really lasted. As soon as I started to feel comfortable, we moved again.

This developed into a self fulfilling prophecy: I didn't feel like I fitted in, and so I didn't. I now know that I actively put myself in situations where I wouldn't be known. I moved away from home as soon as I'd finished A levels and went off to be an au pair in Vienna. When that didn't feel right, I came home. My room had already been given to my sister.

I fell in love with a man who embodied the 'not fitting in'. I told myself it was because he had the most amazing dark brown eyes. Seven years we were together, during which time I walked on eggshells. I became what I thought he wanted me to be. It was a relationship where I felt utterly powerless. He had total control and I guess I just got used to that feeling. I became isolated from everyone. He was never physically abusive to me and I made (so many) excuses for the way he was, based on his upbringing and religion. I believed I would only get out of the relationship if he died.

It's quite amazing really that, despite how unhappy and small I felt, I went on to train and qualify to be a nurse. It seems that all my life, underneath all of this self doubt, there was a strength that kept showing me who I truly was. I just wasn't listening. I got into the habit of building up walls and barriers around my true self, as a way to protect myself. I felt like no one would want to know me for myself. It's been bloody difficult to grow out of that.

I never reached out for help because I felt unworthy of it. I just tried to help everyone else. I put my value in what I could do for others and looked to others for validation. I was a people pleaser to the point of self harm, going out of my way to make sure that everyone else was happy, and more especially that I wasn't. Because only if everyone else was happy was I okay. I'd done my job and I could fade into the background.

I loathed being the centre of attention. Or at least that was what I told myself. Because why would anyone want to hear what I had to say or choose to be bothered with me when there was always someone more important, or prettier, or cleverer around that *was* worth listening to.

I physically kept running away, putting myself in more and more challenging situations where I had to work my arse off to survive. My life has been a history of always working harder, faster, than anyone else, and still beating myself up for not being better.

It's hilarious how I've travelled to the ends of the earth, quite literally, to get away from me and to hide from myself. And you know what? I'm actually pretty awesome! (Can you tell I lived in America for a while?!)

So what has Light Up given me? I've begun to notice that I've started to value myself. I've discovered that I *am* worth something, in fact I'm worth a lot, much more than I ever imagined.

I remember as a small child, in my earliest memories, being able to *be* pretty much anything I chose to be. I had the feeling that I could do *anything*. If I just got the recipe right, I could make amazing perfume out of water and rose petals. If I got that cape right or that jump right, I was sure that I could actually fly. All that was needed was the right take-off. I had no fear, no worry that it wouldn't work out. The only limitations I had were actually non-existent.

And then life got in the way.

I don't know if you remember the programme 'Mister Benn', the black suited, bowler hatted man who used to go into a fancy dress shop, put on an outfit and come out *as* that person. I feel as though I put on so many costumes as I went through school and adult life. They became heavier and heavier and I never felt able to take them off. I fitted myself into all those roles: pupil, friend, student, teacher, worker, nurse, mum.

And with each incarnation the costumes became heavier and I became smaller and more shrunken inside them. And that child was gone.

What Light Up has given me is the ability to take these costumes off. It's given me a way to get back to that child and all her infinite potential. It's reconnected me with the possibility of just being me, with permission to be open, to grow, to be bigger and to be myself again.

I've realised that my people-pleasing was one hell of a habit and that I'd placed my value solely in what I was able to do for others. And you know what? I have the power and I have the strength to be me and not to do that, if and when I choose.

I'm not saying it's been easy, that it's been a magic wand or that I don't go back into those costumes occasionally. What it's given me is a way to take them off again and be completely me.

We all have this strength, this inner super power, this ability to *be* whatever we choose. Every single one of us. And I know that however I'm being, it's okay. It's okay to feel crappy, it's okay to feel fed up. What's *not* okay is to carry that with me and suffer for it and wear it and hold on to it and become squashed by it. Now I can notice how I'm feeling, I can give myself a little nudge, and I can take that costume off again.

It seems now that we are constantly 'on', always at work, always trying, always under stress, always struggling and under threat. Gone are the days when life was simple and our threats were short lived - they arrived, we dealt with them and they disappeared. We fought the bear, we protected our family, we hunted for food and then we relaxed. Now we're constantly under threat, we're 'on' all the time. It's a pressure with no release.

We're brought up and conditioned to believe that we should do all that we can and be the very best we can be. We should work like machines because sleep is for when we're dead. I'm sure now that it doesn't need to be that hard. Even machines don't continue to work when they're constantly switched on.

If we leave our laptop switched on for days, just shutting the lid on it, it will stop functioning after a relatively short time.

It won't switch off or on and we end up forcing it to reboot. We humans are just the same. In my job as an occupational health nurse, I'm finding this more and more. I speak to people everyday who are struggling, burnt out, physically unwell. What else can we expect when we never switch off, when we're completely disconnected from ourselves?

The body eventually shuts down and we become ill, physically or mentally. We're forced to reboot, take time off and download the updates.

I now have the tools to spot this in myself, the awareness to notice it and the power to do something about it. I've discovered the 'off' switch. I have within me all the tools to reboot, download the updates whenever it suits me, and keep myself whole.

What do I mean by all this?

Have you ever noticed how thinking about things, working them out, weighing up the pros and cons, never actually gives us an answer? It's actually almost always a Google search to the worst case scenario. Our brain fills in the gaps, searches out the experience we're looking for and then provides it for us. At best it gives us a stick to beat ourselves with and at worst it leaves us with no hope.

I remember as a child crouching under the bed playing hide and seek. No matter how hard I tried, the more I thought about it, the louder my breathing became. I mean, without thinking about it I breathe pretty well - in fact I'm a bit of an expert at it! Yet laying there under the bed in the dark, concentrating on my breathing, it became impossible not to sound like a steam train. Weird huh?

Everything in life is made harder by thinking about it.

I now know I can go within, to something deeper. Did you know that trusting our gut has been scientifically proven to be the best course of action?

A few years ago my life was thrown into disarray. I was working offshore in western Africa on a twenty-eight-day rotation when I became really ill. I couldn't stop vomiting, I lost loads of weight and I was permanently exhausted. I self diagnosed with an ovarian cyst or an ulcer. Funnily enough I had again gone straight down the Google search to the worst case scenario.

When I eventually went to the hospital after five days of not keeping anything down, even water, I found out I was pregnant.

So we moved back to the UK. I had no job. I found work when my little girl was two months old, working for the nastiest person I have ever had the misfortune to meet, a gold standard sociopath. And she finished me off, she broke me.

After eighteen months I left and began the process of rebuilding myself. I read books. I looked into ways to improve myself. I got into self development. And still I felt crap. I was beating myself up for not feeling better. I'd get all hyped up by things I'd read or listened to, and then just find I still couldn't believe in *me*. I couldn't understand why, no matter how many times I learnt what the cause of my problem was, I couldn't seem to change it or shift myself out of it.

Light Up has helped me to do that. To grow and to find myself, a bigger and better *me* than I've been since I was a child. In fact more me than I've ever been.

Training as a DNA Activator has strengthened me even more. It has deepened that belief that I am someone worth knowing and it's also given me the way to help others to reconnect with themselves too. Hey, now I'm the ultimate people-pleaser because I can show people how to be themselves!

I'm now on a mission to light up the world so we can all know what it is to be ourselves and to realise how amazing we really are.

I'm sure that the idea that we only use twenty percent of our brain is really not the truth. I'm certain that we're using our brains in completely the wrong way. The brain is a beautiful tool ... and it's only a part of us. In fact our head is actually twenty percent of our body, only twenty percent of US. What we are not yet using is *all* of us.

I am now, with Light Up, well on my way to being whole and being me.

SARAH RHODES

Sarah Rhodes Professional Activator

A mum, a nurse, a runner, a woman ... me.

I've been in nursing now for 25 years, from A&E to Occupational Health, via oil rigs and cruise ships. My passion has always been helping others. Often to my own detriment.

As a Light Up Activator, I am confident that this is the right way for me. I can be who I am, and truly reconnect people with themselves. The rest is just plasters, band aids and masks.

My chapter is dedicated to my daughter Charlotte, my shining star, my heart and my world. My greatest achievement will be to have her grow up believing in who she is and that who she is much more than enough.

9

BOLLOCKS TO CONFORMING TO EXPECTATIONS

NOW I TRUST MYSELF AND LOVE MY OWN POWER!

I *was nineteen and living alone in London when I became pregnant. This was 1964 and I was about to become a statistic, 'an unmarried mother'. 'You can't have it,' my friends said. 'It'll ruin your life.'*

Judith's Story

How did it all begin?

In 2012 I was at Jonzac, a beautiful spa town in the Charente, enjoying a three week stay with two hours of spa treatments every day, wonderfully relaxing and great for my arthritis. Mel came down for a couple of days and shared the apartment I had rented. One evening we were playing with 'I am', recognising that wherever we went with it, it always came back to us, that the answer was always there, within us. Was that the beginning? Was that about finding our light?

The journey had begun before then, though. It was in May 2009. I was at a 'Ladies Lunch', not something I would normally go to. I tended to avoid gatherings of English expats in this lovely corner of south west France, but my brother had said he would pay for me, and my lovely French friend, Ginette, had agreed to come. In the event Ginette couldn't make it. She'd just started a course of chemotherapy and was finding it difficult to eat. So I went on my own and met Mel for the first time.

As we sat with our aperitifs, basking in the spring sunshine, we warmed to each other and found, as the meal progressed, more and more things in common. In the normal course of events neither of us would have been there, but we were and I am so glad it happened that way. Just a few weeks before, Mel had split from her husband of ten years and was on a steep and difficult learning curve as she uncovered his sociopathic behaviour.

Some years before I also had experienced the aftermath of marriage to a sociopath. During the healing process I had kept a journal, often turning to writing during sleepless nights. And so I advised her to 'write it out' and she started the blog that was later to become her book, 'I'm Still Standing'.

We had other things in common too, both of us having worked in the field of personal development. I'm twenty years older than Mel and, like her, have always loved working with people, encouraging them, and myself, to stretch and grow and explore where life could take us. In the early eighties, coming back into the work arena as my children became more independent, I found myself working in a residential centre for ex-offenders.

It was here that I first became involved in counselling and personal development work, loving both the training and the work. It was shift work, involving late evenings and weekends, and took a toll on my first marriage. Eventually my husband and I split up and as a single parent it was important to have more regular hours.

I found a new job with the youth service working with young unemployed people in rural Surrey. I became known as 'the lady with the yellow mini-bus'. The lack of a job was often the least significant of the problems these young adults felt and I found that my counselling skills were useful. I took advantage of the training that was offered and undertook a two-year certificate course in counselling at the

HPRG (Human Potential Resource Group) at the University of Surrey.

I loved the work I did with the HPRG and went on to take many more short-courses including assertiveness and the training for trainers in assertiveness. Teaching assertiveness took me in another direction: adult education with the local authority. All the new teachers were asked to attend the enrolment evening and I found myself sitting at a desk watching the queue of potential students file past to enrol in the various courses. This was the mid-eighties.

'Assertiveness!' I heard someone say, 'Isn't that what Adrian Mole's mother does?'

'Heavens!" her companion exclaimed, 'my husband would never let me do that!' I knew I was in the right place.

Last night, thirty years on, I tried to work out why I was feeling so low. Since Light Up I know what to do. My Light is called Cedric – no reason, just the name that flashed into my mind at the moment the switch was turned on. I called on Cedric last night when I was aching and feeling a grey cloud enveloping me. At that moment I didn't find his answer at all helpful.

'Let me go back to sleep,' he said. I couldn't sleep. Cedric usually appears as a cluster of diamonds, bright against a dark blue velvet background. Last night he was a small shrivelled black prune. I didn't argue, I let him sleep and I fell asleep, too.

I dreamed that I was sitting up high in a lecture theatre. Way down at the front was a panel of four or five erudite professors talking about fashion. 'I'm dressed by Alice!' I heard myself say, loudly and clearly. There were looks of shock and horror exchanged among the group. There was, amongst the audience, a rumble of friendly voices that broke into the sound of applause. I was aware that I was shining, lighting up the lecture theatre. When I woke in the morning the grey cloud had passed and I knew again that I was on the right path. Thank you, Cedric.

Throughout my life there were moments when I was guided by my inner voice, by flashes of enlightenment. I know now that that was Cedric before I had thought about him or given him a name.

I love the Robert Frost poem that ends:

Two roads converge in a wood and I –

I took the one less travelled by

And that has made all the difference.

I was nineteen and living alone in London when I became pregnant. This was 1964 and I was about to become a statistic, 'an unmarried mother'. Not just that, the father of my baby was black, an African politician whose country was on the verge of gaining independence. A white wife would not have blessed his career and, as my mother had already pointed out, nice girls didn't date black men.

'You can't have it,' my friends said. 'It'll ruin your life.' In December of that year I gave birth to my beautiful son. My mother was besotted by her first grandchild and supported me in the best way she could. His father was back in his home country. I saw him only once more; he was in London briefly and needed money. I didn't give it to him.

Having my lovely son didn't ruin my life, it just changed the direction. I didn't go to university as I had planned but I did get there, thirty years later. Right then, I needed a job that would allow me to support my son. The pay gap was very real and I needed 'man's' wages, so I went into the Civil Service where equal pay was already a reality. It was there that I met Allan, my first husband. He was kind if not exciting, thirteen years older than me and still living at home with his parents. I needed a husband, a father for Toby, and he needed a wife. He was a good choice at that time and together we made a good, safe and secure home for us all and for Toby's two brothers who followed.

Perhaps it was inevitable that as the younger boys grew to be teenagers and Toby was looking at leaving home for university, we should grow apart. Allan was contemplating a comfortable retirement and I wanted adventure. In 1979 we moved from suburban Surrey to a more rural life in north Hampshire. I was involved, with some success, in showing and breeding dogs and, bitten by the self-sufficiency bug, spurred on by the TV series The Good Life, I longed to have a goat and enough space for the dogs and a vegetable garden.

It was here that Chance (with a capital C) stepped in. That summer we'd been looking for a new place to live within an hour's travelling time from Allan's Whitehall job. It was the end of the school holidays and for a final treat we were going to see the Victory in Portsmouth. Half way down the A3 Rupert decided he needed a comfort break so we stopped in Liphook and, as was my habit that summer, I looked in the window of the estate agent on the corner, Messenger, May and Baverstock. That was how we came to live in Downs Cottage and life was never quite the same again.

The eighties were a kaleidoscope of emotions, trials, adventures and change for us all. Sometimes I chose to ignore my inner voice, to my cost, and sometimes I followed where it led. At the beginning of the decade we were exploring a new area, new schools for the boys and new work for me. For Allan it was just a longer journey to Whitehall. By the end of the decade, Rupert and David were at university in Leicester and London while Toby was at university in Glasgow. Allan and I had divorced. We had both remarried, although my second marriage was short-lived and I was again in the process of divorce.

We had dipped into self-sufficiency after the move. I'd owned a goat, three at one stage, as well as chickens and even turkeys one year. In the September following our move, I went to the newly opened Bohunt School to enrol in an evening class. It was to open a door onto a whole new adventure.

I was trying to choose between a sociology course and an introduction to self-sufficiency. I remember my twin brother Andrew saying 'Self-sufficiency sounds much more fun', and it was. Teaching the course was Susan Dixon. Susan and her husband Tony have been close friends ever since. This year it will be forty years of wonderful, supportive friend-ship both in England and here in France.

At the beginning of the nineties, with the boys all away at university, I left Downs Cottage and my traumatic marriage and moved in with Susan and Tony. I stayed with them for a year before moving to a cottage by the railway at Grately on the Wiltshire/Hampshire border.

For the first time since my teens, I was living on my own. Although difficult, it was a great learning experience and I was able to explore my creativity as never before. I had the space and time now to get more involved in some of the personal development stuff I could only touch on during the chaos of the previous decade.

I had been away for a couple of days on a Gestalt weekend. Having had an amazing breakthrough, recognising and resolving the issues I had with the sister who had died before I was born, I was feeling very much in my own space when I opened my front-door and tripped over the post on the mat. One of the letters was an advertisement, addressed to the previous occupant – a creative writing course at a centre on the island of Skyros in Greece. Within a few days I had organised finance and was booked in. When I came home after that magical holiday I knew that I was a writer.

It was at Skyros that I met Simon, who was to have a profound influ-ence over the course of my life. He taught me so much about myself; he was a friend, a guru, a companion, never a lover. At the time that was difficult for me but so, so important, too. I spent time at his cottage in the Welsh countryside, a few miles outside Aberystwyth.

Walking along the seafront past the Old College one day, I happened to mention that I would have loved to go to university. 'Well,' said Simon, a Cambridge graduate with a PhD, 'It's not too late!' It was another turning point. Two years later, and two months after my fifty-first birthday, I became an undergraduate, and went on to graduate in theatre, film and television studies in 1998.

By this time my house in Grately had been sold and the boys were all doing their own thing. Toby was married and had been living in Japan for some years. David, also married, was finding his feet in the business world in London, and Rupert and his small son, my first grandchild, were living in Ireland.

I toyed with the idea of further study. It didn't fit. I spent time in Ireland, with Rupert and on my own, giving myself space to find the next path to travel. My friends Susan and Tony had moved to France at the same time that I went on to university. I went to stay with them, again and again. In 1999 I went three times. On the third occasion, Susan and Tony picked me up from Poitiers Station. We hadn't driven out of the car park before a new world had opened up!

'Samantha's bought the house at Le Pouyaud and wants you to live in it!' Susan announced. And that was how I came to live in France.

It was a dark January morning, three weeks after we had celebrated the turn of the century, when the ferry pulled into St Malo. I collected my car and drove into my new life in the Charente. I had no money and only vague ideas of how I was to support myself. I had discussed with Samantha the idea of running the house at Le Pouyaud as a B and B. Susan was setting up a business selling houses to the English, who at that time were flocking to France in search of their dreams and I found my role in writing the descriptions of the houses for the English market. I'd found where I wanted to be and, although life was financially precarious, I knew I was in the right place.

This week I begin my twentieth year in France. When in 2004, Susan's daughter Samantha decided to sell the house in Le Pouyaud, I moved to my present home, still in the same commune. Thanks to the help of my twin brother I now own it and live here with my two beautiful dogs while he lives nearby. My sons are still scattered around the world with homes in Japan, Sweden and the UK and I have two grandchildren in each country.

Since going through Light Up in 2015, decisions have been made more confidently and more easily. For me it didn't come all at once. Between

2015 and 2018 I went through Light Up three times, and each time my Light revealed more of itself as I came to understand and know the me that I am.

Looking back at my history, I know that at times there has been confusion, between my head and my heart, between the expectations of others and my own desires. Always with me there has been an inner strength guiding me: call it intuition, call it my soul, call it what you will. Sometimes I've forgotten it's there or chosen to ignore. It takes some getting used to. Light Up has taught me to get to know it, to befriend it, to trust it and to use it.

We all have our own ways of describing our Light. Often there aren't words, not to begin with. That's why we draw it. When I drew mine I found a heap of diamonds in the centre. Those diamonds are my family, my three sons and my six grandchildren, my twin brother and my close friends. When I play the games we learn in the Light Up programme and I grow my Light – wow! How powerful is that! How powerful am I!

JUDITH MACARTHUR

JUDITH MACARTHUR

Judith MacArthur – Professional Activator

I am retired now and living in France. After bringing up my family of three sons I worked with ex-offenders, then with disadvantaged young people before taking early retirement to do a full-time degree in Theatre, Film and Television Studies at Aberystwyth University. To fund my studies, thinking I needed a balance, I looked after rich old ladies, which gave me a different perspective on life. In January 2000, I came to France seeking new adventure.

The property market was booming and having always wanted to write, I found myself writing interesting and hopefully amusing, details of the properties on offer. As the ex-pat community grew bigger, I became aware of the need to become integrated in this rural community and I set up an Anglo-French Association which is still going strong fifteen years on.

I have always, ever since I can remember, been passionate about injustice in any shape or form. As a young woman, back in the sixties, I campaigned against discrimination. I attended anti-apartheid rallies and read the New Statesman, acknowledging in a conservative world that my views were left of centre. Moved by the passion and suffering of the suffragettes, I was determined that I would never waste the vote they fought so hard to win for me and other women. It was an important factor when, in 2010, I decided to take dual nationality so that I can continue to exercise my right to vote in France.

I wish now that I'd recognised the advantages I had rather than feeling weighed down by the labels I felt I'd been given. I wish I'd recognised earlier that I was actually a pioneer with the grit and determination to live by my principles. I knew early on that there was more to me than I dared to show and yet there was always the other part that told me I wasn't quite good enough.

My light has been and always will be an integral part of the me that makes me who I am. When DNA Light Up found me, I recognised how simple and straightforward it could be to reach in to that light and use its strength to be the best person that I can be and that this is my choice.

My chapter is dedicated to all the people who, like me, felt they are 'Not quite good enough' in the hope that they will find their Light too, and know, for certain, that they are quite Good Enough.

10

BOLLOCKS TO ADDICTION, SELF-HARM AND SHAME

I AM MORE THAN ANY OF THE LABELS I WAS GIVEN – I AM ME, AND I AM FREE TO SHINE!

I'd become hell bent on killing myself. I was harming myself every day, using any means available

Emma's Story

My story? What does that even mean? My story? My journey? Finding myself? Who am I? What am I? What is my purpose in this game of life that doesn't come with a rule book?

It's a 'work it out for yourself, make it up as you go along' kind of game. This might not to be a problem for everyone. For me, it meant a childhood framed by fear.

I was born to parents who didn't seem to have been given the rule book either. They were born in the post war era, in an environment that wasn't the most nurturing, and they were dealt some shitty cards. So it's no surprise they gathered some bollocks along the way.

I was born a 'normal' baby, even though they'd suspected I had major problems. What this meant for me, during my childhood, was that my mum was constantly on guard for any signs that I might not be developing like other children. I don't have many memories before the age of age eight so I can't be sure how this felt. I do know that I grew up feeling different, as though I didn't ever belong. I had a constant feeling of fear, of woe, and I struggled to understand people and situations. And I felt misunderstood.

As I got older the label of 'problem child' stuck with me. It seemed I was always causing a problem. I was a strong character and always bucking heads with my parents. They didn't understand me and I didn't feel listened to. I was just a child, struggling with the 'seen and not heard' bit.

One day my parents told us we were moving to a completely different town. This was when my disconnect really started to take hold. We moved to a house that was lovely, in a sought after area. It was unfamiliar and the people spoke in a funny way, not like I did. Their accents were different.

I've never had lots of friends - I was never one of the popular ones. From the moment I arrived at my new school, my weight was pointed out as a problem. And so began my lifelong battle with the number on the scales. Before I knew it I'd begun to collect other people's views and opinions about me and my life.

Around the age of twelve or thirteen my life changed forever. I met a boy who took my innocence. And it changed me. He was both verbally and sexually abusive. His words rang heavy in my head and heart, and I believed them, I soaked them up like a sponge. Deep down I questioned whether those things really could be true, although by this point my light had dimmed to a flicker that simply wasn't strong or bright enough to argue with him. Instead, I became a player in his mind games.

Maybe you can relate to the effect of going along with another person's agenda, even though it goes against every fibre of your being. It causes 'disconnect' both externally and internally. Conforming to fit into his box, I became adept at detaching my mind from my body.

Whilst all this was going on, I was experiencing the usual struggles of becoming a teenager: hormones, conflicts with my parents and siblings, living in a family not gifted at communicating. I began to feel very lonely and started acting out. I was always searching, for what I wasn't sure, always seeking something, anything, to complete me or my situation. I was in total denial about what had happened to me - and what I was still allowing to happen - at the hands of my so-called boyfriend and 'first love'.

To cover up my pain I began experimenting with makeup, wearing enough to compete with a drag queen, and dressing in ways that would make me look older than my age. In fact I was immature and vulnerable. Desperate for confirmation that my reality wasn't just all the bollocks I'd already collected, I became an easy target for another predator.

My next life lesson came in the guise of a man in his thirties. I was not yet fourteen. This man must have been aware of my age - I'd used a child's bus pass to get on the bus. That didn't stop him from talking me into giving him my number. For nearly a year, he was the answer to my prayers. His words were balm to my ears and to my heart. He gave me the strength to stop seeing my 'first love'.

When I couldn't leave the house without my parents questioning me, I lied to him, inventing reasons why I couldn't meet him. His 'under-standing and patience' told me that he must really care about me. Looking back, all the alarm bells were there. He even advised me not to tell my parents anything as they wouldn't understand our 'love' and would do their best to stop it!

Everything in my life was starting to suffer. I wasn't equipped emotion-ally for the experiences I'd gone through - and was still going through. The secrets continued to accumulate and there was no-one I could to talk to. Externally, my education was a major casualty. Internally, my belief system, moral compass, confidence and self-esteem were all driven by or dependent on others.

I developed many different masks, depending on where I was, who I was with and their outlook on life. I've always been outspoken and I learnt to buck against this prison of my own making, walking around as though I didn't care. I pretended I could take care of myself and was in total control of everything. Inside, I was lonely, empty and always seeking to be, look, sound and think more like 'them'. I never actually achieved this and it was a tiring existence, pretending I wasn't wishing anything in the first place and doing my own thing because who wants to follow the crowd anyway! Confused? I know I was!

At sixteen, the predator no longer seemed to speak to me in such a loving way and the relationship was over. It was entirely my fault, he insisted, and I believed him. I left school as soon as I could, much to my parents' dismay. It was never a place where I felt I fitted in and I couldn't wait to get out. I took my mediocre grades and got a job.

I met a boy who was the polar opposite of the others. He was more my age - quiet, softly spoken, educated - and I went straight into the next relationship. In my search for love, to love and to be loved, it was inevitable that I would end up pregnant.

I knew I was never going to abort. I was seventeen when my son was born. I was a baby with a baby, still living at home with my parents. The boy who got me pregnant had left, never to be seen again. This was soul destroying for me. It confirmed everything I'd ever been told or felt about myself.

I discovered alcohol and drugs, and my desire to party far outweighed the responsibilities of being a mother. Whenever I could, I'd find child-care and go out and get drunk. Being drunk meant that nothing bothered me, I was no longer confused and my confidence would temporarily soar.

I was a single parent, struggling with life and all that entails. I never had enough money and was irresponsible with what I had. When I eventually moved out, I didn't have a clue what I was doing. I worked hard, played harder and soon found myself pregnant with yet another baby I couldn't afford, either emotionally or financially. By this point, I was using anything and everything to fill the void within me: food, work, gym, shopping, gambling, drugs, alcohol, tablets, sex and relationships. Anything!

For years, I struggled to balance work life with home life, party life with mum life. Depression, anxiety and eating disorders plagued me. I bumbled along pretending to be exactly where I'd chosen to be, all the while living like a fraudster, playing this game of life. The universe must have heard my silent screams for help. During all those sleepless nights alone in bed, my prayers must have been going somewhere. My life was about to change course in a really unconventional way.

I had a gastric bypass. Desperate times called for desperate measures, and my entire life had been a quest to fit into society's mould, which meant skinny! Skinny was going to solve it all for me. They say be careful what you wish for, because I became skinny. I also became addicted to prescription painkillers.

Fast forward a few months and I found myself in my first rehab and at the start of a new journey. Suddenly my life was under a microscope, every aspect open to being scrutinised. My reality hadn't changed, and yet after therapy, my perception of it had. I came out of rehab and found myself back in the life I'd left behind, back in my old roles. Only this time I was clean and sober.

I felt more lost and out of place than I ever had in my life. Nothing made sense to me. Suddenly I had to come to terms with my past. Owning and accepting my vulnerability wasn't something I ever wanted to do. I was grieving my losses and still not emotionally mature enough to deal with what had happened.

I went through a Twelve Step programme that took me on a journey of self-discovery. I looked at the patterns of behaviour that required changing and I was even more confused. These traits had kept me safe and I'd always considered them my assets. Now they no longer served me and I had to find alternative ways of behaving. It was all too much, too confusing and I couldn't decipher the bollocks from my truth. I couldn't cope.

I was to relapse many times.

In January 2015 I reached another pivotal moment, though I didn't fully understand the magnitude of it until much later. In the run up to this date, I'd become hell bent on killing myself. I was harming myself every day, using any means available: cutting myself, starving then bingeing and making myself vomit, accidental and deliberate overdosing, drinking copious amounts of alcohol and taking a dangerous cocktail of drugs, both illegal and prescription.

It all came to a head on January 5th when I collapsed in pain onto my bed after defecating and vomiting. My last thought was that I needed to get to my phone to call for help. I didn't feel well at all, unable to move or lift my head. My last visual memory was of my outstretched arm and hand. Then it went dark.

I was found by my partner, Ben, the following morning. He called an ambulance and I was rushed to hospital. Eleven days went by before I woke up. I'd been given a less than five percent chance of surviving. I had double pneumonia, heart, liver and lung failure, jaundice, anaemia, vomit on my lungs, and a major chest infection.

The doctors were apparently unsure if what I had taken would kill me, if what I was suffering with would kill me, or if what they had to medicate me with would tip me over the edge. I was put on fourteen different drugs and totally immobilised so that I couldn't move at all. They struggled to get any oxygen into my body.

I came round to bleeping, voices and a ceiling I didn't recognise. I attempted to touch my face and felt what I thought was a hole in my nose. I was terrified about how I'd tell my family this. I reached up again and my hand was stopped by a woman explaining that I was very ill in hospital. My mouth felt dry and stretched and when I tried to speak, I couldn't. The nurse told me to remain still and explained that I had lots of tubes coming out of my body.

The next few days were a blur, in and out of consciousness. I have few memories and the ones I have are bizarre: cats under beds, skittles coming out of my bum and buttons that weren't to be pressed. The day came to have the tubes removed from my neck, nose and throat. It was a very strange feeling and one I don't care to repeat.

I had to learn to use my vocal chords again. My throat was sore and dry. I was told it would take around two weeks and intense physio for me to begin to move out of bed. I wasn't having any of that - within two days I was walking, albeit with a frame, very slowly and very wobbly. I drove the nurses mad, continually asking them to help me get up. I don't know why I was in such a rush, I just hated the idea of my legs not working and that the ease of movement I'd previously taken for granted was no longer there.

I had to use a commode in the ward with just a curtain around me and the nurses had to help me wipe myself. It was very undignified. All I wanted was to shower and they wouldn't let me as I wasn't strong enough. Being washed with a wet wipe and a flannel for a very long time was taking its toll.

I was frustrated and fed up. Reading a magazine I'd fall asleep at the end of a sentence. My brain couldn't take things in. I couldn't co-ordinate a fork to my mouth and dropped food everywhere. I cried, wondering if I was ever going to recover fully. Everything was taking such a long time. There was one bonus - I'd forgotten I smoked! By the time I remembered, I didn't actually want to go back to smoking.

Finally I was allowed a shower, but I couldn't hold myself up. The nurse couldn't hold me alone and I ended up naked on the floor of the shower, crying. I was a woman in my thirties and I couldn't even do the basics for myself. I had to allow the nurses to pick me up! Not having control of myself whilst vulnerable and naked was not a nice feeling. The first time I was allowed to use the toilet and wipe myself was such a milestone that I cried.

From hospital, I went to a detox unit and completed a three week detox in ten days, putting myself in hospital four times because I was detoxing too fast. The pain was immense. I didn't see my family for over a month. I made it though.

Then rehab for four and a half months. There are many stories from my time there, lots of laughter, tears and snotty temper tantrums! I looked like an old age pensioner. To keep warm I had to wear thirteen layers and have a hot water bottle. I was yellow, struggled to hold my head up and couldn't run. (I found this out the hard way after nearly being run over by a bus crossing the road!) Walking upstairs took an age and I couldn't carry anything remotely heavy. I had to fight bulimia and the urge to turn back to cigarettes, drink or drugs.

I had to face demons and parts of my past that I'd denied because I felt haunted by them. I had to be accountable and take responsibility for my life, literally turning a hundred and eighty degrees in my thoughts, behaviours and actions. I had to heal myself and learn a whole new language for my life. What a mountain - one I wasn't sure I was going to manage to climb.

I came out and went back home. Suddenly I was Emma in many roles: woman, sober woman, mother, daughter, sister, partner, and friend. It was so easy for me to slip back into old behaviours and ways of thinking. However, now I didn't drink.

Little did I realise that I'd already made a soul contract with the universe which meant the 'work' had already started. What had felt so comfortable for so many years suddenly wasn't comfortable at all. I'd think and behave as I'd always done and would be left frustrated, confused and with lots of questions I didn't feel able to answer. My anger whilst sober was off the scale and I felt out of control.

I sought help, and attended an anger management course. Who was I? What was happening? Why wasn't life getting any easier? I felt life was shallow and I was searching for something beneath the surface.

By 2017, I was disheartened with life. My relationship with my partner was strained and it felt as though we were moving in different directions. I now understand why I became pregnant again. I was still searching for that missing link and the answer to all my questions.

Having a baby really wasn't the answer and deep down I knew that, and yet I also knew that having the baby was the right decision. After giving birth on my third sobriety birthday, (what a gift), I settled into motherhood again. It was easier than I'd expected and more difficult than I'd prepared for. It was like being a first time mum again, considering the fifteen year age gap between my last two.

I became thoroughly depressed and suicidal. If this was all life had to offer, then I was done! My mental health deteriorated and I got to a point where giving up my baby became an option, relapsing and/or ultimately killing myself was on the cards. What was wrong with me?! After reaching out for support, I sought relief by giving myself a year before reviewing my options.

Never doubt the power in asking the universe for help. Those words spoken in desperate times hold more power than is given credit.

DNA Light Up found me, via a friend who had trained to become an Activator, and I allowed her to take me through. I felt a little disappointed when there weren't bolts of lightning, ticker tape and fanfares and no instant tangible result! Was I really that 'broken' that nothing was ever going to get rid of this void?!

Life went on, and the days passed. After a week and about five different people asking what was different about me, I started to wonder if I'd grown an extra head. Nope, I hadn't lost weight, changed my make-up, coloured my hair or been on holiday. It must be an extra head then!

So what was different? I realised I'd been getting to sleep quicker and sleeping more heavily. I felt calmer, even amongst the chaos I was surrounded with.

How could just five hours (that's all Light Up took) have started to change my life so much and so quickly? Really ... what was happening to me? It felt at times as though I was going crazy. At times, it still does!

The familiar suddenly wasn't enough for me anymore. At this point in my life, I knew I was choosing to break the cycle of financial difficulty. I've always lived from month to month and never had any financial security. The one time I came into a lot of money, I blew the lot on drugs, alcohol and the disease of addiction!

It was suggested that I go to France to learn how to take people through the DNA process myself. I was still suffering with manic depression and feelings of not wanting to be here. I was continually questioning why I'd lived when others had died. Why had I been given a beautiful son, after the damage I had caused to my body, when there are couples out there who are not blessed with even one child? Here I was, an ex-junkie, who'd been given a third blessing.

Against everything practical and logical, I found myself on a plane to France. I definitely couldn't afford it, I was leaving my eight month old son for the first time for a whole week, I was not in the best place mentally and I felt real fear about meeting new people and going through the process. Would I be good enough? What was I thinking? Who did I think I was?

I remember sitting in the car, on the way to the place we'd be staying, and the question went through my mind, 'What the hell am I doing?' Straight after the answer came the reply: 'I am doing exactly what I am meant to be doing'. I felt in exactly the right place and calm in my decision.

Little did I realise that my time in France was going to change my life forever. It changed *me* forever. I confronted all of the bollocks I'd collected over the years, head on. No going round, I went through. I faced and felt it all. I was presented with opportunity after opportunity to be comfortable in myself, in my skin, authentic and true, without justification or apology.

On the plane home, I knew something magical was happening within me. And I chose to embrace it.

Once home, I found that setting boundaries, making decisions and speaking my truth was becoming my first language. My focus had shifted. I found that I could sense the disruption in others in my presence. I knew people could sense something was different and that I'd shifted.

I began taking people through Light Up, and with every experience I knew exactly why I'd been saved. My purpose in life was suddenly crystal clear. After being licensed and acquiring one label I *did* want, that of Professional Activator, I set to work.

What a journey it continues to be. It's a beautiful, difficult, painful and emotional journey of self-discovery. One I cherish, take very seriously and yet wear very lightly. I've found a simple joy in my life, and a peace I've never known. I have a softness and vulnerability about me that I've sought my entire life. I share laughter, genuine belly laughs, that cause my face to ache and my belly to wobble. Every day I grow more in my confidence and ability.

My mental health had held me back for so long and I'd lived in fear and darkness. I'd wasted precious time, wondering if I'd relapse or not cope and yet, year on year, I feel I am getting stronger.

I am forever grateful for what happened to me, because I wouldn't be where I am today without it. I discern who, what, when and where, choosing to surround myself with soul nourishing people, places and things. I have the power and control and I wear that unapologetically.

I am more than Bipolar, EUPD, Morbid neurosis, OCD, Unipolar, self-harmer, and addict/alcoholic. I, for sure, am more than the labels I have collected. I am me!

I have never been so certain that my purpose in life is to empower others to be their best self. To search out the 'broken' misfits who feel life to an extent that it hurts them and the others around them, the 'hopeless causes'. I'm going to work with people who are stuck, who know they're worth more than the boxes society insists on shutting them in. The ones who are trapped in life choices that lead to darkness and judgement, guilt and shame.

Together we will capture those moments that have to be felt to be believed and connect on such a deep level, that there is no doubt of the limitless magnificence within each of us. I will assist ANYONE in walking their authentic truth without question, and I will do this via the Twelve Steps and DNA Light Up.

For years, I lived in the dark, continuously in pain behind closed doors, desperate to fit into a box that wasn't me. I wore masks and lived in guilt and shame, pretending I was okay. Now the light is on and I intend to shine bright everywhere I go, lighting up as many people along the way as I can.

I see you, I am here, I will hold you. And together we will light up our world.

EMMA CHAMBERLAIN

Emma Chamberlain Professional Activator

I've worked in many roles over my working life so far, most notably in fraud prevention in an insurance company.

I have been searching my whole life for something that was within all along.

My passion and purpose is to share my light in a world that can be quite dark, searching out other lights, one person at a time.

Near death experiences can prove quite a game changer. Mine was, and yet whilst I could say I wish I knew then what I know now, I also know that my journey to this point is one I cherish. I could have done with knowing not to collect other people's bollocks or allowing it, or them, to dim my shine. And yet here I am, resilient and tenacious.

It's my life's mission to get this "work" out there, far and wide and I will not stop living this work. Its message is too important.

To all those little people, both in age and those trapped within grown up minds and bodies, disconnected from their limitless power, this is for you.

11

BOLLOCKS TO PANIC ATTACKS AND FEAR

LIFE IS NOW PEACEFUL. IT'S KNOWING, FEELING, BELIEVING AND LIVING MY TRUTH.

As a young person I had panic attacks and passed out when quite normal situations became so overwhelming that I went into meltdown.

Elaine's Story

I've come a long way in my forty-four years from the talkative and terrified girl I was during my childhood and adolescence. I was the child that had panic attacks, went into meltdown and passed out when quite normal situations became too overwhelming.

My background wasn't unhappy or tragic. My parents and all my family members were, and still are, amazing. I had, and still have, amazing friends, some of whom have stuck with me since childhood. I've experienced the highs and lows of life, like any person does. I've just processed things in my head differently to the majority of others! I remember how I had to force myself to do things that others would look forward to, because I'd be fearful that something would go wrong, something embarrassing would happen or I might even die!!!

Without me actually searching, people and situations were put in front of me to help me move forward, to allow me to choose a different way of reacting and living. The inner desire to re-find and use the confidence inside me was strong. I never blocked the help shown to me, even though at the time I didn't recognise it as help.

A school project prompted me to find an unusual subject to study, and mum said her friend Judy was a homeopath ... and so my first mentor and earth angel arrived in my life.

Bit by bit, situation by situation, I re-found myself and the courage I'd always had and just didn't feel at the time. Sometimes I amazed myself, especially when I did the hard work and won three international scholarships. After huge deliberation I accepted them and spent a year working in four different countries, including three months in the USA.

That was for me a huge decision, and a defining moment, because although lots of things went wrong, nothing embarrassing happened (well nothing I'll admit to here!) and I didn't die. What fun I had, what a truly amazing experience it was, and how many fabulous people did I meet. I might have missed out on all that if I'd let myself re-remember the younger days when I was too scared to take any risks at all.

So the quest to rediscover more of me was, and still is, a priority in my life. I mean who knows what might happen ... how hugely exciting is that!

Another amazing mentor in my life, Bernie, has said to me more than once: 'Your brain could power a small country - you've so much going on in there!' Therein lies my biggest challenge: to get out of my 'head' and to 'feel' what is important.

It took me over a year to make the decision to train to be a Bowen therapist in 2013. Self-doubt and over thinking nearly stopped me. Luckily that inner power that was always inside overrode my fears and I committed myself to one of the most amazing professional and self-development experiences of my life. Have you ever heard the expression 'fast and painful or slow and painful'? I always seemed to go for the slow and painful way of arriving at a decision! I now believe there doesn't have to be any pain at all.

It was, and still can be, a busy old place in my head when I regress to my old ways. I can be full of self-doubt, fear and low self-esteem. And there's also a large dollop of fabulous fun, a can-do attitude and lots of other wonderfulness - it's not all doom and gloom in there!

Another chance meeting at a charity event in 2017 was to take me into the 'world of me' like never before! It turns out that the amazing woman I met was a DNA Activator - and so my Light Up journey began.

Of course, true to form, it took me ages to make the decision to move forward with Light Up. Thankfully that inner pull was there to override the nonsense going on in my head. I'll never forget turning to my husband in the car on my way to my first session and saying 'I'm going to hand over money today and I've no idea what for. I don't know what's going to happen. And it feels important that I do this!' Already change was happening.

Life after Light Up is peaceful: it is knowing, it is feeling, it is believing, it is strong, it is powerful. It is living my truth. And it's not a magic wand - we don't live in a fairy tale Light-Up Land where nothing ever goes wrong because magic dust falls from the sky!

Now, when faced with situations where in the past I'd have got stuck, I have a new set of tools, and they always work (when I remember to play with them!). I find myself making decisions much more quickly - I tend to just 'know'. And when something requires more attention, I play with the tools I now have. I overthink much less and so the exhausting confusion isn't there. The fear that stalled me in the past is turning to excitement. It feels like I have the ability to process things differently in my brain because I've changed habits and now I feel before I think. It's brought a great deal of peace into my life.

Light Up has also been a tremendous help professionally. In Bowen therapy there are a huge amount of different movements as well as combinations of those movements, and it's always important that I give the best possible treatment to every client. Somehow through Light Up things have become clearer. I'm more concise in my decision making process in this area, and I believe it's because I feel and know, rather than just think!

I can also help clients on a different level using the tools I've been taught. As well as treating physical pain and conditions, I work with people with anxiety, depression and stress, and these new tools have become a part of my treatment process.

I've found myself being more direct in all areas of my life. I communicate powerfully when the situation requires it and I speak my truth. Sometimes in life it's important that things are said, important to take a stand and not allow ourselves to be walked over. Before Light Up I would have suppressed the urge to say what I felt for fear of upsetting the person who was actually upsetting me!

Now I have no fear in these situations and I say what I feel is important for me to say. I believe strongly that we all have different characters, different traits, and we won't always see eye to eye. For me, it's not about convincing others that my way is the right way. It's about standing my ground regarding my own beliefs, what is right and true for me.

ELANE CRONIN

After having an intense career in the poultry industry I finally found my passion in the form of Bowen Therapy.

Helping people heal is a very special way to spend my day and earn a living. Bowen and DNA Light Up work in harmony with each other helping the healing process on so many levels.

There are so many opportunities out there to help us now, there's never been an easy time to shine.

Don't hesitate to invite DNA Light Up into your life and experience the magic and sparkles - and try Bowen therapy, you'll be amazed at how you feel.

BOLLOCKS TO BEING DIFFERENT AND NOT BELONGING

NOW I WALK IN THE FULLNESS OF MY POWER.

People were a different matter. I didn't notice splinters of ice in their eyes straight away, but I knew I didn't belong.

Yuliya's Story

A life story is a potent form of magic. We have the power to erase, rewrite and transmute any and all of our experiences. Whatever story we tell ourselves becomes true, becomes us.

My own heart lies with adventure - daring voyages, halls of mirrors, losing and finding my way, and epic battles between light and darkness. For me, a tale worth sharing has to brim with courage, imagination and dreams written in the stars, so it can better serve to inspire our inner noble heroes.

I was born in the middle of a stormy night, as blizzards roamed the indigo sky sprinkled with faraway lights. I must have landed on the Snow Queen's sparkling coat tails as she was rising above the clouds, because for a few hours I was flicked back and forth between emerging into the life I was determined to have and returning into the infinite space as a spark of light. I stubbornly kept pace with the dream of opening my eyes in this world that swam in an ocean of stars, and no one was more surprised than my parents that I managed to hold on to the blizzard's tail and defy the Snow Queen's playful winds; especially as my twin sister didn't make the journey.

And so here I was, innocent freshly fallen snow, shimmering quietly and keeping hidden all the gifts that would grow within me. Loneliness would never be a problem - stars sang, books whispered and trees held my hands.

People were a different matter. I didn't notice splinters of ice in their eyes straight away, but I knew I didn't belong. My light bounced off their wall of mirrors, getting warped as it returned. The distorted image of me I was offered didn't feel true, and I knew then that something lived in me that did not fit in with the biases and beliefs of the world I encountered.

I was different. I had met the Snow Queen. From that time, like a pale new Moon, I only ever showed a fraction of my face and made a habit of always turning to the Sun in the way that reflected my light to the best advantage.

Around me life was hard. My parents' unhappy marriage, grandparents' nightmares of war, constant uncertainty and being unwanted in our own country were dragging on the heels of my family. Walking on black ice, they saw hardship and restriction everywhere. None of it had a home with me while I walked in tune with my memories of light, and for a while I was able to escape into the world of heroes and legends, and watching the stars at night. My real life happened away from the 'real' world.

Innocence unguarded eventually shatters. Soon it was time to test my resolve. Having made a few dramatic close escapes from crossing over the veil, I duly confirmed to the Universe that I was happy to stick around for a lifetime. Finally I engaged with the messy human experience and started getting bogged down in conditioning.

With no boundaries set, I found myself battered by squalls of resentment and unresolved conflicts that blew in from the ages and places belonging to those who walked before me. Slowly and surely I was pushed further off course, forgetting my power and magic and trading in luminescence for density. Sticks and stones slipped in between the gears of the engine to upset the balance at the appointed time.

Next to me, lights were going out - every few years one of the family walked through their final gate on Earth. As I turned twelve, my father unexpectedly followed them. My feelings were mixed, my mind blank.

As my mother picked up the pieces, life became about riding a thin sheet of ice on a turbulent sea. I started looking around for stable footing, fixing my eyes on the slippery ground rather than trusting in the hands that had already carried me over the abyss more than once. It was then that I learned to fear and freeze still the water of life. Living was hard, and now there were shards of grey ice living in my eyes, too.

Fortunately, what the eyes don't see the heart continues to recognise. At fourteen, light knocked on my door again and the encroaching wall of ice parted. I landed in the country of druids, philosophers and eccentrics and I knew, before my feet touched the ground, where my destiny made her home. I took everything in - the nature, the castles, the stained glass windows, the ancient music that swung open the doors on the deepest memories I could not trace, like a gust of wind knocking down a bale of hay that rolls through endless fields under the biggest sky I could ever get lost in.

I spoke freely, wore the biggest smile and knew it wouldn't be used against me. I fell in love with the soul of this land and left a coin in every fountain.

Coming back every summer, I studied, lived and went away to what used to be home. I became obsessed with education as my ticket to the dream land, studying all day and dreaming all night. The ground began cracking between my mother and I. She scolded me for looking tense and pried my hands apart when she happened on a panic attack. I continued to be a model student, running on the fire in my heart while the ice in my eyes was slowly conquering my mind. It was too bad that where I came from mental illness didn't exist, only weakness of character.

Fast forward a few years and I was packing a suitcase. My family quietly resented my choice; chances are they didn't know any better. It mattered little; I was already beat-up, gathering material for my apprenticeship in spiritual alchemy, and I had no bag space for any more family heirlooms.

In my mind I was steering my ship towards freedom; curiously, I didn't see that a blind sailor couldn't make a skilled captain. I was ready to pick up where others left off and disempower myself. Soon enough I cut myself off from my roots and created a new family, hoping to eclipse the shadow and keep the grey ice from reaching my heart.

Ten years and a few nosedives later, I arrived to my starless night of the soul right on time. The stars were there alright, eternal and resplendent as they first greeted me, but now invisible behind the storm clouds I fashioned out of my pain. My ship lay wrecked at the bottom of a frozen lake, enveloped by the deep arctic sky - a blanket of glacial stillness that muffled everything it touched.

Going with the flow of life was now a distant memory. I was a prisoner under the ice, a river bound by her own frozen waters. I wasn't going anywhere, and lying there in shards and pieces I couldn't make fit together, I had no choice but to simply stare into the night and start remembering - back to the beginning, to meeting the Snow Queen, to loving life and knowing who I was.

Giving up was out of the question, and not just for the sake of the pair of curious blue eyes fixed on me. There was other work to be done, and I persistently woke every day and summoned memory to my service in order to go full circle to joy and freedom, so I could teach the next girl in line to own the power that was her birthright.

Dark nights are beautiful things. When they pass, the light never loses its magic again. They are the ultimate test of our will to live on and transmute everything to light, that we may return to our original brilliance and genius, never again innocent of our creative potential.

With everything laid bare under the onyx sky I was once again able to travel light. Like the Sun in mid-winter, after a moment of stillness my trajectory swung inexorably back towards awakening. Leaning on a broken sword, I began tracing my way by the constellations in the back of my mind to the forgotten crafts and tools that would hammer my fragments back into shape.

The stars never gave up on me despite my blindness, and a while later the Sun rose high enough to show the path. I found my true family and the key to unlocking the potential entrusted to me. Out of nowhere, giant hands ripped my ship on its frozen chains from the glacier that had buried it under solid darkness, and for the first time I witnessed the true size of my vessel.

To welcome back the gifts breathing under my skin, I set about healing and realigning my sails. Nothing escaped the purge as I tossed overboard all that did not serve my True North, while my Divinity patiently led my Humanity by the hand back to where I belonged all along.

As transmutation became a habit, the trapped water of life began thawing and the weight squeezing my heart into a cage retreated day by day. Facing the mirror again and again without flinching, my mind regained its nobility and broke through the wall of unspoken lies that had separated me from my God-given power decades ago. My ship was ready for the adventure of a lifetime, this time with a captain guided by true-sight - a wizard, a shipwright and a guardian with no compunction about crossing blades with a wayward storm.

Leaving the old shores under a golden flag greeting the sunrise, I saw how far I had travelled. Stumbling through the starless night on instinct had been the making of me. Like the Snow Queen, I could now ride storms without holding on and recall winds from every corner of the world to aid my voyage. I learned to stand alone as a Woman and as a

Soul, and became my own Tree of Life reaching to others across the River of Change.

The more I fought for my right to the Light, the more I realised that creating with joy and wonder is our only option in the face of fear and darkness. I made a promise to carry forward this knowledge by embodying the magic that walked by my side eternally, holding its invisible hand around me when I thought the stars were going out.

The Snow Queen, the Keeper of the Gate of Ice and Light, once smiled at me and decided I was strong enough to do this work. She helped me to my destiny in harsh and beautiful ways and taught me to free the water of life and reflect starlight by lighting up every particle of my being.

As I skate with her under the northern lights, leaving a trail of living water where my blades touch the ice, I wave to others I see on their way through the silent arctic night, looking for their lost stars. No longer a pale new Moon, I walk in the fullness of my power and control the tides of my life. I laugh and shine with those who helped me remember that magic was never hard work and that we could reignite the Sun over our heads by choice.

This is the story I choose for myself from all others, and my prayer is that one day we all share in a tale of empowerment as one voice echoing endlessly on the wind; that our unchained light reaches our ancestors and those who will inherit this world. Whatever legend you are creating today, may it lift you to your highest potential. The power lies with you. Believe it.

YULIYA RUNNELS-MOSS

Hi, I'm Yuliya, and like most of us, I am many things. I'm a certified practitioner of Tama-Do Academy of Sound, Colour and Movement, and a budding bard (or so I'm told!) of the Light-Up family.

I tread my path as Warrior, Healer and Wordsmith by turn, and sometimes all at once. The all-consuming passion of my journey is attaining my highest potential and helping others to their brightest light.

This work has led me to my current apprenticeship in the Magic of Life, and I am determined to inspire as many fellow travellers as I can.

My greatest hope for this story is that it reaches those who are journeying through their dark night of the soul and are searching for strength to emerge on the other side.

There were many things I didn't know when I faced challenges that seemed overwhelming - that my truth was always the best guide; that eventually all trials make sense and build us up if we can extract every ounce of grace from our experience; that in the end there was never anything but light.

This tale is dedicated to everyone who is rewriting their story and looking up and out of their present boundaries to the yet unknown stars on the horizon. May you see a new dawn flying fast your way!

With light to each of you.

BOLLOCKS TO BURNOUT

NOW I LIVE MY LIFE WITH AUTHENTICITY AND SELF BELIEF.

The perfectionist in me was a hard and unforgiving task mistress. She would dismiss insecurities and anxieties, telling me to suck up the responsibility, the pressure, the desire to do the best job possible for clients, regardless of personal sacrifice or cost.

Nikki's Story

Overpowering heat, still air, the acrid stench of stale sweat mixed with desperate hope. Those are my abiding memories of my thirtieth birthday in March 2004.

I'd spent the morning talking to an inmate in a shadowy Jamaican gaol. He was nervously chatty, at times breaking into incomprehensible Patois. He appeared in a hurry yet with no place to be. He'd spent longer on Death Row than I had been alive, his sentence eventually commuted to life. He was being rehabilitated ready for release. I felt, with him, the chance of freedom and an end to a lifetime of psychological suffering.

In my diary, I'd simply written 'Goblin Hill', the name of the remote tourist spot where I'd spent the rest of the weekend with friends. We'd sipped Appleton rum and coke beside the ice cool Blue Lagoon, surrounded by lush, tropical greenery. No reference to the earlier prison visit, although that's what will remain etched on my brain.

I was a volunteer barrister working in downtown Kingston, at that time the murder capital of the world, assisting in the defence of capital cases for the Bar Human Rights Committee. I normalised being in that cell at that particular moment because that was what I did. Just part of the job, given all that I'd already seen, experienced and been personally affected by.

It was an extraordinary assignment, at a seminal moment in my history, and one of which I remain immensely proud. Barrister colleagues in Bradford asked whether I was worried about the impact that such a placement might have on my practice in Yorkshire. I wasn't known for taking the easy or expected path in life so the short answer was no, I wasn't.

I'd been right. My profile, and consequently that of Chambers, was raised. More significantly, at least two lives were saved.

And it also revealed an internal conflict in terms of how I felt I 'should' behave professionally. The things I witnessed there, and at home (dealing with child sexual abuse cases on a daily basis), were enough to make me weep, warping my ordinary sense of right and wrong. Yet over the years I learnt to adopt the requisite impassive, emotionless veneer.

Pondering how I came to be there, in that prison, I reflect on my childhood. Travel, the outdoors, making human connections - these have always been significant influences in my life. I read law at Balliol College Oxford and quickly discounted the 'city slicker' London solicitor career path, opting instead to become a Criminal Barrister. Fighting hard at the coal face for the underdog felt to me more worthwhile, raw and real. After Bar Finals, I secured pupillage, then tenancy, in Yorkshire.

In and around developing a successful career, I now see that I'd forgotten what makes my heart sing. The perfectionist in me was a hard and unforgiving task mistress. She would dismiss insecurities and anxieties, telling me to suck up the responsibility, the pressure, the desire to do the best job possible for clients, regardless of personal sacrifice or cost.

Escapism was my coping strategy, and it set me on course for an unconventional career path. When a rare scholarship opportunity presented itself, working alongside a Silk (Queen's Counsel) in Wellington, New Zealand, it was an absolute 'no-brainer'. Many Bar colleagues didn't 'get' this approach. They were on the career progression treadmill, hobnobbing with Judges and taking on as many cases as possible on a clear upward trajectory, without deviation or let up. I was happy to lap up the opportunities for the here and now, without too much thought for the next best case. Whilst others raised eyebrows, I remained authentically me.

On my return, it soon became apparent during my annual practice review meetings with clerks, that I wasn't moved by the 'expected' career path of a fledgling barrister, and I didn't share the common career goals of Silk, Recorder (part-time judge) or Judge.

Instead, I avidly pursued my passion for travel, frequently on my own, visiting Australia, Brazil, Thailand, Tanzania and America, to name but a few. Every time my over-packed purple (fake) snakeskin trolley hit the baggage carousel ready for another exciting excursion, I experienced an immediate and all-pervading sense of relief. Job stress and responsibility melted away.

It was only whilst away that I was able to appreciate just how unhappy I was. The intense pressure was hard to handle; the subject matter of the cases I was dealing with wasn't just unpleasant, it was downright unpalatable, skewing my own moral compass. The working conditions, with unpredictable and antisocial hours, added to stress levels.

It was on one such trip, to St. Lucia, that I met Melanie Pledger. Her passion and enthusiasm for life were as infectious as they were energising. I was working hard on myself that holiday, to live in the present, without regrets for the past or fear of the future. I was helped in this task by reading The Power of Now by Eckhart Tolle. Inadvertently I was learning to practice mindfulness. Little did I realise how influential and important a trip this would become.

The first time I went to Jamaica was different. Uncomfortable even. Usually I'm talkative, irrepressible. I arrived at Manchester Airport with my parents, about to embark upon the latest in a long line of travel adventures (albeit on this occasion for work), and sat in stunned silence. Mute through fear. I was scared. Scared of the unknown, scared of the negative reports about life out there: guns, gated communities, violence, murder. During my 'WTF' airport moment, it took my deepest reserves of determination, perseverance and courage to fight back tears and actually board the flight.

My Jamaican exploits could fill a book of their own, and maybe one day they will. During the initial placement, thankfully, with caution and a willingness to take sage advice from my local hosts, my fears subsided. In eighteen months, I re-visited that beautiful, troubled and contradictory country many times.

I felt compelled to continue working to assist in the defence of those caught up in the most shocking cases of injustice I had ever witnessed: inadmissible evidence being presented to the jury, third-rate legal representation, judicial bias, media interference, violent attacks on defendants whilst incarcerated, even the murder of a recently released former death row inmate. As a lawyer, I couldn't fail to be moved and inspired.

I was in my element. The pressure was intense but the difference was that the work was voluntary, I was doing it because I was passionate about the cause, AND I worked behind the scenes in a supporting role, as opposed to the buck stopping solely with me.

Progressing in my career on returning home certainly wasn't the problem envisaged by the more senior and traditional bods in the profession. Nearly two years on, I was experiencing real success. And the daily diet of sexual abuse trials, particularly relating to children, created within me a conflict as to the worth and value of my UK practice. I was dealing with heavyweight cases so, on the face of it, had a great job and income. In reality, I had no time or head space for anything else. I was becoming cynical; my thoughts were becoming warped by the day to day reality of some of the individuals I was dealing with. And my mistrust of others grew.

In 2008, I experienced coaching for the first time. As a result, I examined my values and beliefs and came to understand the benefits of going, as Jim Collins put it, 'from good to great.' My work at the Bar was, as a direct consequence, revitalised. I discovered a new sense of purpose, vigour and personal congruence. Coaching got me back on track in a career that otherwise, I could well have left. It would have been twelve years too early. Instead of resenting the job and feeling trapped by it, I resolved to make it work for me. And so I did.

Such was the profound effect upon me of coaching that between 2010 and 2012, I qualified to become a Corporate and Executive Coach and NLP Practitioner. During that time, with a clear goal and an action plan to achieve it, combined with lots of energy and enthusiasm, I surprised myself how easy it was to motivate myself to work hard on additional projects over and above an already demanding professional job. It also gave me a glimpse of an alternative course: my own coaching business.

Around the same time though, late 2010, I met my husband. Relatively swiftly we started a family. Any thought of launching a new business was almost immediately shelved. Instead, reluctantly, I returned to full-time barrister work after six months with my first child. This felt too soon, and yet the expected norm is around three months. There's a lack of flexible part-time working options at the Criminal Bar and the continued risk that stepping out of practice for too long makes any return harder.

Before her first birthday, my daughter was twice hospitalised for over a week, directly as a result of the childcare choices we'd made – once at seven months old, (causing my husband and I to postpone our honeymoon), then at ten months old (the ill-fated honeymoon was cancelled altogether).

On this second occasion, I was already pregnant again. I have a vivid recollection of an overwhelming, near suffocating, sense of 'mother guilt' engulfing me. I'd placed my baby in full-time childcare purely to service a career that I'd worked hard to achieve yet which had, by then, become unfulfilling, draining and downright depressing.

Like a brick to the face, it struck me. I was at court, defending a part-heard jury trial. The judge was mid-way through his summing up. My baby girl was miles away from me in the hospital hooked up to various wires, tubes and machines. My notes of proceedings became less ordered and sensible as my sight began to blur. I had a fiery red burning sensation in my ears. Turmoil raged through me - the intuitive feeling that I was needed elsewhere. What the hell was I still doing in court anyway??!! Some things were just more important.

In that instant, I understood how the most compelling goals are those kept under constant review. Outlooks alter and priorities change to flex with prevailing situations. Career decisions made almost twenty years before shouldn't define me or keep me shackled to them forever. I'd worked hard to achieve all that I had in my career to date, yet all that melted into insignificance in the face of my daughter's hospitalisation.

With my middle child, I made changes. I took longer maternity leave. I went back when I felt ready, having enlisted the services of a nanny. She played mum while I paid her for the privilege of returning to work.

Having been out of the court environment for nearly twelve months, channels of communication between myself and the clerks who managed my diary broke down. A request to 'ease me back in' to the job as part of a phased return was interpreted as a free-for-all on any case, anytime, anywhere.

For me? A baptism of fire. A wounding with intent case where the defendant had broken a glass and twisted it into the face of the complainant, who as a consequence suffered life-changing injuries; a murder trial; a rape trial where the client I represented was just thirteen years old. This was the beginning of the end. The relentlessness of the criminal bar had me running on empty.

Having a career challenge brought about by significant changes in personal circumstances is of course not unusual. What is more uncommon is the ability to accept, or get comfortable, with them. This for me was the start of looking internally for reassurance, rather than focusing outwardly towards a specific goal or solution.

When I was seven months pregnant with my third child, a last-minute case was returned to me from another set of Chambers. It was a serious sexual abuse re-trial with multiple complainants. Papers more than two feet deep, the pink brief ribbon barely holding them together due to their sheer weight and volume, were couriered to my home address late after the close of business. I had to be ready for a clean start the next morning in a non-local court.

I wrestled professional ethics, guilt, anxiety and a deep sense of obligation. And then I said "No". For the first time in sixteen years of practice, I refused to take a brief.

It was the most liberating experience, a coming of age. As David Bowie said: *'Aging is an extraordinary process where you become the person you always should have been'.* In that single moment, I embraced a momentous change. I learnt to say no.

This became the catalyst for something far greater. Less than a month later, I was back on maternity leave. I'd worked full time on returning to work with both of my first two children. Now, with three children under the age of four, and a husband working away mid-week, I wasn't in a rush to repeat my most recent return to work experiences. That said, being self-motivated, determined, resilient, resourceful, independent, and formerly the family breadwinner, I certainly wasn't going to sit idle, waiting for the hubby to bring home the bacon.

It was then that I realised I wasn't alone, either in the challenges I'd faced battling personal demons within my career around confidence, internal conflict and stress, or with the obstacles re-surfacing around the ease or otherwise with which I could return flexibly. Highly successful and hugely talented women are leaving the legal profession 'mid-career' in droves.

In 2017, while on extended maternity leave, I experienced Light Up. A short course akin to coaching, and yet with an entirely new emphasis: quietening distracting thoughts, focusing on a calming sense of internal wisdom and knowing, and a resource to call on at any given time, in any given situation, to remember with confidence our own ability to choose and decide. It's not about seeking answers, it's more about knowing them.

Empowered, full of confidence and excitement, I re-embraced the world of work. And so my new business launched. The Bar was no more.

I 'get' the responsibilities, pressures and expected career paths of women in law. I empathise with clients describing frustrations with their job, the overwhelm due to overwork and minimal financial reward, the lack of life balance, the need to more effectively manage time and increase productivity, and confidence issues around pursuing a promotion or returning to work after a career break, or starting new roles after promotion.

I also know from personal experience how effective coaching is at increasing personal performance in every aspect of life. Doing things differently, working from the inside out, for me has been the key to success.

I recall the day I was almost immobilised through fear at the airport en route to Jamaica. I realise now that it led, without question, to the most influential period of my life. Having the courage to live a life true to myself, not the life others expect, gives me the opportunity to live a life in which I am the best that I can be.

For the sake of my independence and sense of pride, and to be a positive role model for my children, that is precisely what I now do. Every night when I tuck them into bed and reflect with them on their day, I ask myself specifically: how have I inspired, motivated or acted as a role model for them that day?

As my experiences in Jamaica taught me and Light Up helped me to remember: with authenticity, self-belief and an excellent, supportive team, the most challenging of obstacles can be overcome and goals can be achieved.

NIKKI ALDERSON

Nikki has 19 years' experience at the Criminal Bar in Yorkshire, working from Broadway House Chambers, Bradford and Leeds. Nikki now works as a specialist Corporate and Executive Coach: supporting law firms and Chambers to attract and retain female talent; and empowering female lawyers to achieve career ambitions whilst creating congruent lives.

Nikki has learnt a lot from her successful career as a barrister, having gained great insights into the responsibilities, pressures and "expected" career paths of those, particularly women, working in law. She sees a challenge within the profession to retain talented female role models, given the dearth of women in senior partnership roles and within the judiciary, and is passionate about addressing these issues through the coaching services she provides.

Nikki specialises in 3 areas of coaching, whether for individuals or for law firms/ Chambers:

- Enhancing support for career break returners and those in career "transition"
- Providing a benefit for those recently promoted in the first 100 days of their new role
- Increasing awareness around workplace confidence, wellness and resilience, and mental toughness.

Although Nikki's work is focused predominantly on 1-1 coaching within the workplace, she also offers bespoke workshops and speaker events.

3 simple lessons learned in Nikki's professional career, business and personal life:

- People don't look back at life wishing they'd spent less time with their kids
- "The key to success is to start before you are ready": Marie Forleo
- "Whether you think you can or you can't, you're right": Henry Ford

Nikki lives by the mantra: live a life true to yourself, not the life others expect.

14

BOLLOCKS TO OVER-THINKING AND FEELING INADEQUATE

NOW I KNOW THAT LIGHT AND POWER COME FROM WITHIN ME.

I was abused at a young age and when I was finally able to confront the abuse it caused my world to crash. Everything I knew to be true, wasn't, and it caused me to question everything.

Jack's Story

I had what I believed to be an idyllic childhood in Durban, South Africa. It was a complicated background. I grew up in a house of seven with lots of cats and dogs and a caring, loving mother, who often struggled with daily life and knowing how to respond to things. My mother was remarried and my step-father has children of his own. I also have two sisters. My father and step-mother lived in England. They're now divorced and I'm still close to them both - I see my step-mother as a second mother.

I was abused at a young age. When I was finally able to confront the abuse it caused my world to crash. Everything I knew to be true, wasn't, and it caused me to question everything. To survive, I chose to leave South Africa and move over to England to live with with my dad and step-mom.

I struggled to find what I wanted to do and who I wanted to be. After some more years of questioning, I ended up studying Psychology at university, where I still am today.

Light Up came into my life through my step-mom, who is one of the amazing Activators. I'd seen the amazing effect Light Up had had on her - she seemed to glow and shine. I knew I wanted to experience what she'd experienced.

I've struggled greatly with how my life 'should' be, feeling inadequate and as though things should be different. I've often felt unsure about myself and what I'm saying and if it, or even I, mattered. I've always been a big reader and love learning, which led to me over thinking everything.

I don't believe in a higher power, I don't believe in a life after this and I've never had spiritual experiences that I've truly felt. I do believe that people have power and there is more going on than meets the eye. I've always believed in the power of people.

I went into Light Up without expectations and excitedly nervous. The process was a lot more than I ever anticipated. Going through it truly felt like coming back into myself. The strength, light and power I experienced were unlike anything I've ever felt before - probably the closest I'll ever come to a spiritual experience. The sense of calm and clarity were powerful. It allowed me to see my strength and feel secure in myself.

Touch has always been a powerful and grounding sense for me. I like to feel, to know what things feel like. My light is called Zen – it's a tall piece of wood that looks a bit like a kidney, smooth, firm and cool to the touch. Feeling what Zen feels like and experiencing that sensation connects me instantly.

Since Light Up, I find I'm able to do things I never would have thought possible before. It's helped me realise the negative impact that over-thinking was having on me. I've never felt as strong or as sure in my life. I use the tools of Light Up all the time and they're truly helpful.

I've also learnt that it doesn't mean that I'm going to be happy all the time or that life will always be easy. Life is complicated and full of surprises. Life is also made of interactions with people, who bring their own energy into our space. I've learnt that I can't control everything and that's okay.

What has changed is my response to life and to other people. I no longer feel weighed down with the idea of how things 'should' be. I know now that the Light and Power comes from within and from me. It's my hope that one day everybody is lit up and we can all shine together.

JACK COLBOURNE-FLITTON

Jack was originally born in England and moved to South Africa when he was a toddler. He spent his childhood and teen years growing up in a large family and moved back to England to live with his father a few years ago.

Jack is currently in his final year at Nottingham University where he is studying Psychology. He has always been fascinated by people, and latterly it has become his passion to understand and help people who suffer from mental health issues.

Jack is lucky enough to have two mums and was introduced to Light Up via his English mum, Beth. He is really keen to help spread the Light Up word, and hopes that his contribution to this book will help others who are going through similar issues.

15

BOLLOCKS TO DEPRESSION AND BREAKDOWN

I'VE RE-ACTIVATED MY POWER AND RESTORED MY HOPE!

B*eing on antidepressants filled me with shame; this I added to the shame I carried from all that had happened to me as a child.*

Heather's Story

It was a warm African day; the sun was high in a beautiful blue sky and the bustling cafes, the lilac-pink flowers of flourishing Jacaranda trees and hopeful black and white faces enjoying their lunch breaks flashed past me as we drove out of Pretoria. It was the early nineties and change pulsed through the South African air.

Tears were streaming down my face. These were not the recent tears of utter anguish and pointlessness that I had been feeling; these were tinged with hope.

Just an hour before I'd sat in front of a plump, kind and obviously very clever woman. She was the neurologist my doctor had referred me to after he'd been unable to get to the bottom of the awful, almost daily, headaches I'd been suffering. I was also continually exhausted and unable to fight off recurring infections, so I was constantly ill. One doctor in our small-town practice had diagnosed me with ME, commonly called 'yuppy flu' as so many high-achieving young people were suffering with it. The weekly Vitamin B6 injections into my bottom didn't seem to be helping and, as a teenager, I found each painful encounter with the gorgeous young male doctor particularly humiliating!

After a few hours of tests, the clever neurologist told me I was depressed. I remember feeling a little flabbergasted. Depressed? I was the happiest person I knew! I was doing well at my studies at the world-renowned University of the Witwatersrand, had lots of wonderful friends, was living through the most exciting time in my country's history, had a loving and supportive family, and had shown incredible resilience in surviving some truly horrific childhood experiences. I certainly wouldn't have called myself depressed!

The clever neurologist had explained that it was all to do with my brain chemicals and 'a little tablet each day' would make me okay. I'd walked out of her office armed with a prescription - and so much hope!

And so began my nearly thirty year old relationship with antidepressants. And with the big black dog.

I only very recently came across the analogy of depression as 'the black dog'. I'd been reading around mental health issues and a very simple and poignant cartoon popped up on one of my searches. It described my experience of depression so perfectly: it showed depression as a huge black dog that sometimes lies over our head completely blocking the senses and weighing us down with its all-encompassing, all-engrossing, cumbersome weight. At other times the black dog is more medium-sized and lies closely and tightly on our chest. We feels its weight and it catches our breath, but at least our head is free. At other times the black dog trots quietly by our side. We knows it's there, and that it could jump up at any moment, but for the time being it's at arm's length.

Although I love this analogy, I understand that it is simplistic on many levels. For one, comparing depression to a dog simply does not in any way describe the physical agony of depression. For most of us dogs are loving, loyal, life-enhancing pets. Depression is none of these, although it might be described as doggedly loyal in its attachment to sufferers.

Secondly, the cartoon implied that depression, like the dog, is always with the sufferer - forever. I now know that this does not have to be true. If you've come across this cartoon, or indeed played a part in creating it, and see it differently, thank you for entertaining my interpretations!

As I look at my younger self, sitting in that car filled with hope (and huge relief) that one tiny pill taken daily would 'fix me', I feel very sad. I was on the brink of adulthood, about to graduate and begin a career in teaching. I would finally be earning my own money and be able to build a secure, and hopefully successful, future. And I thought I needed fixing. At no point over the next years did any professional ask about what might have caused me to be depressed, and no-one offered any other solutions - other than the little green pills. More than sad, I feel angry. I am one of millions of people diagnosed with depression in their teen years who were told it was a chemical problem with our brains that needed fixing, and a tablet would do the trick.

I've done a lot of reading around this, and although there's a chemical change in the brains of depressed people (lower levels of 'the happy chemical' serotonin, for one), the effectiveness of antidepressants prescribed in their millions to treat this chemical imbalance is actually far less well-documented than one might imagine.

And so I embarked upon the new chapter of my life excitedly, optimistically - and knowing a part of me was broken and I would only cope well if I took a daily dose of my new happy pill.

Unfortunately being on antidepressants filled me with shame; this I added to the shame I carried from all that had happened to me as a child. It was at least a decade before I told the people closest to me that I had been diagnosed with depression and took antidepressants. Thirty years ago there was a far bigger stigma attached to mental health problems, and this was definitely a factor for me. I felt like a complete failure for not being able to cope without medication. It would take almost thirty years before I'd address my low self-esteem.

As for my childhood, I still haven't told my nearest and dearest those tales; they'll have to keep for another day.

My little green pills worked a treat at keeping the black dog at bay. Well mostly, anyway. On the surface, I was doing well. I'd built a strong reputation as a good teacher in the 'new South Africa'. I cannot describe the joy of teaching classes of children from every culture and background when only four years earlier I'd matriculated in a 'whites only' school. I'd always wanted to travel, and I was battling to support my mother and myself financially on my South African teacher's salary. So the lure of adverts to teach in London was very powerful.

I took the leap. And oh, how I loved London! I planned to spend a couple of years in this incredible city, to travel as much as possible, and then return to my beautiful homeland.

Life had other plans. After meeting my husband and having our son, London became my home. Teaching continued to be my passion. I was promoted and took on more responsibilities, and then decided to move to work in a Pupil Referral Unit, where children are taught who for various reasons are unable to access education in a mainstream setting. I absolutely loved my new role, even with its challenges, which were many. I was making a difference, and it felt good. Well, it felt good some of the time.

I also took on a chair of governors role at a school where I'd been a governor for years. The school was experiencing difficulties, and it fell to me to move our head teacher 'on' and appoint a new one, at a time when London was facing a head teacher recruitment crisis. It took three rounds of intense interview processes before I could fill the post. I had to do this with almost no support from the local authority. It was an incredibly stressful process - and my green pills were not doing such a good job anymore. I ignored the signs that I was in distress by doing more and saying 'yes' to more; this was how I'd always covered the fact that I could feel things were beginning to fall apart.

It was a crisp April morning in 2015. I was working at my desk in my classroom before school began when I experienced the strangest sensation: it was as if I was watching myself from outside of my body. I felt completely numb and disconnected from myself. I just knew it was important to get out of the building before any children arrived. My head teacher, who was hugely supportive over the next days, months and years, sent me home with an instruction to see a doctor as soon as possible. It would be four years before I could even contemplate entering a classroom again.

This was a huge shock. I'd fully expected that I'd have a few days off and then get back to normal. I had not anticipated that for the next six months I'd be literally hiding under my duvet, nor the paralysing fear I'd experience as I sat on the edge of my bed unable even to select a pair of knickers to wear.

The doctor said I'd suffered 'burnout', or what years before they might have called a nervous breakdown. It certainly was not how I would have imagined a 'breakdown' to feel: I was still myself - I was just completely numb, paralysed. Of course my limbs could actually move, my brain just couldn't decide where or how to move.

My green happy pills were no longer doing their thing. I was petrified. We'd been part of each other's life for so long. Changing antidepressants is no picnic. It is brutal. It was my experience of these drugs over the next few months that made me recognise their power. It is frightening. I was put on the first alternative and it did not suit me at all: I turned into a wild, wailing witch! My family was distraught. You cannot just swap one antidepressant for another. If one pill does not suit, you're 'weaned off' it and then started on another until one is found that seems to be working. It takes weeks and weeks and is a painful process. I was shocked at the effect of these drugs on my mood and my personality.

Eventually I found a new happy pill that seemed to suit me - with only minor side effects like wanting to sleep all the time, and suffering excruciating headaches twice-monthly! At least I was able to get out of bed and function (I use the term 'function' very loosely!).

My 'breakdown' or 'burnout' was accompanied by more shame. For someone who thought they coped well, and HAD coped well ever since she was a little girl, this very physical unravelling, that forced me to step back from life indefinitely, was horrifying.

Looking back, however, I had seen it coming; the signs were there. For a long time I'd felt I had lost myself. I'd been so many things to so many people and I honestly couldn't remember who I was anymore. I had forgotten what I believed, what I stood for, and sometimes didn't recognise the person I'd become. I had been feeling disconnected, hopeless and directionless for a long time before that fateful morning in my classroom.

Just six months before the morning when things finally fell apart, I'd started a home-based business. Yes, I hear your cries of surprise. Among all the other commitments I had, I'd decided to start a business! Looking back on this decision, I now believe one hundred percent that this saved my life.

As a new business owner I embraced a huge amount of training which included hours and hours of personal development. It was on one particular course I attended that I first encountered a tiny figure, a powerhouse of grace, light and life-force. Turns out she was a DNA Activator.

It was this connection that was to begin my healing. She introduced me to the force of nature, full of love and wisdom, who 'birthed' Light Up. These two incredible women have become spiritual mothers, best friends and inspiring mentors to me.

I thoroughly enjoyed the DNA Light Up journey. It was short, fun and more powerful than years of self-development, hours and hours of counselling and thirty years of antidepressants! It allowed me to reconnect with myself, re-activate my power and restore my hope. The journey following these sessions has revealed startling changes in me. I cannot begin to describe the utter relief of knowing beyond any doubt that I was never broken. My brain was never 'broken' and it was simply years and years (a lifetime, in fact!) of BOLLOCKS BELIEFS that I'd learned from life's experiences, other people's poor decisions and appalling behaviour, and society's expectations and pressures that made me believe I was broken.

I continue on this beautiful journey, still unlearning the BOLLOCKS, shifting forty-seven years worth of habits and beliefs, and embracing my power, limitless and magnificent. I'm not saying that every day I feel these incredible truths all the time. And I'm constantly aware of the power I have to choose my focus. There are still battles, and I now have the power of my beautiful light, and a raft of simple and transformative 'tools' and strategies to keep me connected with it.

The black dog still sometimes comes yapping at my feet; on a couple of occasions it has jumped up at me quite powerfully. It's a tiny dog now, and most days I can't see it - or even remember what it looks like.

It's my absolute privilege and joy that I now get to share this beautiful work with others.

HEATHER MARGRIT JONES

Heather Margrit Jones Professional Activator

Originally from South Africa, my background is in education. After fifteen years in mainstream education, I acknowledged that my passion lay in working with the more vulnerable, disengaged and 'hard to reach' children and moved to a Pupil Referral Unit.

Whilst I absolutely loved my years in alternative education, I found myself frustrated by government policies that insisted my very damaged students must be assessed in exactly the same way as high achievers across the country. After what felt like literally bashing my head against a brick wall every day, attempting to meet my students' needs and empower them to reach their full potential, I finally left education in 2015 to set up my own businesses.

Light-Up was quite literally 'the missing piece of the puzzle', and after the work transformed my own life, I trained as an Activator in 2018. I love sharing this beautiful work with people of all ages and from all walks of life, knowing it is 'the secret' to empowering them to live their best life.

16

BOLLOCKS TO SEXUAL ABUSE

I'M STRONG NOW. WITH A CHOICE AND A VOICE.

"*S ilence" he said, "speak nothing to folk,*
For bad things will happen." I started to choke.

BG's story

A massive weight upon my chest,

I couldn't breathe, I couldn't rest,

The weight pressed down, the air squeezed out,

I couldn't scream, I couldn't shout.

"Silence" he said, "speak nothing to folk,

For bad things will happen." I started to choke.

I wanted to tell and the nightmare to end,

But reality was different, no wounds could they mend.

On and on he came, back for more.

I learnt to go numb and stare at the door.

I shivered, I shook, I started to cower,

My tiny body exposed, a slave to his power.

Nearly three years went by, then one day, the end.

We moved far far away, did not have to pretend

about the double life, my journey to hell.

But I held onto my memories not wanting to tell.

The pain is still there, what he did to me,

Took away my childhood I'm beginning to see.

But now things are different and I've reached out my hand,

Friends picked me up and allowed me to stand.

I'm stronger right now, as I have a choice.

I open my mouth and I have a voice.

The feeling of anger is fading away.

He no longer exists, he has had his day.

I owe my rescue to a certain few,

Who have taken their time from the things that they do.

They have listened without judgement and loaned an ear,

I will always be indebted and hold them so dear.

So my reason for writing is to all those in despair.

Hold on and reach out, someone will be there.

My journey has been rocky, but one hell of a ride.

All it has taken is the right friends by your side.

A tiny weight upon my chest

It's now my time to sit and rest.

The weight has gone, the elephant small.

I'm shining bright above them all.

FEAR

What is fear to you or me?

Let's look closer for us to see

FEAR is the unknown and being out of control

FEAR is being frightened right down to your soul

FEAR is a hurdle which we can overcome

If we look deep inside, (not easy for some)

Its triggered by a sound, memory, traumatic time

Sweating, nausea, there's a physical sign

FEAR can paralyse us, strike us down anywhere

A powerful state of emotion (if only we'd share)

It stops our dreams, shuts us down

Turns a smile into a frown!

We have a choice … do we run … do we hide

Do we bury ourselves under a mountain side

Bollocks to that!

we stand up and be counted, open our eyes,

Face Everything And Rise

.   .   .

A MESSAGE TO MY NINE-YEAR-OLD SELF

If I could write a message to my nine-year-old self

And not leave my past story on the dusty wooden shelf,

I would start by saying how amazing you are,

A strength you haven't yet found.

Just stop for a minute, take it all in, listen to every sound.

Your life is about to go down a path, a choice you will not make.

It's dark, it's scary, you should not be there (you're a child for goodness sake!!)

But through it all your inner light will never be put out.

Just hold on tight and don't give up.

You will eventually speak and shout.

The power is yours, don't ever forget, not his to take away.

You should just be laughing, dancing, do nothing all day just play.

But that's not the journey you'll have,

It makes me sad to say.

Believe me when I tell you, you will find yourself one day.

This day I speak of has finally arrived and now I shine so bright.

I don't dread Thursday coming around as now I've learnt to fight.

I've taken back my life, my thoughts, I'm totally in control.

I'm feeling truly happy, which reaches to my soul.

So just to reassure you, even on your darkest days,

You will beat your nightmares and rise above the evilest of ways.

You are stronger than you'll ever believe and I'm proud to be 'grown up' you.

I'll always be by your side and help to get you through.

BG

I'm self-employed, running my own business from home so I can be there for my gorgeous ten-year-old son.

Having only very recently spoken about what I went through as a child, I'm choosing, for now, to remain anonymous.

I wish I had started this journey many years ago, knowing what I know now, having the amazing support I have discovered, realising I've always had the power to choose - all of which would have changed the last thirty-five years of my life. I am now determined to make 'the rest of my life, the best of my life'.

I have realised that talking about the childhood trauma I experienced is only the beginning of the healing process. It's now about the here and now and about the future, rediscovering who I am and what difference I can make.

Sharing these poems with the outside world is utterly terrifying and liberating at the same time. If nothing else, I hope they reach out to just one person to let them know that the support is there, the tools are there, and your light is already there … you just have to look for it.

I am dedicating these poems to my nine-year-old self.

17

BOLLOCKS TO SEXUAL ABUSE AND KEEPING QUIET

NOW I EMBRACE WHO I AM. I AM POWERFUL. I ALWAYS WAS. I HAD JUST FORGOTTEN.

efore the age of ten I'd tried to hang myself. I just wanted the hurt and pain to stop. I didn't want to be the kid who cried every day at school because they didn't want to go home.

Danielle's Story

We're all born with so much potential, so much light, so much hope. I was desperate to be an Olympic gymnast as a child and spent more time walking on my hands than on my feet. I was sure that I could soar effortlessly through the air like Nadia Comăneci, using the sofas as vaults.

Life got in the way and circumstances beyond my control quashed my dreams.

As children we have little control over the environment we inhabit and the people we encounter. A negative, fraught environment breeds anxiety, sadness and terror. The people around us as we grow have such capacity to help or hinder our view of ourselves. Some will enable us to bloom with nurturing love, kindness and a warm touch, others will have a more negative impact, shattering and destroying our confidence and self-belief.

As a child I experienced sexual abuse at the hands of multiple perpetrators. I grew up feeling dirty, confused, expecting every man I met to abuse me. Key figures in my family unit were absent and I lived in a home where violence was the norm and experienced emotional and physical abuse regularly. My self-worth and self-esteem were at rock bottom.

With no-one to turn to I felt alone and isolated. I figured that death was the easier option. I wanted out. Before the age of ten I had tried to hang myself. I just wanted the hurt and pain to stop. I didn't want to be the kid who cried every day at school because they didn't want to go home. I wanted to be like my friends, with mums who met them from school with a smile and a hug and made them feel safe.

As I write this, I feel sad for my younger self and all that I went through. Yet I wouldn't change one thing. What I experienced enabled me to develop my resilience and hope. It made me tenacious and determined. If I hadn't known hardship, how on earth could I be grateful for the beauty in my life or find the skills to climb the mountains which I faced as an adult? If I hadn't experienced these terrible things, I wouldn't be ME!

We've all had one moment which defined us, fuelled us and made us realise who we could be, haven't we?

As a kid I lived in a half-finished bedroom for many months. I had to climb over a rolled up, half fitted carpet and it drove me crazy. I was fastidiously tidy and super organised, and the carpet represented all that was disorderly in my world. One summer holiday I decided that enough was enough. Tired of waiting for my father to fit the bloody carpet, I decided it looked simple enough and that I could do it myself. Using rudimentary tools: a saucepan, a Stanley knife and a butter knife, I somehow laid that carpet and regained control of my own environment. I can't describe the euphoria that such a small achievement gave to me. It shaped my personality.

There was nothing that I wouldn't attempt. I became a master at experiential learning. Even if I was clueless I would find a way. I was determined to succeed. Now I'm not saying that this gung-ho kind of approach always works. And ... I've demolished fireplaces, taken down walls and murdered multiple power tools in my attempts to 'just get on and do it'! I've taught myself to build a website, run a podcast and write a book. The ability to just try it and see what happens has stood me in good stead.

Practically I felt that there was little I couldn't do, yet emotionally I felt flawed, broken and inept. It was another thirty something years before I experienced the next personality defining moment in my life. This one set me on my journey to losing the bollocks in my life, consciously, and finding my brightest light.

I was terrified of getting to forty. I recall being nineteen and thinking that forty was practically dead! I laugh when my kids refer to 'that old teacher in school' who is close to my age. I remind them that I have the power to disinherit them should their ageist slurs continue and that one day, God willing, they too will be mid-forties and nearer the death side!

Joking aside, my forties have proven to be the most revolutionary of decades, both in the changes in myself and in the circumstances of my personal life. At the beginning of my fourth decade I was at a crossroads, unable to decide which was the right path for me. My inner sat nav was refusing to work efficiently, and I was petrified of committing to one path or another. Each route seemed fraught with dangers, frightening mysteries and trip hazards. I struggled to see sunlight through the dark trees and my intuition, which I'd relied on through many years, seemed useless.

I'd faced the demons of my abuse through counselling with a specialist sexual violence service. Opening this Pandora's box, which I'd kept nailed shut for so many years, had been emotionally harrowing. Admitting to myself that I'd been abused and that I wasn't mad, crazy or psychotic, was a feat in itself.

Yet still I felt a fraud as I sat in the chair week after week. I knew that so many women had experienced much worse than I had endured, and I tried to give my abuse a score out of ten. I had witnessed, in my work with survivors of domestic abuse, how people play down what's happened to them. I had no idea that I was doing the very same thing!

In my head, I'd totally minimised the abuse I'd been living with for all those years. I was perplexed by the counsellor's shocked face as I sobbed my way through telling her about what I'd endured as a child. It wasn't really that bad, was it? Over and over I apologised for wasting her time. Patiently, she took me through her view of it. No child should ever have to endure what I had been through. I was a survivor of horrific abuse. I'd made it this far alone and now, having addressed my past, I felt free to move on with my life.

I began to insert boundaries into my personal life and allow a little time for me. Both things were challenging, to say the least. I was used to accepting poor behaviour from members of my family and now I began to question their treatment of me. I took time out for myself, in amongst the daily havoc that life with six children brings. I allowed myself time to read and to run, me-time that gave me important head-space. Putting myself and my feelings first was liberating. And it took practice.

I'd anticipated that instilling boundaries within my personal relationships would be the most challenging. I was not wrong. When I began to question and push back, I was told I was being difficult, prickly and hard to be around. It seemed that as long as I was subservient and remained quiet, I was easier to get along with! With every passing scenario I gained strength. My eyes opened. It was as if I was waking up from a bad dream. The more I began to question, the louder my voice got and the more I was labelled difficult. As a result I became even more isolated.

I realised that this is what had stopped me from openly challenging anything before. In my heart of hearts, I knew that in standing up for myself I'd be forced either to back down or run the risk of being ostracised by my family. I couldn't back down now. I'd come this far and

I could see the difficulties in front of me. I surrounded myself with those who championed me, saw my strength and respected me for being me.

Without the shackles of labels, my confidence began to grow. I began to share openly with people that I was a survivor of sexual abuse. Some chose to disbelieve me. Some looked uncomfortable and muttered that it was a long time ago and I should get over it. Some never spoke to me again.

That hurt. It hurt a lot. Yet I knew my truth and I no longer needed to convince anyone else of it. Their opinions were theirs and not mine. Once I'd mastered this perspective, I began to feel freer, lighter. I saw the beauty around me and was grateful for those people who filled my life with joy. I observed so many others in my work and around me who desperately wanted to put boundaries in place yet were afraid of the consequences if they spoke out.

Many said to me that I was brave, others that I was foolish. I felt neither. Merely that I was being the truest version of me and beginning to value my own worth for the first time.

Many parts of my life seemed so glorious, yet I mourned for my past and all that it could have been. I felt at times like an island, alone in a vast sea. Occasionally dark waves of blackness would come crashing down around me as I came to terms with all that had gone before. This healing process was at best a roller coaster ride and at worst felt as if I was riding an uncontrollable tsunami.

Outwardly it seemed that I was functioning, achieving and thriving. I had a good job, six beautiful children, a home in an enviable location and a fabulous relationship. Inwardly I was traumatised. My dreams were horrific, filled with people who hated me, my own self-loathing and the sensation of falling. As long as I was busy, I didn't need to think, so I occupied every waking moment. Being busy filled the void in my heart.

Being a great believer in the power of the universe and the Law of

Attraction, I started to focus on manifesting something that might help me to feel more like the person that I knew I could be. I had no idea what it was that I needed nor even what I wanted, yet I asked for it anyway.

In May 2017 I met, by chance, a woman who would help me to change my life, enable me to say bollocks to this and choose to shine! I attended a training day at work. I wasn't really in the right frame of mind to go but had gone nonetheless. That morning I sat riveted listening to an inspiring speaker tell the auditorium how she'd chosen to focus her energy into working with children after experiencing sexual abuse herself as a child. Her courage and willingness to contribute and give back impressed and empowered me.

I felt shaky and emotional as I sat through the rest of the training session, detached and deep in thought. Half way through the day I popped out for a pee. Desperate to clear my head I made for the shopping area. It was there that I saw the same woman who'd given the presentation earlier that morning. I stopped for a chat and before I knew it, had spent an hour telling her about my past abuse and the isolation that followed. I sobbed unashamedly.

At her side appeared a tiny effervescent woman who exuded warmth. I trusted her immediately. My intuition, like a large beacon, drew me to her and before I knew it, I'd signed up to a programme I knew little about called DNA Light Up. It promised to reconnect me with the brilliant light inside me and to help me find ME!!

I was game for anything. I felt so lost, alone and out of touch with who I was that I had nothing to lose and everything to gain. We arranged to chat that week. One phone call and a few days later I found myself sitting in her comfortable lounge. Unsure of what I was about to do or experience, I felt completely at ease and trusted her implicitly.

She explained that this programme wasn't therapy and it wasn't counselling. It was an opportunity for me to re-connect deeply with who I was, find my light and learn to tap into the innate powers that I'd had since birth and which had been crushed and nearly extinguished by the trauma around me.

She asked me about my life up until that point. I recall thinking, 'You are so going to regret asking me that'. Yet she sat and listened as, for the first time ever, I poured out every snippet of my past, from abuse, loneliness, neglect, bullying, mental health issues and shocking family revelations. She passed me tissues as I cried buckets and gently checked my language as I used 'you know' instead of 'I know'. I was not used to owning my feelings and thoughts and it became apparent I was sabotaging my subconscious thought processes.

At the end of this epic Jackanory session, we worked through a series of exercises which left me feeling lighter, freer and more energised. We addressed my habit of self-deprecation and my deference to others. I learnt to tap into my deeper intuition and to detach emotionally from negative relationships that had ceased to serve me.

Bizarrely, yet unsurprisingly, I was given a box of art and craft paraphernalia. Glue, glitter, stickers and paint. When she asked me to draw what my inner energy looked like I thought she was bonkers. I had come to heal me, not take part in a messy play session. Ever the obedient student though, I dutifully sat on the floor and connected with the energy I felt flowing through my veins. It was bubbling, swirling, fizzing and bright gold. I felt it as it rushed through my body, coursing around and shining brightly. It was no longer a tiny ember within me. It surrounded my soul as I stood upright and I felt taller (not a bad thing when you're a mere five foot two and a fag end). I felt stronger, as if I could fly. My ability was unlimited, it was formidable. I was a superhero in the making.

My rational brain was telling me that it felt too woo woo, too spiritual, too deep! Yet I cannot deny what I was feeling that day and have felt every day since. I'd made a conscious decision to allow my light to shine, brighter than the darkness of my past and the dark forces who sought to do me emotional harm. And I was powerful. I am powerful. I was always powerful. I had just forgotten how to be.

One thing that she said to me that day sticks with me. I told her I wanted to write my story down, to have a voice and inspire others in the process. 'It's important that you tell your story,' she told me.

I'd been given validation by someone that I trusted and, with a flush of gold glitter in my veins and a surge of energy in my belly, I rushed home to start writing that afternoon. I'd toyed with the idea of writing my memoir for so long but had been paralysed by fear. What if others thought that I was a crap writer? What if my book failed? What if people laughed? I had no idea practically about the technicalities of writing nor how to get my musings into print. And suddenly none of my reservations mattered at all. I didn't care if I hadn't a clue about book deals or publishing or if anyone ridiculed me. I was going to tell my story and help others to heal too.

That evening, high on my glittery endorphins, I began to write. As if controlled by some alien force words flowed onto the paper effortlessly. By the end of the week I'd written five thousand words. It was not cathartic, nor healing. It was as if I were telling the story of someone I knew intimately. It felt right, and for the first time in a very long time I knew that I was on the right path. My gut instinct told me this. I felt settled, calm, like a woman on a mission.

Each day as I put into practise the things that I'd learned during my Light Up, I felt my energy grow and my inner strength and light become stronger in magnitude. I told my children about my gold energy, trying to explain to them that I felt like Spiderman with a golden web which could help trap darkness underneath it. I could see they thought I was nuts. 'Are you going to wear a leotard and fly like Spidey then, mum?' my youngest child asked.

'I draw the line at the tight jumpsuit leotard' I replied, 'but as regards the flying, anything is possible!' When fuelled by golden glitter and a love of life anything is infinitely possible.

Six months rolled by and I wrote daily, watching my word count grow towards fifty thousand. I had still told no-one about my writing. In those six months I noticed a shift in my thinking patterns, my self-belief and my self-esteem. I was calm, yet exuded inner strength. I didn't dwell on the negativity around me (because of course it hadn't left my life). I was choosing to shine despite it, I was choosing to make my light brighter than their darkness. After all, one candle in a dark room illuminates and suppresses the darkness. My light gave me power and warmth, strength and determination.

Fast forward to May 2018 and I was nearing the end of my book. Writing the closing chapters was tough. I'd nurtured this baby for nearly a year and grown attached to it. And I knew that the time was coming to let go and share it with others who might well need the healing even more than I did.

I was still clueless about getting my book published and was too much of a coward to send my manuscript off to publishers to try to get a book deal. What if they thought it was a load of bollocks? Should I put my manuscript out for publication? I pondered for hour upon hour and decided that I didn't want to invite rejection and criticism. I would find another way to get my book in print. I would wait for the path to become clear.

I sat for six weeks with my manuscript gathering dust on the desk. I stroked it and imagined a glossy cover on it. I visualised it being read by other survivors and those enduring suffering and offering them hope too. I was still absolutely sure that my book would be published as I intended. My intuition told me as much. I just needed to be patient and wait for the universe to answer my request.

The answer came one day as I scrolled on FaceBook, procrastinating, finding any distraction I could not to do the thing I should have been doing. Up popped the profile of a friend of a friend, someone who runs her own company helping authors to get their books into print. Seizing the moment, I messaged her straight away and thirty minutes later she was talking me through my options. The universe had delivered as I had asked.

The wheels were now in motion, I set a launch date and the preparation began in earnest. Cover photos, blurb, press statements and publicity. Months flew by and suddenly in a flash my launch date was here. *'It's No Secret, Thriving after Surviving'* was real, larger than life and hitting Amazon. Within an hour it went to the top and knocked the beautiful and talented Oprah off the number one spot in the biography category.

It was the icing on the cake, a true testament that from adversity can come success and from challenge can come light.

The feedback from most readers was heartwarming and amazing, validation that I'd done the right thing. The dream stealers and energy vampires in my family came out fighting, labelling me a liar and shouting loudly that I'd only written the book to further my business interests. Nothing could have been further from the truth. I knew my truth and the reason that I'd written my book and it was never about money. I knew that with my decision to heal and move on with my life, I could help and empower others who faced challenges. I could inspire them to keep moving ahead, to keep looking for the positives and to appreciate their strength and resilience. In saying 'Bollocks' to my past, I was able to shine brightly to lead the way for others.

I know that with one in four women facing sexual violence at some points in their lives, and many others who come through bereavement, isolation, mental health issues and anxiety, my book can and will continue to help many.

In the light of decision to speak out and share my truth I realised that it was important to build a community for others who have faced sexual abuse, violence and domestic abuse.

When I was coming to terms with my abuse, I felt so alone. I was desperate to find the 'sisters' who might relate to what I had experienced, yet didn't know where to find them. This is how my Facebook group, Speak Out Sisterhood (SOS) was born.

Within this group, this band of survivors, warriors and victims, we have created a safe community which honours a woman's right to share her story should she wish, to seek support and friendship, safe in the knowledge that in coming to terms with her own past and her own truth, she too can free herself and reclaim her future. For many women, admitting to themselves initially that they have been abused, sexually or in an abusive relationship, is the first step in Speaking Out and coming to terms with their truth.

In becoming a trained Light Up Activator, delivering this vital work, it is an honour to work with all manner of people, many of whom have faced past trauma, challenge and adversity. To see people relearn, reconnect with and remember their innate power, to help them shed the bollocks which kept them caged for so longed, to watch them flourish ... it makes my soul sing loudly.

I choose to lead a life where I shine so brightly and thrive so well that I'm able to illuminate the darkest recesses of my mind. When life throws those inevitable curve balls, I can get myself more quickly back on an even keel. I am living, breathing proof that we can decide to change our thought processes, our attitude and beliefs about ourselves and our situation in order to change our future.

I'm not saying that it will or has been easy, AND I can tell you from the other side that it is worth it. We can make a conscious decision to begin work on ourselves TODAY, on our mindset and attitude. We can turn our 'I can't' into 'I can' and our 'I might' into 'I will'. As the title of this book so eloquently says, we can choose to say 'Bollocks to that, I choose to shine'. And we will.

DANIELLE DOWNEY

Danielle Downey Professional Activator

I'm the best selling author of"'It's No Secret".

I've worked as a midwife and an Independent Domestic Violence Advocate. I'm passionate about empowering and enabling women to have a voice and am a fervent champion in improving government and agency responses to domestic abuse and sexual violence. In speaking out passionately about abuse we break the stigma and chains which help to keep us silenced. I undertake speaking work and training for organisations using my experiences and professional knowledge.

My own experiences with overcoming adversity allow me to empathise and speak loudly about what it can be like in the aftermath of sexual abuse. I want others to know that with determination, focus and some luck, they can overcome the seemingly insurmountable. My journey has allowed me to be a light for others who have suffered and to help them to feel less isolated and alone.

I live in Devon with my two youngest children, an ill behaved Newfoundland cross dog, two squeaky guinea pigs and my patient husband. I enjoy writing and running, although not at the same time!

I dedicate my chapter to my children and my husband. Without their light and warmth my world would be grey and lonely. They bring out the best in me and make me a better version of myself, even when I lose my shit and shout like a crazy fish wife! They give me hope for tomorrow and their presence in my life makes my soul sing. I love you all so very much, round the moon and back again.

18

BOLLOCKS TO BEING STIFLED BY CANCER

MY ONCE DIMMED LIGHT IS NOW BEING ALLOWED TO SHINE BRIGHTLY.

That night, not even sure if I would wake up from the anaesthetic, I wrote a letter to each for my three beautiful girls.

Rosanna's Story

When I'm even older, greyer and more fabulous, I will look back at my life and laugh. Because I survived. Because I had the audacity and courage to do some of the things I did. I will be grateful for every single day that I survived.

Having had a very difficult childhood, I'd hoped that life as an adult would be plain sailing. But in 1993 everything changed.

I was married to a lovely, kind man, with three beautiful healthy daughters, aged eight, six and two. I had a comfortable large house and my own coffee shop which also did outside catering. My life was full to overflowing. I was juggling an awful lot of balls and sooner or later I would let an important ball slip, but from the outside looking in, it would seem that I was very lucky.

The reality was different. I was seeing a psychotherapist, the wonderful Dr Meg Robertson, having been diagnosed with postnatal depression when our youngest daughter was one. My beloved mother was slipping away from me with terminal cancer. All the pressures of everyday life were bearing down heavily on me. Being a hard taskmaster and liking to do things well, I was constantly pushing myself, never taking the time to relax. Relaxation was limited to watching the television for a few minutes before I got up to do one of the many jobs running around my head.

In November 1993, a month after my mother's funeral, I went to my local hospital Outpatients to have a swelling below my right ear examined. I was referred to a hospital forty miles away for surgery as soon as possible. Tired, frightened and still mourning the loss of my mother, I was admitted at the beginning of January. My husband was working shifts, the girls had school and nursery to go to, the house and business still had to be run. My father, barely coping with the loss of my mother and drowning in a sea of grief, was another burden on my already heavy load. All these concerns had to be left behind.

That night, not even sure if I'd wake up from the anaesthetic, I wrote a page for each my three girls. I find writing very cathartic and necessary. It was the thought of them growing up without me that spurred me to keep going throughout my illness.

The operation over, and with a big unsightly scar, nerve damage, and a partially shaved head, I was grateful to be going home five days later. The surgeon's prediction of an eighty percent chance that the lump was benign proved unfounded. It was malignant, I *did* have cancer. I'd only just been holding things together - losing my Mum had been one of the most unbearable things I could ever imagine. Was there no justice in this life? I trusted God enough to thank him for giving me my Mum for thirty six years. Would I be able to trust in him again? My deep faith would be tested to the limit in the following months and years.

The first step was to check if there was any other source of cancer. When the consultant came out of the radiographers' room, I knew he must have found something. He had - a larger tumour between my left kidney and spine. The next course of action was explained and I was handed a leaflet about Non-Hodgkin's Lymphoma.

I was referred to Patient Services to be fitted with a wig - my hair would fall out as a side effect of the drugs I'd be given. A fairly classic bob hairstyle meant it was comparatively easy to match up. I even managed to wear the wig while I did a few days supply teaching in a local comprehensive. Only when a pupil asked if I was wearing a wig did I decide it was time to step off the hamster wheel and spare myself the indignities of such questions. It was eventually used to finish off a 'Guy' that we burned ceremoniously on Bonfire Night!

My treatment went swimmingly. My hair did fall out. I didn't, unfortunately, lose weight. Life carried on as before. Rainbows, Brownies, swimming lessons and music lessons were all attended, bills paid, washing, ironing, cleaning and dusting all completed.

My mum's Macmillan nurse, Hazel King, was a great source of inspiration and comfort to me through this time. Hazel was one of life's 'special people'. She has since lost her own battle with ovarian cancer and the world really is a lesser place without her.

The Macmillan nurses not only provided me with help in the psychological, spiritual and emotional sense, but also practically and financially. When the going got tough they were there for us in every aspect. The financial grants we looked on as loans, and vowed to repay the kindness when I returned to good health.

After five sessions of chemotherapy, my husband and I were able to leave the girls with family and go to Tenerife for a week. Just being able to relax and not worry about ordinary parent and household problems was lovely.

On the last day, I banged my head on a sun umbrella. I thought nothing more of the incident and we flew home the next day, keen to see the girls. The following morning I woke up with blurred vision in my left eye. After a phone call to my consultant, I decided it must be a problem with my sight and duly booked an appointment with the optician who, after extensive tests, suggested a detached retina caused by the blow to my head. Four days later I had a session with Dr. Robertson. By this time I'd lost three quarters of the sight in my left eye, and she immediately picked up the phone and dialled the Eye Department, describing me as 'a lady who doesn't like to make a fuss'. I was seen that same afternoon and a few days later was at the Royal Eye Hospital in Liverpool for more detailed tests.

All I kept hearing was 'strange, rare, and unusual'. At the end of a long, tiring, intense day we returned to Wrexham Hospital where I was told that the cancer had grown and started to metastasise. A microscopic tumour had lodged itself in my left eye. The treatment I'd had over the last five months had not worked.

It was a big blow, not just to me but to my husband and all the family and friends who'd been praying for and supporting me. I wanted to be alone with my thoughts and prayers and needed time to think and see where I went from here. I asked for no one to come see me that evening but my request went unheeded, and my visitors jovially tried to establish a sense of normality in a life that was fast caving in around me. That night, in the sanctuary of my hospital room, I started to write. The emotions that were going through my head were too intense to share with anyone so I wrote them down to give me more space in my head.

With the dawn of a new day things seemed better. The treatment I'd been given was obviously the wrong type for me, so they went back to the original histology of the tumour and changed my treatment. A long awaited trip to Lourdes was cancelled and I embarked upon a new regime of very intensive chemotherapy. This time I responded well, the tumours shrank, and the one in my eye was removed by a single dose of radiotherapy.

My whole life revolved around my girls and the hospital treatment - visits, four night stays and blood transfusions. Family occasions came and went and all in all we coped quite well. I was so relieved just to be alive that I made the most of every day.

I was thoroughly spoiled by my friends and on one occasion was taken out for a day trip to a village called Pennant Melangell, where I met a counsellor called Evelyn Davies. She was inspirational in helping me through those dark times, teaching me that tomorrow doesn't exist, it's only a figment of our imagination - and if it doesn't exist then there's no need to worry about it. We were also able to have a short break away, paid for with a Holiday Grant by the Macmillan Cancer Fund. It gave us a chance to get away from everything: the visitors, the telephone, the hospital, everything, just to have some quality time with our girls.

By Christmas, my treatment was finished and we brought in the New Year with fresh hope. I was free of disease, my hair had come back curly as a corkscrew, and I was happy to get back on the hamster wheel of life, which became even more hectic and busy than before. An inspiring visit to Lourdes to say thank you was followed by a very emotional trip back to Italy where my parents came from. A scan in July 1995 showed that everything was fine.

In September I returned to work as a supply teacher. Another Christmas and New Year came and went and life was just grand. Then in February 1996, just as I was due to have a second routine scan, it started to snow and didn't stop for twenty-four hours, sending the whole country into total chaos. The radio was saying that only emergencies were to attend hospital. I thought: 'Well it might not be an emergency for anyone else, but it's important for me to have my scan as scheduled today'. A lift in my brother-in-law's four-by-four car and a trek home in a foot of snow, and I was scanned as planned.

Three days later my life was plunged into pitch-black darkness. My cancer had come back, a new tumour in my left lung. I was devastated, more frightened and angry than ever before. I have a deep faith and I can honestly say it was tested to its very core. I fell into a big black hole with sheer sides that I could see no way out of. All the hardship of fourteen months earlier, the tears, fear, pain, anger, had been for nothing. The depression got a firm grip of me and the nauseous sensation gripping my very being wouldn't let go.

The Macmillan nurses and our network of friends and family supported me and very quickly re-grouped to help me face this new battle, not least with prayers. We lost a few close friends along the way but realised not everybody could fight our battles with us. Considering the battering I'd taken over the last few years, a psychologist in the Christie Hospital told me that I was doing remarkably well to crawl out of my big black hole using my own resources.

On our youngest daughter Verity's fifth birthday in March, the Dunblane tragedy happened. At home I watched the news breaking and spent the whole day crying. It was as much as I could do to stop myself going to our daughters' primary school and bringing them home to protect them.

Cancer, when it strikes the parent of young children, brings all sorts of practical and financial problems. Up until now I'd been able to afford to pay a cleaner for three hours a week, but I had to ask her to stop coming. Even though I had a battle for my life on my hands, bills still needed paying. I was unable to work for quite a while but was deemed 'not ill enough' to qualify for benefits. A Macmillan hardship grant took the pressure off and helped immensely through those dark days, and we were grateful for help from family and the various funds that social workers from Christie hospital gave us. My Mum used to say that God is good and God will provide. I try to apply those philosophies in my life whenever the going gets tough.

Another Hickman Line was fitted for the heavy chemotherapy to follow. Preventive measures were taken to reduce sickness and nausea, but the drugs caused high temperatures, great discomfort, aches and pains. Every time I closed my eyes, an endless stream of pictures coursed through my brain, like a twenty four hour film festival in my head. At the time this was very disturbing and some images vividly remain with me to this day. Two have since happened in real life and sometimes I wonder if they were prophetic.

I coped as best I could, set myself targets, and the milestones came and went. Intensive chemotherapy ended and a mid-term scan showed that the tumour was shrinking. The treatment was working.

There was a few months' respite while I waited for a radical new treatment called Autologous Stem Cell Transplant. Injections in my tummy stimulated the growth of stem cells which were collected by an amazing machine which pulled all of my blood out of my system through a vein in one arm, stored the necessary cells until the end of the procedure, and sent what it didn't require back into my body via my Hickman Line. The stem cells were frozen until I needed them later in the year. A trip to Lourdes was cancelled and hastily rebooked: this time I was going back to say please.

In August, another routine scan revealed microscopic shadows on both lungs. So in September I went for a lung biopsy, returning home a week later with instructions not to iron, vacuum or drive for six weeks (a silver lining at last!). The surgeons had cut through some ribs to get to my lungs and any repetitive movement would prevent the rib from knitting together and healing itself. Luckily the biopsy showed that the shadows were simply tissue damage. I was facing the final straight, waiting at home for a date for my stem cell transplant to be started.

Our eldest daughter Chiarina went up to secondary school, another milestone. I was due to go into the Christie Hospital on December 1st for at least three weeks and hoped that with carefully planning and good behaviour, I could be home for Christmas. I would miss Melissa's tenth birthday but it was unavoidable. The treatment started in the form of tablets four days before leaving home. I hadn't anticipated the strength of these and hadn't yet packed for my three-week holiday! Planning and shopping for Christmas had to be left to my husband.

With heartfelt good wishes, Mass cards and many, many prayers, I set off to scale the final mountain. The Stem Cell Transplant would hopefully cure me so I had no choice but to face it. It was the only way of extending my life. I was thirty nine, had three children aged eleven, nine and five and I had to persevere. A new Macmillan nurse Carol Roberts came into my life and remains a friend to this day.

Each hospital stay was for me like a little holiday - thinking of it in positive terms helped me through it. I would pack favourite things, be pampered by family and friends and cared for professionally by the nurses and doctors. My three-week stay in the Christie Hospital felt more like imprisonment. The indignity of having to collect everything that passed through my digestive system, the nausea, fatigue, fear, loneliness, despair and the fight to survive all took their toll on me.

I like to know what's going on and why things are done so I'd read up as much as I could about Stem Cell Transplants. They say knowledge is power, but in this case I think less may have been better. In an article by the editor of American Vogue Liz Tilberis, who has since lost her battle with ovarian cancer, she wrote that they take you to the point of death and bring you back again. I now know that she wasn't using journalistic licence.

On the night I was admitted, I was very frightened of what lay ahead. I was extremely sad at leaving the girls, scared at being alone forty miles away from home in a strange miserable place, and already sick from the chemotherapy tablets. For the first and only time in my life I had a panic attack and put my back into a spasm. 'Come on girl!' I thought, 'get a grip'. The nurses gave me a Valium tablet to calm my nerves but all it made me do was hallucinate and have psychotic dreams. My husband had gone home but rapidly made arrangements to come back and he slept on a camp bed by my side for four nights. Beyond that it was dangerous for him to stay as I would have virtually no immune system and infection and germs would be very dangerous for me. A phone next to my bed was my only contact with the outside world. I was on my own again.

The nurses had expressed concern over my state of mind and the resident psychiatrist came for a chat. Satisfied with my answers, he left never to return, which was a pity in a way because he was rather dishy! I lost my hair and my nails started to come away at the root as the doctors had warned me. My skin took on a false tan look and it was many months before it returned to normal. Time moved slowly, and with Christmas preparations advancing all around the world, I was stuck in my ivory tower. I wasn't allowed any flowers because of the possibility of infection, but I had numerous cards and letters and phone calls and all of these kept me going.

My sister and I had a game that we'd buy each other presents and always try to better what the other had bought. Never in my wildest dreams could I have guessed what she had in the pipeline for me. She'd asked for a photo of my girls and I'd thought that she planned to have it transferred onto a plate. When a parcel arrived I didn't pay any attention to the unusual postmark. The box was elaborately wrapped with beautiful ribbon and expensive wrapping paper. 'She's gone upmarket!' I thought, when I saw the name of a London firm embossed in gold on the front of the navy box.

There haven't been many times in my life when I've been speechless. This was one of them. In the box was a monogrammed frame with a photograph of the Princess of Wales with William and Harry. Knowing that the Princess was one of my heroes, my sister had written to her to see if she would send me a message of encouragement. This was her response. A lady-in-waiting also phoned my sister on behalf of the Princess to tell me that the Princess was thinking of me. I didn't have the strength to wash or feed myself at the time, but I felt I had to write to the Princess to thank her. I feel that had she been in Manchester in that three-week period, she would have come to visit me.

I had many visitors in those three weeks, including my middle daughter Melissa on her tenth birthday. I was thrilled to see her and aware it must have been frightening for my girls to see their mummy so poorly. Years later I came across a piece of work Chiarina had done for school. She describes the interminably long hospital corridors she had to walk down when she came to visit me. She thought the further down the corridor a patient was, the more seriously ill they were and 'my mum was always in the second to last room'. I also found a piece of work by Melissa called 'Wearing a Mask', in which she describes how she pretended everything was fine but would cry herself to sleep in the privacy of her own room. Very frightening for a small child and I can't imagine how difficult it must have been for them all.

Nativity plays, carol concerts and Christmas parties were all going on without me, whilst inside that cold, stark, gloomy room I was having the fight of my life. Finally on the 22nd December, I was released to start rebuilding my life.

I've now been in remission for over twenty years and am living my life as fully as I can. My own personal journey took me to five excellent hospitals, under the care of two professors, some brilliant doctors, marvellous nurses and invaluable other professionals. I had a fabulous family and tremendous friends. The network from church supported me with soup, cakes, balloons, books, magazines, gifts, fruit, flowers, chocolates, smellies, cards and letters, countless phone calls and last, but most definitely not least, prayers. Without them I would not be here now. I'm praying and hoping that it's an experience I never have to repeat.

Looking back on some of the things I've written about, my experiences don't seem as bad as they felt at the time. Having to make any change in our life, through no fault of our own, is hard for whatever reason. It saddens me that despite having gone through all of that, there is still disharmony, acrimony, deceit and unsettled times in the world, not least in my own life. Despite my experiences, I know that some of the most important people in my life can show me rancour, disdain, jealousy and disrespect. Having said that, I've learnt that it's about what's happening in their lives, rather than what's occurring in mine. There's a survival instinct in us all - the thought that my girls could grow up not knowing me was one that I hung onto through thick and thin.

Having the Stem Cell transplant has meant that, since then, I've had the opportunity to take part in the London Marathon in 2002, as well as swimming a mile for the Macmillan Nurses. On my fiftieth birthday I was on the Great Wall of China doing a charity trek for the Marie Curie Nurses. I later secured a job at a great school where I am still working with top quality colleagues, some of whom have become dear friends, and I've been privileged to teach some amazing young people.

I had my account of dealing with Non-Hodgkin's Lymphoma published in Woman's Realm. I've been through the sale of my lovely little coffee shop, the intense pain of a divorce, the fear of a solo mortgage at fifty four and the end of some very precious friendships. A minor skirmish with Cervical Cancer in 2011 culminated in a hysterectomy. I vented my creative spleen by organising and playing a major part in a Flower Festival in my beloved church. I gained a Graduate Certificate in Education at Glyndwr, and started my Masters. Then another devastating and arduous battle, this time with Breast Cancer, entailed minor surgery, more chemotherapy and radiotherapy and I now have been discharged from the hospital, six years later.

What doesn't kill you makes you stronger, doesn't it? When new people come into my life I think: please don't look at the woman I've become. Look at the woman behind the arduous journey I've undertaken to get here.

I've had the joy of my eldest daughter's wedding and being here to see all three of my girls in settled established loving relationships and full time employment. My amazing daughters are now thirty-three, thirty-two and twenty-seven. All healthy, beautiful, vibrant and lovely young women. I look on them as my greatest achievement so far, I'm very proud of them and I love them with all my heart. I get to see my beautiful granddaughters growing up, my dad reach ninety-two years old, and I have spent precious time with my much loved siblings and their families. I've been blessed to spend quality time with some of the strong wise dependable men and women who I'm lucky enough to call my friends, and we've raised over £28,000 for cancer charities.

Every birthday is a milestone, as was being present at the birth of my adored granddaughters, Lily and Amelia, both of who bring immeasurable joy into my life. I've been able to indulge my passion for travelling by visiting some fabulous far off places, with the promise of being able to visit many more.

I had my cathartic Light Up experience with the brilliant Melanie Pledger in her beautiful home in France. The lessons I learnt on my personal Light Up journey have since proved to be invaluable and have helped me through some painful times. It's meant that now nothing and no one can ever hurt or affect me again. I don't tolerate or accept disrespectful or intolerable behaviour any more. I've unhooked, separated and dispatched any demons that try to cross me. I deserve and have earned better behaviour and relationships. My once dimmed light is now being allowed to shine brightly.

I still have many ambitions to achieve, new plans to make and hopefully many more years of good health. I am truly blessed. Was falling ill and having cancer the best thing that ever happened to me? Of course not. Did it change my whole life? You bet. It has altered my whole outlook and even though I know there's a chance it may come back, I'm not hanging around waiting for it.

ROSANNA JONES

I live on my own in Wrexham, North Wales, which is where I was brought up by my Italian parents. I have three grown up daughters and two beautiful granddaughters. I teach Food Studies three days a week, a job that I still love. I've got a large circle of great friends and spend time going to the cinema, live shows, eating out as well as dabbling in antiques and collectables with regular visits to car boot sales in the summer and spending time with my 92-year-old dad. I also travel whenever my bank manager allows. I'm passionate about Italy, love all aspects of it. I'm not lucky, I am blessed.

Having had major life experiences since an early age, I wish I'd known that all troubles eventually pass. I wish I'd recognised that people have unrealistic expectations of me, probably mirrored by my expectations of them! I wish I'd been more protective of myself and the gifts that I have.

Everything happens for a reason and I'm thrilled to have been given this opportunity to share my story in the hope that it will help anyone who facing a similar journey.

My chapter is dedicated to my beautiful mamma, Chiarina who died aged only 65. My life has never been the same since. To my amazing daughters Chiarina (she was named after my mum), Melissa and Verity and last but not least to my fabulous granddaughters Lily and Amelia who I thank for all the love and joy they bring into my life.

19

BOLLOCKS TO LOSING MYSELF TO MASKS

I'M RECONNECTED WITH THE BEAUTIFUL GIRL I WAS BEFORE ANY OF THE DAMAGE HAPPENED.

I was completely exhausted after twenty-five years of hiding, being someone else, and believing all the things that the abusive relationship had taught me.

Alison's Story

My name is Alison Ellis and I'm a Light Up Activator. I love saying that: I feel so proud to be part of this amazing work.

I was born in 1969 into what I perceived as a normal family. Me, mum, dad and a brother. Mum and dad worked full time and I went to school, had lots of friends and generally enjoyed life. 'We only know what we know' is a brilliant way to describe my perceptions of my early life. My mum (bless her) protected my brother and me from the reality of what was really going on.

Mum asked my dad to leave when I was fifteen. He'd been having affairs for the twenty-one years of their marriage, had children by other women and had been in a relationship with one woman and her children for the last eleven years. Wow, that was a shock! So the BOLLOCKS had well and truly begun.

Of course, the mandatory system bollocks had been happening too. The 'be still, be quiet, don't act the fool, follow the rules' stuff that we all endure and see as normal. That too had been running its course and doing its damage along the way.

Also when I was fifteen (yes, it was quick!), mum announced that she was marrying again. We moved into my new step dad's house and I gained two step sisters who'd recently lost their mother through cancer and really weren't looking for a new family. For mum's sake, we played the game. More bollocks, more not being myself, more acting as though it was all okay and desperately wanting to leave and start my own life.

Then college, and more of the systemic damage. And A WAY OUT. I moved to London and started my life independently. I wasn't scared, I had so much to give and there were no 'fun suckers' telling me to abide by the rules.

At first it was fun. And then it was hard. This adult life was tougher to juggle than I thought. Here's where I formed my model of financial struggle - how to make ends meet and how to feel guilty when I bought something I thought I needed. So yes, I was like most people, following society's rules and slowly forgetting the excitement and joy I'd first felt when leaving home. Life started to leave its marks.

And then disaster struck: a relationship that was abusive, manipulative and criminal. I fought to keep my identity throughout the rapids of 'I must survive'. It was this that subsequently began to form the template of who I believed I truly was.

My new perception of myself was that I now had to be careful, be alert to danger, stay respectable and follow the rules. Or bad things happen. The fun was truly gone from life. Unless I got drunk, let go and pretended I was free.

Pretending to be normal was my new occupation. Being responsible and respectable was the new me. And yet it wasn't me at all. I'm naturally loud, outspoken, fun. I love to giggle. I now knew from my experiences that being like this led to disaster.

Joy entered my life again when my children were born, three years apart. Being a mum is the most amazing job in the world and the times of freedom with my children when we would play and laugh helped me through the years of drudgery.

I'm telling you all this because I know what it's like to live in this world, to suffer the mandatory damage that's put on us by the system and by the perceptions of others, and the things we do to help ourselves survive some rather massive traumatic events.

I went to church, brought up my kids well, worked really hard. And still there was always something missing. *Me.*

I decided at the age of thirty-six to change my life. I'd met and married my second husband, the love of my life. I felt joy again and I was now in a position to help others. In 2013 I was privileged to go to Cambodia on a mission to work with agencies who supported victims of human trafficking. I met children who had suffered horrendous abuse and my heart broke. I felt guilty about my own situation and the hugest pull to help. I researched trafficking in the UK and was appalled at the lack of support for women who had been coerced into the sex industry. Many of the women were UK nationals and it was clear that they were not being recognised and supported.

I worked tirelessly to create a charity to support survivors of human trafficking. I built the business up and opened a house to support survivors. I had found a place that needed me. And I needed to feel needed.

I ran this charity for over four years, and it was exhausting. It felt like a constant cycle of trying, pushing, struggling to help and fighting for recognition. Don't get me wrong, we did some amazing work and helped save the lives of young women who were victims of the heinous crime of modern-day slavery. And yet there was always something missing. Yes, you guessed it: still *me.*

In 2017, one of the volunteers at the charity told me about a friend of a friend who was doing this thing called Light Up. We discussed it and I thought it could add to our programme for the women we were supporting at The safe House. So we arranged to go over to France to experience Light Up for ourselves. All the time my focus was solely on the charity and how Light Up might bring some positivity, mindfulness (or whatever it was) to the company.

Boy was I wrong ... and right!

The most surprising thing about Light Up for me was that it was all about me. *Me*, eh! - what's all that about? I was so fixed on doing the 'right' thing, helping others, being respectable, being a good mum, being a good wife, being a good leader, that I'd never really looked at *me*. I mean *really* looked at *me*. It was the bit missing. It felt wrong to look at *me*. Vain and self-indulgent.

At first, I have to admit, I thought the whole thing was bonkers. I really enjoyed that, I loved going through the process and just believed that I'd forget all about it once I got back home. I was also really concerned that I was going against my faith and that it was *wrong* to look at *me*. I struggled with this and when I got back to the UK I continued to struggle.

What I now understand is that without knowing me and without the whole thing being about me, who would I be helping? Because I am part of everything that I do, every relationship, every conversation. I can affect my own life and other people if I know ME. Christians are commanded to 'Love their neighbour, as they would love their self. If I loved my neighbour how I loved myself, I'd be saying "oi you're too fat, you're stupid, you never do anything right". It's only when I loved myself that I was able to love others.

It wasn't until a few months later that I started to notice different things about myself. And they weren't all good (or so I thought - 'thought' being the correct word).

I realised I was completely exhausted after twenty-five years of hiding behind masks, being someone else, trying hard and believing all the things that the abusive situation I was in when I was younger had taught me. I'd built a life around an image of who I 'thought' I was, based on a short period of my life.

Going through Light Up reconnected me to the girl I was before any of the trauma, before life 'happened'. It took me back to being ME. My image of myself today is not based on the things that happened to me, the bollocks that life taught me. Don't get me wrong - I don't regret *any* of the things I've done. I only know for sure that if I had done them truly being me, I would have enjoyed them so much more.

Today I am able to be that little carefree girl again, playing in the back field, making up games in my imagination and rejoicing with the sun on my face. Today I am giving myself a break and just being. Being me, I am powerful, I am all the things that I have always been and just forgot or squashed down to allow me to fit into the world.

My light is Joy and I know for sure that I have missed her and that finding her/myself is joyous. I have Joy with me constantly, because that is who I am, who I have always been.

In 2017 I decided to go through the Activator Training course so that I could start to support others to reconnect with themselves through Light Up. I was unprepared for the huge surge of inner growth as the course led me even deeper into knowing myself. There were some scary, dark places there and at times it was painful. Beneath the darkness though, there was, is always, my light, always my Joy, ME.

I began to look at my life and what truly brought me joy. I decided it was time to turn the page and start a new chapter. I chose to have relationships only with people who brought me joy. This too was painful, as I dredged through all my old habits of helping everyone else before myself, all the old reasons why I did the things I did.

One morning I got the kick that I needed, and it came, of course, from ME. During activator training we were invited to write a letter to ourselves about the truths we'd discovered. This would be posted to us in six months' time. I'd totally forgotten all about it. It's funny how we humans remember the bad stuff and forget the really important personal stuff. Anyway, the letter arrived, in my handwriting, addressed to me, and this is what it said:

- You've done enough, close the charity and let others pick up the mantle.

- Do what you've always wanted to do. Just choose it - and move to Cornwall.

- Deliver Light Up to others from your house in Cornwall and provide residential retreats to people who choose to stay for a few days.

My husband's dreams were the same as mine. We closed the charity down, put our house up for sale and yeah, we just did it. We moved to Cornwall.

I am happy. I am me. I spend many days walking my two gorgeous dogs down at the beach and looking out to sea. I love it here and the waves remind me that it's all about now. Each wave, like us, is unique. It's there once, crashing in the very moment, and there are never two the same. Each wave is magnificent in its own way, just like all of us.

Now my new plan, being me and living totally and freely as me, is to open my home to others who would like to get to know themselves again. The time is 'now', the only time there is, and I am filled with joy daily. I choose to share the beautiful surroundings that I now live in to offer a residential stay to anyone who has forgotten who they are and would like to reconnect.

People sometimes say to me 'it's alright for you, life is simple and easy for you' and yes, that is now so true. AND it's taken me a long time to get here. It doesn't have to take that long. Light Up is here now. Grab it with both hands.

ALISON ELLIS

Alison Ellis Professional Activator

I'm passionate about helping people enjoy life to the full. I believe that it can be a challenge to achieve the delicate balance between enjoying life to the full and fulfilling all the roles we are assigned by society. It's a lesson that I have learnt after I spent many wasted years 'thinking' and believing society's, and my own, mixed up views of who I 'should' be. Since finding Light Up I have sieved through my beliefs and find that I am at last being true to my authentic self. This is what God made me to be.

I love being a Light Up Activator and receive so much joy when I help others to find themselves again. Reminding and prompting others to become all that they are is such a privilege and the best job in the world.

20

BOLLOCKS TO BULLYING, ABUSE AND KEEPING QUIET

THE GHOST HAS FINALLY BEEN EXORCISED AND I CAN FINALLY LIVE OUT MY DAYS IN PEACE AND LIGHT.

I was programmed, or 'bullied' if you prefer, to look at things this way. This is just a fact of life, right? Boys don't cry about 'silly' stuff.

Warwick's Story

When I was asked to write my story for inclusion in this book, I was thrilled. But also, if I'm honest, a little apprehensive.

In the fifty-four years of my life to date, like most of us I'm sure, I am thankful to have experienced many amazing 'highs' and joyful experiences. But there have also been many periods of deep depression and despair which at times have risen to the forefront.

On reflection, and looking back in particular at my time spent at an all-boys boarding school in the 1970s, aged eight to thirteen, I could also describe what would now immediately be recognised and classified as abuse, although at the time and in the environment I found myself, this was considered 'normal'.

For anyone (boy or girl) who was ever sent to boarding school as a young child, and who suffered as a consequence, I would thoroughly recommended a book called 'Boarding School Syndrome' by Joy

Schaverien. It 'turned my head' when I read it - it was as if it had been written just for me.

I personally find that joyful experiences have imprinted fond memories in my mind, which reside quietly in my subconscious and I can recall at will, while the abusive or negative experiences have left scars that tend to surface in my conscious mind, especially at times when they are unwelcome or uninvited.

Many people who have experienced emotional turmoil find it cathartic to discuss it openly and in depth with others. I take my hat off to them, especially given the courage this takes. Personally, this isn't something I'm comfortable with and therefore choose not to go into too much detail here. That said, I did reach a point where I needed to put my demons to rest. I was unable to do this until I found Light Up.

So how then do I describe my story and what Light Up has done for me? The process of going through Light Up and the life changing effects it has afterwards can be quite complex to put into words!

Also, as far as I'm aware, more women than men seem to have sought out what Light Up has to offer, and that's a shame. We all hurt equally and can all benefit from this incredible gift. I want therefore to try to make my story and journey particularly relevant for the guys, because in my experience it works just as well for both sexes.

It dawned on me that of the many of the stories I'd heard about the Light Up experience had been highly emotive (not surprising, considering the amazing effects). If I restrain myself and describe my experience using the 'H and T principle', then it might hopefully appeal to people of both genders who prefer to look at something in a less emotional and more analytical manner. So what is the 'H and T' principle?

In my career as a commercial pilot, and latterly as a registered Emergency Care Practitioner (ECP), there are many key aspects that have to be recalled rapidly and accurately from memory alone, to ensure passenger or patient safety and in order to reach an appropriate and robust analytical decision, often in highly challenging and emotive situations.

The memory method of emergency training is very similar in both aviation and medicine (and of course in many other careers as well) and is largely achieved by the use of mnemonics. For example, as an ECP practitioner dealing with a patient in cardiac arrest and without time to refer to a text book, we MUST remember the possible REVERSIBLE causes, remembered as the five 'H's and six 'T's. Hypovolemia, Hypoxia, Hydrogen ions, Hyper (or Hypo) kalemia and Hypothermia. Tablets (or Toxins), Tamponade, Tension pneumothorax, Thrombosis, Thromboembolism and Trauma.

Being able to remember these 'off the top of the head' and then use drugs and other techniques to treat any reversible causes rapidly, we stand a much better chance of getting a successful resuscitation outcome. Happy days then for the patient, their family, and us, and we all get to go home for dinner!

Thinking about how I would document my story, I remembered that during my Light Up experience, along with the 'H's and G's' (Heroes and Gremlins - I can't say too much more here or I'll spoil your experience!), there were also my own 'D's and L's'.

I like to think that I'm a man's man, a typical English bloke, more than capable of dealing with the inevitable blows and crap that life dishes out to us all, and able to handle it all on my own thank you very much! I really don't require or welcome 'expert' help and I certainly don't trust so called counsellors, self-help gurus or other 'airy-fairy' groups.

I have an avid dislike of the victim culture. Some people seem to feel they can hide behind or blame others for the problems they have in their life, including their own failings. They use this as an overarching excuse for not getting their act together and taking responsibility for their own well being, which also then affects (mostly negatively) those who love and care about them.

I recognise of course that others have caused me considerable distress and pain over the years, but I grew up in a 'man-up' culture, from when I first started boarding school in the seventies at the age of eight. I was programmed, or 'bullied' if you prefer, to look at things this way. This is just a fact of life, right? Boys don't cry about 'silly' stuff.

My Four 'D's

Denial. If I'm so confident and capable of handling this alone, why then have I struggled so much?

Delusion. If I'm so strong, why haven't I actually paid attention to what my inner-self has been SHOUTING at me all along, and acted upon the incredible natural self-defence instincts that my own body has given me?

Dread. As I got older, the fact that I *still* hadn't found peace and was still wondering who I really am started to weigh more heavily on my mind. Would I ever get this sorted?

Disbelief. While I mistrusted counsellors, voodoo, self-help groups, airy-fairy solutions and victim culture, perhaps I did need to explore this more. What could Light Up really do?

My Four 'L's

Light. Light Up came into my life, I won't explain exactly how or why here, but I will be forever thankful that it did. It isn't counselling, it isn't victim culture, it isn't self-help, it isn't religion, it IS hard to explain! If you'd like to know more about my experience with Light Up, please feel free to email me.

Laughter. Laughter and happiness have come back into my life, which I had never thought would be possible again.

Lies. Lies - to myself, and those to others, albeit 'white lies' made in the spirit of self-defense - have gone. No more.

Longevity. No matter what length of time I have left on this earth, my 'D's have finally been sorted and it was these that I now know were dragging me back into darkness. The ghost has finally been exorcised and I can now live out my days in peace, light and love.

I'd like to share this beautiful piece that I recently happened to find. It's an essay written in 1987 by American author and social activist Emily Perl Kingsley, about having a child with a disability. It's given by many organisations to parents of new children with special needs. For me, it beautifully encapsulates what life in general is all about. I hope it speaks to you as much as it did to me.

"Welcome to Holland" By Emily Perl Kingsley, 1987.

I am often asked to describe the experience of raising a child with a disability - to try to help people who have not shared that unique experience to understand it, to imagine how it would feel. It's like this. When you're going to have a baby, it's like planning a fabulous vacation trip - to Italy. You buy a bunch of guide books and make your wonderful plans. The Coliseum. The Michelangelo David. The gondolas in Venice. You may learn some handy phrases in Italian. It's all very exciting.

After months of eager anticipation, the day finally arrives. You pack your bags and off you go. Several hours later, the plane lands. The stewardess comes in and says, "Welcome to Holland."

"Holland?!?" you say. "What do you mean Holland?? I signed up for Italy! I'm supposed to be in Italy. All my life I've dreamed of going to Italy."

But there's been a change in the flight plan. They've landed in Holland and there you must stay.

The important thing is that they haven't taken you to a horrible, disgusting, filthy place, full of pestilence, famine and disease. It's just a different place.

So you must go out and buy new guide books. And you must learn a whole new language. And you will meet a whole new group of people you would never have met.

It's just a different place. It's slower-paced than Italy, less flashy than Italy. But after you've been there for a while and you catch your breath, you look around.... and you begin to notice that Holland has wind-mills....and Holland has tulips. Holland even has Rembrandts.

But everyone you know is busy coming and going from Italy... and they're all bragging about what a wonderful time they had there. And for the rest of your life, you will say "Yes, that's where I was supposed to go. That's what I had planned.

And the pain of that will never, ever, ever, ever go away ... because the loss of that dream is a very very significant loss. But ... if you spend your life mourning the fact that you didn't get to Italy, you may never be free to enjoy the very special, the very lovely things ... about Holland.

CAPTAIN WARWICK PLAYER

To all intents and purposes, I suppose I'm what could easily be described as a professional man who has done well for himself. I am currently a UK State Registered Paramedic and Emergency Care Practitioner. I am also a qualified commercial pilot and flight instructor.

And yet ... my reason for sharing my story here is that like me, so many people in life have struggled to find true inner peace and happiness. Unexpected and unwelcome events happen to us. Life doesn't work out as planned. And we often choose to bury the bad stuff, hoping it will go away. I finally found my peace by admitting what happened, accepting myself through it all, and choosing to search for the light in the darkness.

I wish that when I was younger, I had been able realise how special life is and been able to focus more on what really matters – this isn't a rehearsal!

I dedicate this chapter to all my family and friends, immediate and extended, and especially to my grandchildren Riley, Oliver and Ethan.

21

BOLLOCKS TO SHAME AND LOW SELF ESTEEM

NOW I AM CONNECTED WITH MY TRUTH AND POWER.

I sought external validation from everyone and everything, doubting my abilities, living life as a chronic people pleaser, allowing the circumstances around me to determine my happiness, confidence and ability to achieve.

Lucy's Story

We are here for a reason. Each one of us has a unique purpose and a message to the world that only we know how to share.

I spent years stuck in the notion that I had to look outside of myself for the answers. It wasn't until I was able to see that I had everything I needed within me that I uncovered my own way of finding what makes my soul sing. I started to recognise the things that gave me a complete sense of fulfilment, certainty, and freedom - when I remembered to tap into them.

It was a journey that meant I finally felt like I could breathe. I was no longer searching for the answers, and was able to show up with more confidence than ever before. This journey enabled me to walk away from toxic and unsupportive people that before I had allowed to dominate my world and take advantage of my vulnerabilities.

Everyone deserves to live this way, and my mission is to help you to uncover and share your greatest purpose with the world and build the foundations of the life you so deserve. As an entrepreneur, Affiliate Marketing Professional, professional Activator and with a background in teaching, Light Up gave me the confidence to trust in me and my own decisions, ultimately supporting my career success.

We spend so much of our lives trying to fit in, to be liked, to be good enough, that we forget our true selves, the power that is already within us and the unique contribution we have to bring to this world. It leaves us feeling unfulfilled, meaningless and very far from home. This is how I lived for most of my life.

I had an inner knowing that I was born to do more, give more and be more and yet I always found myself falling short of achieving my greatness. I sought external validation from everyone and everything, doubting my abilities, living life as a chronic people pleaser, allowing the circumstances around me to determine my happiness, confidence and ability to achieve.

I would experience days of feeling burned out, full of anxiety, drowning in financial debt, and living a life that was compromising my values. With this came a tremendous amount of guilt and frustration, because I was surrounded with so much to be grateful for, and yet I never felt fulfilled. I continued to long for the day when I would achieve my 'big break' for success with the vehicle that would get me there. The world had disconnected me through years of conditioning.

Light up permitted me to forgive myself for previously allowing my external world to dominate my internal one. It was time to align myself back to being unapologetically and authentically me.

I know for many of you, reading about this for the first time, you might be thinking 'it all sounds a bit woo woo.' I get it. For many of us, we've been conditioned for so long and social media has created a pressured environment to always show up a 'certain way', and it can cause us to lose sight of who we really are. As much as I am on my own spiritual journey, this isn't about any religious or spiritual teaching, this is about remembering and being *ourselves*.

When we're able to harness what has *always* been there, we can live life on purpose, fulfilled, aligned with our values and what's important to us, protected from unsupportive or toxic people. We have the opportunity to overcome any challenge from within with more confidence than ever before.

I appreciate that my story, my life and my challenges will differ from your current reality. So I hope they inspire you to see how you too can utilise the power that is within you to come home to yourself and be the change in the world you were always meant to be. When we live from a place of being empowered in our own skin, we can create purpose and meaning, and avoid external corruption of our truth.

I know what it feels like to be a dreamer, a believer, and at the same time feel overwhelmed and daunted by the gap between where I was and the person I chose to be, the value I longed to give to the world and the life I wanted to create. A life lived not just for me, but for the people who mean something in my world too.

This will be one of the first times I've ever shared my truths to the world. For so long I felt ashamed of my failures, my struggles, my mistakes, my low self-esteem (which allowed negative people to shape my world), my failure to pick myself back up when things went wrong and how hard it was to make any change. I share this with you now because it may be that my message, my experiences, trials and tribulations will give you the confidence and belief that you too can overcome any challenge and change your current circumstances and life... it starts with YOU.

I know that everything before now has been happening FOR you. So my message is: don't ever be ashamed of your journey to date, the goals you didn't reach, the mistakes you made, the people you trusted who let you down, the feeling of being lost and never quite making it. Your time is

NOW, and everything has been leading you to this the next part of your journey. This I promise you.

A constant battle for me has been living with that burning desire to be more, achieve more and give more. I thought it was all in my mind, but in truth it was my intuition, my inner calling reaching out to me. These feelings would often leave me distracted in the day job, feeling disappointed as each day passed and I was no closer to the life I longed for and the dreams I created in my mind. There was a constant internal nudge that there had to be more to life than just this. I knew I had the potential to achieve all of my goals yet I found myself getting in my own way consistently.

The truth is, most people don't ever pursue their dream, even when they're capable of it, because they haven't taken the time to find out what to do or explore the possibilities. I spent my whole life believing that reaching the next goal was about 'pushing further, working harder'. And this kept me stuck. I invested so much money over the years into the wrong people and the wrong things, seeking external validation to give me the confidence that I was worthy of success.

The truth is, I needed to trust in myself to be confident in my own decision making, trusting in my own imagination and creativity and action that potential in my own authentic way. I see the world through very different eyes now, the way I was born to see the world.

I'm a firm believer that everything happens for a reason. The people we meet, the challenges we face, the failures and successes we encounter: it's all part of a bigger plan for us, even if we can't see it in the moment.

I don't believe it's any coincidence that you have picked up this book. Perhaps you feel you've lost your place in the world, and your life experiences to date have made you feel like you're not good enough. That feeling of not being in control is paralysing and can keep people stuck for their entire life.

The reality is that all of us will at some point come across difficult circumstances, negative people and experiences that we can't control.

It's these moments that will, if we're brave enough to put ourselves out there, shape our character and reveal what we're really capable of. We can't control everything that happens to us, but we can control the meaning of everything that happens. Remember, nothing in life has any meaning except for the meaning we give it.

Light Up found me when I was ready, after a lifetime of allowing people into my world who took advantage of my vulnerabilities; something we are all familiar with. There is a great lesson in every heartbreak and betrayal, people aren't always who we would hope them to be. Listen to your intuition, she knows before they can act. I've been so fortunate with many people in my life, but one or two have left me completely paralysed to the point where I was experiencing anxiety. Isn't it awful how the actions of someone else that have nothing to do with us can actually cause us to lose our own confidence?

When things happen to us, when people do us wrong and we can't make sense of it, we often start questioning if *we* are the problem. Are they right? Did I deserve it?

Relationships can either make us or break us. I've kissed many 'frogs', many who have encouraged me to doubt my own worth.

Looking back, I know the universe was protecting me from living a life with the wrong people who absolutely were not right for me, and at the same time allowing me to feel the feelings to teach me what it was important to learn.

For all of those people, experiences, and events that led me to where I am now, I will be forever grateful. They taught me that sometimes we have to face our darkest times to find ourselves.

During those times of struggle, when I was longing for change, hope and reassurance, my beautiful friend who was a DNA Activator reached out, and Light Up came into my world. The experience of Light Up enabled me to feel wholly heard, safe, empowered, healed and with an ability to find this inner strength, guarded with tools from within to overcome anything life could throw at me. When I came home to who I really was, I allowed myself to love and trust again.

It was also the start of bigger things for me.

Looking inside myself, I realised that there was actually a lot about my life that wasn't making me feel fulfilled or in alignment with who I really was. I was just doing it to fit into society's expectations and please the world before myself. I know for many of you reading this, there will be areas in your life that are not where you want to be. In fact, things may be so far away from your expectations that it's causing pain, disappointment, resentment, and feelings of helplessness, trapping you in your current reality - whether it be in your health, finances, relationships, career, spiritual connections (or lack of) or life circumstances. All of these things can take us so far away from the person we are, the value we are meant to give and the purpose we're intended to fulfil that we forget to even listen to our intuition, to what's guiding us home.

This is what allows most people to settle for an average life rather than reaching their true potential. It's what keeps people trapped in stressful or unfulfilling careers because they think they have no choice. It's what kills so many dreams and allows people to believe they are worthless. It's what encourages the negative people of the world to manipulate those being brave because they're not brave enough to pursue their own dreams (our struggles, failures or lack of success actually cause us to start believing them too!) It's what makes us feel frustrated, confused and totally paralysed.

The worst part of it all is living with that deep down feeling that we are absolutely capable of doing more, becoming more, achieving more and giving more, but feeling totally trapped by the circumstances of 'life'. We too often get gripped by the overwhelm of too many things we can't control. This distorts our view and makes us believe we can't influence the many things that we actually can. What we focus on and the meaning we give a particular event or situation will hugely impact how we feel about it. The truth is: we can change our instant reality.

If you're anything like I used to be with life problems, worries, pressure, and pain, it's easier to stay on the treadmill of life, waiting for that 'miracle' and looking for change externally. The truth is nothing ever did change for me until I made the decision to actually start trusting in me. It was then, in that moment, that everything shifted.

Emotions really are just a habit. When we're questioning how to pull ourselves out of our own 'funk', we first need to own the fact that this is the way we've been choosing to live. We get what we tolerate. And the way we look at life is just a habit. In any given moment we can choose to respond differently, to feel stressed out, sad, overwhelmed and anxious or happy, passionate and strong.

Before Light Up the feelings of overwhelm and anxiety, in so many areas of my life, kept me stuck in my current reality. My past financial situation (being in debt and having no money), my lack of knowledge and skills, comparing myself negatively to successful people, the lack of time around all of my commitments, negative people and relationships that over time left me feeling demotivated and unworthy, worrying too much about what others thought of me. Not to mention the pressure I put on myself to be a certain weight and look a certain way, which would send me into the overwhelm of the 'exercise and eating' regime. Life problems eh! Well, everything is relative, and for me these were real feelings that prevented me from ever taking the time to really get to know myself.

Maya Angelou said: *'People won't always remember what you said, but they will never forget how you made them feel.'* I actually can't remember the exact steps of the Light Up experience I went through. And yet I will always remember how it made me feel.

Knowing how Light Up has shaped my world and the impact it's had on others who have experienced their own journey, I will continue to share the magic that it is. It's not about teaching us anything new, it's just about REMEMBERING. We all have a beautiful, unique gift; Light Up helps us sing the song that has always been inside of us. Light Up shows us how, from any given situation, we have the power to find our light every day.

If any of my stories have resonated with you - perhaps you too have struggled with your own inner confidence, or lived outside of yourself as a chronic people pleaser, or perhaps you're a female in business or a struggling entrepreneur feeling stuck or unsure how to find your break-through - you are it. Reach out anytime.

LUCY CRANE

LUCY CRANE Professional Activator

A glow-getter from the UK with a passion for supporting women all over the world to take advantage of the Digital marketing world and create the financial and time freedom they are seeking through Affiliate Marketing.

I am also the Operational Director for Authors & Co - a book publishing company for Female Entrepreneurs and Professionals. We support women to write and publish their own book so that they can be known as the expert in their field, become a bigger influencer in their industry, share their message with the world and leave a legacy.

Light Up allows me to embrace who I really am. If there's anything I could have told myself before Light up it would be this: to trust in my intuition, my gut instinct - because *she knows*. Too often I made decisions based on 'logic' and not what 'felt' right - it shrank my confidence and self-esteem for years. I struggled to trust in me, continually seeking reassurance externally and changing who I was to fit into the vision others had for me. I believe everyone is unique and I'm on a mission to help women avoid years of emotional struggle and see their own power, beauty, and abilities from within. I'm so grateful to be able to give people the opportunity to 'Light Up' in their own way and avoid some of the many challenges that I allowed to negatively affect me in my life.

I dedicate this chapter to my wonderful mum and dad, Tom and Jacqueline Crane, my biggest heroes and cheerleaders, the ones who supported me with every fall or failure, and celebrated every win and achievement. I will be forever grateful to you both! You are and always have been my blessing!

22

BOLLOCKS TO STRUGGLING AND PUSHING PEOPLE AWAY

NOW I'M JOYFUL, LOVED AND FREER THAN EVER.

From the moment of my birth, I learned that life was difficult, it was a struggle, it was a fight and it was often unfair.

Anita's Story

From the moment of my birth, I learned that life was difficult. It was a struggle, it was a fight and it was often unfair.

My birth was traumatic, both for me and my mother (almost a year after my brother's birth and nine months after his death). I was not expected to survive. Nearly fifty years ago, being born six weeks early, at only three pounds and with a collapsed lung, was far from ideal. My mother didn't see me for a week because I was taken to another hospital to be placed in an incubator (in those days not every hospital had one.) When I was returned to her, I was still essentially on my own as she was so ill, fighting to survive herself. When I think about it now, this was pretty much the blueprint for how I would view and experience life.

The first ten years of my life were happy. I was the quintessential 'daddy's girl' and we lived a life of prosperity and comfort. My earliest memories are of Saturday afternoons when my mother closed her shop and she and my father would discuss how well the business had done that week. I remember feeling worried that perhaps it hadn't done well. This, combined with the fact that my parents were saving for a new house so we lived on a strict budget, I translated to mean that we didn't have enough money. I was conditioned from a young age into a scarcity mindset.

When my parents' marriage fell apart, I was completely unprepared. Nothing in my hitherto charmed life had equipped me for how quickly my reasonably safe world would be demolished, and become one I didn't recognise at all, with a father I no longer knew. A man who'd always seemed to me loving and devoted became a stranger. I went from knowing nothing about domestic abuse to witnessing it on the odd occasions he'd visit. It was as if he wasn't there to see me but to abuse my mother.

The divorce took a long time to complete and was incredibly acrimonious. My relatively prosperous childhood (scarcity mindset notwithstanding) turned into one where scarcity was all too real. My father took all the savings we had (including the money from the sale of my mother's business) and stopped paying the mortgage, which we didn't know about until the bailiffs came calling.

My mother was working part-time then, and didn't earn anywhere near enough to pay my school fees, the mortgage and all the other bills that were piling up. I remember seeing her crying over another bill coming in and I learned to hide from people who knocked on the door. It very successfully cemented my scarcity mindset.

My father eventually stopped seeing me – after some very disturbing events – and I went from daddy's girl to abandoned daughter in the space of six months. So a sense of real unworthiness was added to the scarcity mindset. And all of this confirmed in me that life is tough, it's brutal, it's unfair and we have to fight every day just to survive.

I was bullied at school (the only child in the school at that time from a single parent family). My mother worked several jobs to make ends meet, which meant I spent an inordinate amount of time alone during my teenage years. My grandparents were marvellous but we both wanted to spare them as much pain as we could, especially as my grandfather had a weak heart.

My mother remarried when I was fifteen. This brought me great relief in one sense, as it meant she wouldn't be alone when I eventually decided to leave home. There was also an additional income coming in. By now, though, my poverty mentality felt hardwired.

Just three months after my mother remarried, my grandfather (the one constant male in my life) died suddenly from a heart attack. I was devastated. And I did what I always did with difficult emotions – I buried them and carried on with life. I was starting to expect loss and rejection, feelings that I carried into every relationship I had with men for the next twenty-five years.

My comfort zone was to be with people who would reject me, men who were in no way right for the real me, but perfect for the damaged Anita, the one who didn't believe she was worthy of love and who, as time went on, was becoming incapable of feeling love from anyone. I expected rejection in every single relationship in my life and perfectly created the opportunities where that would become a reality. I was a control freak, making sure, at a subconscious level, that I was controlling my relationships to ensure my perfect outcome.

My career thrived, the one area of my life where I was comfortable around success. I earned good money but always managed to feel poor, despite all the evidence to the contrary. I spent money like water. It literally flowed through my hands and yet there was little if anything to show for it. I didn't look after myself, I 'yo-yo' dieted and didn't exercise consistently. I would, as my grandmother would have said, 'let myself go' regularly, and I often shut myself away from the world, going through periods of being alone and barely socialising outside of work.

All the time I yearned for stability, security and a loving relationship with the opportunity to have children – clearly all of this at a conscious level, not at the important subconscious level. It wasn't that my light was dimmed; over the years it had been switched off.

I hit rock bottom at the age of thirty-seven when I had an affair with a married man. I despised myself for this - it was something I'd said that I'd never do. Needless to say, he was wrong for me on more levels than just being married to someone else. I switched off and became incapable of feeling.

Then somewhere deep within, the real me decided that enough was enough. I finally went for therapy. It helped, a lot, especially understanding that I was the one repeating negative behaviours, and it wasn't the fault of others (i.e. the men I'd had relationships with). I was confirming my subconscious beliefs about myself. I felt liberated!

Two months later I was diagnosed with breast cancer. It knocked me hard and I felt I didn't know what I'd done to deserve it. I'd fought hardship all my life so surely God would give me a break from this? Interestingly, it became one of the most positive experiences of my life. I realised that life was beautiful, that the world was full of beauty, especially natural beauty and that material things were unimportant compared with family and love. I realised that my career wasn't important if there was no one to remember me when I was no longer around. I swore that this would be the line in the sand for me: the past thirty-eight years were gone; the next thirty-eight were in front of me, and they would be positive.

My recovery was tough, but I fought hard. I was yet again confirming my belief system that life is tough and we have to fight to survive. I fought my way through the treatment (more brutal than the disease!) and through the inevitable depression that followed. It is an oxymoron that cancer survivors become depressed; quite often it is due to a 'survivors' guilt'. There's also a grieving process, and this covers every imaginable emotion, including anger. It's fair to say it was a roller coaster!

During my cancer battle, I discovered that two of my exes were engaged to be married. This hit me very hard at the time – there was I, with a reconstructed boob and no relationship, while they had been able to go on and get engaged. It did wonders for my sense of self-worth. I fought through these emotions (yep, still fighting!) and carried on with my life.

I trained in NLP and Hypnotherapy - which I loved, but I was too scared to give up my comfortable income and branch out on my own as a therapist, with all its financial uncertainties. I moved house a couple of times and eventually ended up living next door to a therapist who helped me with all my remaining issues around relationships. This included helping me to face up to my passive-aggressive tendencies, and to see that this stemmed from an unwillingness to rock the boat and risk being rejected (whilst subconsciously waiting for – and therefore willing – it to happen).

So when I met the man who's now my husband, I was ready to welcome him in. It helps that he's a force of nature who wouldn't take no for an answer and who decided the first time he met me that I was 'The One'. He wasn't going to go anywhere and for once I didn't turn away from that obvious devotion. I welcomed it. He accepted me, even with my scars and dodgy boob, and the confirmation from the doctors that I couldn't have children.

We married five months later and, two weeks after that it was a real shock to discover that we were pregnant. I didn't really know how I felt about this - the way I describe it now is 'detached'. I didn't dare let myself hope that this could be happening for real. I conditioned myself: if it didn't happen and something went wrong, I would move on.

My son Henry is like his father. He is tenacious and wasn't going to accept anything other than being born healthy and beautiful.

I've always struggled having anyone or anything depend on me. It makes me feel smothered and claustrophobic and I end up walking away because it's more than I can cope with. Henry didn't give me that option and neither did his father. I was *committed* to both of them and neither of them were going anywhere, no matter how I tried to push them away. At some level I knew I loved them, of course I did, but I wasn't sure how that felt inside me anymore. Looking back, I can see that I've always been an 'actions not words' kind of person; I would smother them with love, a complete contrast to the overwhelming fear of rejection that caused me to push away people I loved.

I was the main breadwinner in the household and I came to the acceptance that this helped me to feel secure: I would *not* be in the same position my mother was when my father left. I could pay all the bills on my own so that meant I would never be destitute. This became even more important after Henry was born: my son and I would be fine financially, no matter what happened. Yet I still had a scarcity mentality; I still worried every month about the bills, and still spent a lot of my money mostly servicing debts.

Then, when Henry was almost three, I sustained a head injury at work. I suffered a severe concussion that left me feeling depressed, in pain and completely unsure of anything anymore. I struggled with everything – my concentration levels, my memory, pain, depression, fear of what on earth was happening to me and, eventually, fear for my job. The organisation I was working for at the time treated me appallingly, which I now know has meant my brain has never quite come out of the concussion mode which affects many aspects of my life. They made me redundant, in a very unprofessional way, just three months after my return to work, and the stress levels were immense. But I fought them and, for a time, ignored what my body was telling me.

My husband repeatedly pressed me to go back to the GP, but everything I told them was 'pooh-poohed'. I decided it was psychosomatic and I just had to get over it. I'd secured alternative employment and it was time to move on.

Two years after the accident, I was still feeling the same pain and still having issues with what I now know is vertigo and tinnitus, a consequence of the accident. When I'm going through particularly intense episodes, I'm the most unpleasant person: short-tempered and sometimes spiteful. My anger comes from nowhere and literally explodes. At other times I cannot summon the energy to speak to people or really engage with life. Knowing it's the head injury and not 'me' doesn't help. I often felt that 'me' had gone forever and Henry will never know who I really am; he'll only know this sometimes hateful person - who isn't the real me, not deep down.

Over the last twelve months, I've struggled with many things, including the effects of my head injury, allowing it to narrow the prism of my world. Also I sense that the work I do (the thing that's identified me since leaving university) is no longer fulfilling or sustaining me. I've realised it's destroying my soul to simply go to work to pay the bills. I've taken up running as I read that it helps with mental health and, indeed, it has. It's helped me to realise that there is another way to live and it's the way I choose to live – authentically.

I choose to dig deep to find my true self and to switch my light back on. I've started to read books that are more spiritual in tone and to find the rhythm in all of them. I'm finding the link that brings all together in my mind how we live, and how I choose to live.

I've chosen to explore a different career, one where I can be in service and help people through my own life experiences to awaken their true selves. I'm not saying I am now one hundred percent serene all of the time, but I've noticed a difference in me which is coming from deep within. I'm prepared to engage in life again and to reject completely the notion that it's a struggle that must be fought through.

Going through the DNA Light Up process has been a big part of that journey, one that will continue and will lead me to being an Activator. I'm choosing to give something back (part of the reason why I've written my story here), and to help myself grow as I help others to do the same. Life is to be lived in joy and authenticity.

I'm immensely grateful for my husband and son whom I adore. I choose to give myself, the authentic me, to them at last, to cement our happiness as a family and to strengthen it. I have my light back and I choose to be open to opportunities – and they're coming my way. I'm being sociable again with my friends, some of whom I haven't seen for a while but who are still there for me in ways I'm immensely grateful for.

I'm now choosing to see that I'm a lucky person and I *expect* joy in everything I do. It's liberating, I'm feeling freer than I ever have and I know that the world is my oyster. I'm starting to live to my true potential and to realise that I'm choosing, not to fear, but to embrace.

And I know now, deep inside, that all my 'truths' about how hard life is, that it's a battle to be fought, together with my scarcity mindset, are all simply beliefs that no longer stand up to scrutiny. I am changing those beliefs and it feels marvellous!

ANITA BOULTON

I am a Chief Executive, passionate about my family, about helping people and living life authentically.

As a younger me, I wish I'd known that I am enough, that I am worthy and that I could love myself, as I am lovable. Sharing my message is important to me because I feel that I've overcome many obstacles in my life, mostly created through my own belief patterns, and if I can help someone else to see that it is indeed possible to overcome limiting beliefs, then it was all worth it.

I am dedicating this to my Mum who has been with me all the way (naturally!) and whilst she may have inadvertently helped with some of my limiting beliefs, I know it was only ever done with love.

23

BOLLOCKS TO CONSTANTLY FEELING AFRAID

NOW I KNOW WHO I AM AND I'M AT HOME IN MYSELF.

O*f everything that happened in that time, what I remember the most is the feeling of fear. So deep in my body. It was at times totally paralysing.*

Simone's Story

As a child, I was often told that I had an 'old head on young shoulders', along with other labels like clumsy, silly, imaginative, uncoordinated, backwards, slow and creative. Quite a mixed bag, often heard in whispers from a variety of adults, teachers etc.

I was aware my parents were worried that I was struggling to learn to read and write like a 'normal child', at the 'normal rate'. This resulted in me receiving a lot of unexpected attention from them.

Little did they know that the extra attention they were now giving me was what I had really needed the year before I started school. Sadly they were completely unaware of the very tough year I'd had.

As my parents wanted to move my sister and I out from a London council estate, my mother went back to work. And so I was placed with a childminder who had three sons.

My memory does not serve me a single happy thing about my time with this family. I have flashbacks of being suspended upside down, having my legs repeatedly slapped and being dropped on the floor head first. I frequently wet myself because I was too terrified to ask to go to the toilet. There are flashbacks, too, of having to eat food that I had just vomited. To this day I cannot eat chicken soup or rhubarb.

Of everything that happened in that time, what I remember the most is the feeling of fear, deep in my body. It was at times totally paralysing. Added to that was the pleasure her sons got from seeing me get beaten. I vividly recall my sister watching with an expression of complete help-lessness. She couldn't help me or the same thing would happen to her and I would never have wanted to witness that.

Most of the time I was on my own with this vile woman, as the other children were often at school. I don't know how I coped. I had horren-dous nightmares which often involved my mother not being able to rescue me. In dreams I had a weird power that when things got too bad, I could rise up into the corner of the room and watch what was happening below me.

Despite all the physical and mental abuse, I knew deep down inside that I was *not* the names they called me. I never felt I deserved what they did to me. In my very young head, the only words that I could attach to their behaviour was that they were being very unkind. I knew right from wrong - and this was *very* wrong. I knew this deep down inside me, where my Light is.

I went on to really enjoy school and eventually I caught up academically, much to my parents' relief. It never worried me because I knew I'd catch up. I was willing to do the hard work it took although it didn't come naturally to me. I sensed that belief inside, not in my head.

This period of my life made me a people pleaser and gave me an exhausting need to be ahead of the game when planning my life, in order that nothing bad would happen to me. It was a survival technique more than a coping mechanism and at times it was exhausting. I would play any situation forward in my mind so that I'd be prepared for any eventuality, and so that I could protect myself from getting scared or hurt.

I have also struggled to have good relationships with the strong women that were either my teachers or my bosses. I felt so threatened. I took their assertiveness as dominance, when really they were trying to bring the best out in me. People saw me as super organised, reliable, trust-worthy and a great listener. I always gave my time when people were having problems as I didn't want them to suffer. I rarely said no to anyone. Self care was never a priority.

So life moved on. I had a successful career. I am married twice with two fantastic grown-up children. Twelve years ago I moved to France and my only regret is that in being a full time mum and supporting my husband in his business, I lost my career. Along with that I also lost the sense of who I am outside the roles of wife and mother. I felt thoroughly stuck and disconnected. And that's when I came across the opportunity to go through Light Up.

It has reminded me that I always have a choice, that I choose my experi-ence. For me, my past is just 'is-ness'. I cannot change it and so I decide how much it's going to affect me in this very moment. I have learnt how important it is to honour my inner knowing, not in a selfish way but in a way that means I am even better for others.

Taking responsibility for myself and what happens next in my life has taken away all the ugly resentment, which sat like a huge knot in my stomach. I am free of all the labels and beliefs that I've carried for many years and that were not serving me. I know who I am. I am 'at home' in me.

SIMONE PERRYMAN

SIMONE PERRYMAN Professional Activator

I am a Professional Activator and am delighted to be able to spread this beautiful work to help people live in the moment and be free of experiences and beliefs that hold them back; to help people discover and experience their own magnificence.

It felt important to share some of my life's story in the hope that someone may connect with it and realise that they too were incredibly resilient. We cannot control everything that happens to us; we can choose how much our past experiences impact on our daily lives. This is where our power lies. I wish I had known that the words I heard that labelled me as a child did not need to define who I was growing up. It is wonderful to be free from them.

I would like to dedicate my chapter to my beautiful sister Michelle who witnessed some of the events in my story and was powerless to help, and yet I knew I had her love and support in those dark moments. And still do today. I am very blessed to have her in my life.

24

BOLLOCKS TO PEOPLE PLEASING

MY LIFE IS ENHANCED FOREVER AND I HAVE A GLOW ABOUT ME THAT WASN'T THERE BEFORE.

M*y world fell apart in the space of twenty-four hours.*
Suzanne's Story

When I was asked if I'd like to write a chapter for this book, I thought 'What can I say that'll interest anyone?' Some of the contributors have been through dreadful journeys and mine seemed tame in comparison. It was rightly explained to me that we all have a different journey to share and someone out there thinking of finding their light might just resonate with my story.

I appear on the outside to be a very confident and outgoing individual. On the inside that's not always the case. I get nervous in new situations and I'm not keen on stepping outside my box. I've been involved in training and development for many years. When I first started in it, my mentor told me that as a trainer you have to become an actor. You put on a persona for the day and you come across as confident and knowledge-able no matter how you're feeling. I have kept that up in and out of work.

I've always been a 'pleaser'. I performed well in school and constantly had good school reports. I never gave my parents anything to worry about (unlike my brothers!). I'm also a perfectionist – I was brought up to give everything one hundred percent.

I had the idea before leaving school that I'd like to be a teacher. My mum had always wanted to be a domestic science teacher or work in hospitality and she and my dad persuaded me to go to the local college to study hotel and catering management. I didn't really know what the course was about. I went along with the idea because I wanted to please them – it wasn't really what I wanted to do, I didn't know what I really wanted to do but I felt I couldn't tell them that. With my own children I've instilled in them the importance of following their dreams and doing whatever excites them;not me.

The huge bonus of college was that I met my best friend there. I'd always felt like the spare wheel at school, never having a best friend as such, always the extra person to a pair. Helen and I clicked and that was the start of a friendship for life.

I moved to Germany when I was eighteen to be an au pair – another idea of my parents. They thought it would be good to learn a language (I hadn't studied German at school). They had been stopped from travelling when they were younger by their parents and they didn't want to do the same to me. I went along with it. I have *never* been so homesick. If you've ever been homesick, you'll know the physical pain that goes with it. My parents told me I'd be fine and that I'd get over it. I didn't; I just learned to live with it.

Whilst I was there one of the children I was looking after died from a cot death and I was the one to find them. It sounds horrendous and for the parents it was. For me it wasn't the death that gave me pain (I wasn't a parent then so didn't appreciate the full impact of it); it was the fact that my parents didn't ask me to go straight home in such awful circumstances. They left me to cope alone because they thought it was the right thing to do - on the outside I appeared to be in control. They believed I was strong and I could deal with anything. As a pleaser – I did exactly that. I was lonely and dreadfully unhappy so I ate to compensate –

putting on three stone. Fat, homesick and lonely – not the best experience. One that followed me for a long time.

Through the good and the bad times I now realise I was already using my light, I just hadn't realised it. I had lots of gut feelings, although I didn't always listen to them. I was stuck in the habit of pleasing, focusing on other people's desires not my own. And I was in the habit of eating when I was lonely.

After a year I left Germany and moved to Guernsey in the Channel Islands. Another idea of my parents – to work in a hotel abroad. I lost my weight relatively quickly and loved Guernsey. I fell in love and my best friend Helen joined me to make it even better. We had a ball; it was the eighties and life was really good. After that I went to work in London, then travelled to Australia and New Zealand. I decided to go back to university as a mature student at the ripe old age of twenty-five. *My* idea this time!

During my time at university I spent a year in the US working for Marriott hotels. I had an amazing time. Again I put on weight but this time it was due to a very healthy social life and not loneliness.

I left university and got a job as a trainer/mentor for the ferry company Stena Line in Holyhead, North Wales. I met my husband and we got engaged within a week (my gut told me it was right, even though it was so quick), we married after eight months and I was pregnant three months after that. Another baby came along two years later.

Everything happened so quickly and my husband and I hadn't had time to really get to know each other. We had our ups and our downs - in fact some downs led us to counselling - we still muddled through. My gut told me we were meant to be together.

My husband went through a spate of illnesses and it seemed to me that anything that could happen to a couple happened to us – illness, job loss, car crash, death. I lost my best friend Helen to cancer too, which was devastating. I used to ask 'Why me? Why does it always happen to us?'

Does this sound familiar? The glass was half empty for me, not half full. I was constantly focusing on the negative. I took myself off to counselling because I believed our relationship was cracking and I was becoming more and more resentful about my husband's illnesses (focusing on the negative yet again).

I thought many times that I would be better off divorced. The more I did that the more I focused on how awful my marriage was and it literally started to disintegrate in front of my eyes. In Feb 2018 my husband told me that he didn't want to be with me anymore, that he didn't love me and he wanted to separate. I was supposed to be the one who made the decision about our marriage – not him! The next day I was told my dad was dying and had weeks to live. My world fell apart in the space of twenty-four hours!

We split up. My focus was work and it got me through – well, some of the time. My husband moved out and my life changed forever. I have never known grief like it - grief for my marriage and at the same time grief for my dad.

My gut kept telling me that it wasn't right. Friends and family told me I was strong and I could do anything I put my mind to. I was so scared of being lonely – let's go back to Germany and being eighteen all over again. I had counselling; still my gut (my light as I now know it to be) told me we should be together. I asked it what to do and it told me to write a letter to my husband telling him how I felt. I did.

Fast forward twelve months. After family counselling and lots of hard work, we are back together. We're stronger than before and we talk to each other, even if we feel the other doesn't want to hear it. In the last twelve months I've been to hell and back but I've also learnt so much about myself and I'm stronger than I've ever been. Who knows what will happen in the future; what I do know is that I am equipped to deal with it.

My brother has been friends with Mel for over twenty years and it was he who told me about Light Up. Given that I now work as a lecturer (I eventually got to be a teacher!) and a coach, he felt that Light Up would be perfect for me. My other brother also went through Light Up - it's a proper family affair!

In January 2018 I met my DNA activator (who will be a friend for life!). I absolutely loved the sessions and loved finding my light and learning about the four pillars.

Afterwards I didn't really feel fireworks explode for me or that I'd found the Holy Grail. I just felt a sense of peace and calm. That is where the magic begins.

Having been through Light Up I now realise how important focus is and how we can change our life by refocusing. Aged eighteen I was focusing on homesickness instead of the amazing adventure I was having. In my marriage I was focusing on the negatives instead of looking at the amazing friend I have in my husband. I believed that I always needed to please people – I don't! Don't get me wrong – I haven't suddenly become an awful, uncaring person; now I know I don't have to please everyone all of the time. I can now look after me.

Light Up works everywhere. I had a student last week who was going for an interview and was incredibly nervous. She was focusing on everything that could go wrong, so together we switched her focus onto everything that could go right. She got the job. We talk about habits in my coaching sessions - how we can change habits that are harming us and how some habits are good for us. My daughter had to give evidence at a coroner's inquest and she was extremely nervous. Before she went into court, in the toilets, we played with another of the Light Up tools; Hara and before my eyes she grew in confidence. At the inquest she came across clear, confident and concise – I was so proud of her.

DNA Light Up has enhanced my life forever. Friends and family are saying that I have a glow about me that wasn't there before. I want to share that glow with others. I have now trained to be an Activator because I want to share this journey with colleagues, friends, students, businesses and with individuals who get the nudge just like me.

We all have different lives and we all take different journeys – some are easier than others. If we can find the tools to help us travel those journeys, why not use them? My life has a sense of calm now and I look for the positives everyday instead of the negatives. It's amazing that spending just a few hours on ourselves can change our life forever and that of those around us. Don't give into the BOLLOCKS - come find the light!

SUZANNE PROFIT

Suzanne Profit Professional Activator

I'm a Lecturer in Human Resources and Coaching and Mentoring, currently working for a college in North Wales, Grwp Llandrillo Menai.

I'm passionate about: Uplifting others; Beach huts (I have one in my garden – some people call it a shed; it most definitely isn't a shed – it's my sanctuary. There's something really magical about one.) My family – time together with them making memories; Glamping – I absolutely love it.

Three things I wish I'd known earlier in life: We always have a choice; Everything will be fine;

Failing at something doesn't make us a failure.

Sharing my message is important to me because what we see on the outside isn't always what is going on in the inside. Sometimes we become actors and cover up what we're truly feeling. I want people to realise that it's okay to do that at certain times (it's our armour) and then sometimes we can choose to 'take the face off' and own up to who we truly are and be thankful for who we are 'warts and all'.

I'm dedicating this chapter to my lovely dad Michael Ryan who passed away last year and my gorgeous friend Helen Galsworthy who passed away three years ago – I know you are both always there for me – butterflies, robins and feathers are everywhere.

25

BOLLOCKS TO BIPOLAR

I'M A WARRIOR GODDESS, HERE AGAINST ALL ODDS, TO SHINE AND GUIDE OTHERS!

With bipolar I go from deep depression to absolute euphoria. It decimated my memory and processing functions.

Tracy's Story

My story has been difficult, heartbreaking, soul destroying. There have been many times when I didn't think that I could continue. And then I found something more and I did.

I found the courage to leave my emotionally abusive husband. I got back into making art and poetry. This has been my therapy. I am still here. I am Trace.

The Girl on the Bed

The girl on the bed hides her eyes,

Her heart is breaking, she cries and cries,

Things that have happened, her world has turned blue.

She has no idea about what to do.

Her family scattered and torn apart

Has left a scar so deep in her heart.

A foreign land to where she's come

Is strange and new and she knows no one.

The bullies who taunted and called her names,

To them it wasn't real, it was just fun and games.

A family new, that she was not a part,

Continues to torture and deaden her heart.

She found a friend, a soul mate for sure,

Then he walked away. For that there wasn't a cure.

And so all her life she has struggled alone,

With no family to care and no place to call home.

She lies on the bed and covers her eyes.

Are you really surprised

She cries and she cries?

My mother took my brother and left me with my father when I was seven. When my brother joined us, I promised him I would look after him. That opportunity to uphold my promise was taken away from me. It is now forty-six years without seeing each other and I cannot see a way for us to meet again.

Ode to my Brother

My life!

spinning through time and space

I'm destined

never to gaze upon your face.

Wanted to see you

was my desire

with a longing

that burns like fire.

Wish I was in

another time and place.

Feelings now

like I'm such a disgrace

never getting

to join the human race.

Wanting things

it seems to me

that were never in

my destiny.

Dreams

I'll never catch, I seem to chase.

All I want

is to see you one more time.

Surely not

a very major crime.

What did we do

that was so bad?

That left me feeling

so very sad.

Is it such a crime

this dream of mine?

So I let you down

again my friend.

We must keep fighting

to the bitter end.

The one thing

I must surely do

is somehow find

my way to you

so this nightmare

can somehow finally end.

My father decided to relocate back to England from Australia when I was ten. This was a major culture shock for me. As far as I was concerned, Australia was my life and my homeland. And I thought that I would never see my family again. Not only my brother and mother but also grandparents and mum's cousins.

Red Earth turned to White Snow

The hot red earth beneath her bare feet turned to

cold white crystals of snow under her wet boots.

How did she get here? she asked a world that didn't care.

Once upon a time

she had never owned a coat,

never seen snow,

never felt the cold.

In fact it never even rained.

This was a brand new world and there were

so many people,

and they seemed to live on top of one another.

She could no longer see the horizon,

just houses,

just people,

so many people,

all strangers.

She felt so small,

she felt worthless,

she felt lost and alone.

Where are we and why? She asked herself.

There was no reply.

We came back because my dad had family. These strangers had known me before we went to Australia so they just accepted me as family. I had no idea who these people were. My cousin came to live with us and to watch over me while my dad worked. For that I'm truly grateful. She included me in her families activities, so I experienced much more than I would have if it had just been my dad and me. This, however, didn't last long because the money ran out and the cost of living was so much higher in England. We moved away from the family back to the town where I was born. Having looked after myself before without incident, I was left to look after myself again, after school and when dad was doing his hobbies. I was eleven years old.

That could have been fine, if someone hadn't tuned into my dwindling self confidence. Although I was good at everything, I was different, an outsider. The headmaster pointed me out because we had a similar name. Then, to top it all, a teacher decided to use me to split up two girls who were a bad influence on each other. The same teacher thought it would be better to isolate me from the playground bully, instead of punishing the bully or helping to resolve the issue with me.

I was cut off from support at every turn. The bully knew I went home to an empty house and so followed me with most of the girls in our year. They shouted and threw stones, then stood in the road shouting, some knocking on the door and shouting through the letterbox. When I phoned dad in tears, he told me not to bother him at work. Again I was on my own left to cope.

I do remember one good point. As the girls followed me home, a boy who hadn't joined in with them asked if he could hang out with me. I wanted to say 'as long as I can bring my friends,' pointing to the bullies. Instead I said 'no', not wanting to burden anyone else with my troubles.

Recently, when kids in my street started playing knock down ginger, banging on the door then running away, I had to deal with this trigger. I wrote this poem.

Childhood Memories

They ...

are still out there.

Voices of children,

taunting and teasing,

whiny voices,

laughing,

mocking without reason.

Petty calling of names,

just childish games?

They ...

are still out there,

hanging on my gate,

tension fuelled by hate,

as I watch half hidden

by the curtain.

All I know for certain,

is the memory of

a time long gone,

when

they ...

sang their songs

and taunted me.

All I can see,

knocking on the door,

they ...

are still out there.

Footsteps run away.

Children at play?

My anxiety rushes back

inside my head,

pounding out a rhythm

feeling dizzy and sick.

They ...

are always out there.

My father went to court to divorce my mother and sort out custody so he could remarry. I was asked where I wanted to live and I chose my dad. After he remarried, I didn't feel like part of the family, constantly being told that I had to share my dad's time, that I was selfish. Eventually I'd get my step sister to ask for things I needed like a new school bag, because if I asked, the answer was always no. If she asked, then I could say 'I need that too' and they would say yes, okay.

After we all moved in together, my father asked me if I wanted to see my mother. Yes of course I did. 'I only have enough for a one way ticket. Do you want to go and live with your mother?' Having been asked who I wanted to live with in court, I said 'No.'

'Well I'm only responsible for you until you're eighteen, after that you'll have to find your own way.'

What a shot through the heart. I was sixteen by then. I would have left soon enough with support. Now I was being rejected and ejected from the tiny world I knew. On my own again.

At eighteen I met the love of my life. We were best friends and someone said they were surprised we weren't an item. Neither of us disagreed and a few months later we got together. We made plans for the future. I spent most of my time at his house. His mum wasn't impressed with my parents' attitude.

Then we went on to further education. The distance was an obstacle but we did what we could to see each other. There were no mobiles then and we were lucky to talk once a fortnight. The best surprise was on Valentine's when, having not received a card, he rang in the afternoon and pretended to be far away. Then he knocked on the door a few minutes later. Any surprises were happy surprises. Until he told me he'd met someone else. I was devastated.

This was my first mental breakdown. I'd been ill for many years but until I actually reached the point where I couldn't cope with life, no one took any interest in my mental state.

I couldn't go home. This resulted in me trusting a man who would take advantage o my poor health and become my emotional abuser which lasted for twenty-five years.

Meeting up with the love of my life again twenty years later triggered another breakdown. There had been other factors at work which were causing a state of anxiety and uncertainty - the bosses were deciding if they were going to sell our club or not, re-interviewing us for our own jobs so they could reduce our wages and hours. So when the love of my life arrived my head started to imagine all these scenarios where he'd rescue me and we'd live happily ever after.

Life doesn't work like that. Not for me.

With this breakdown I had psychotic episodes and lost all sense of reality. Eventually I pushed him away and told him I wouldn't contact him again. I was devastated, alone again, trying to cope with mental health issues when no one would listen to me. Too ill to be able to communicate or fight for my life.

A past love

When you broke my heart the first time,

My heart, it didn't understand,

But when we met again that day,

Another heartbreak wasn't planned.

But my heart saw your happy face,

And warmed to your embrace,

It remembered happy times,

It thought it had found its place.

You didn't know how much I cared

Or how I cried at night.

You weren't interested in my woes,

You did not feel my plight.

I could not tell you way back when,

I cannot tell you now.

My heart remembers painfully,

It wants to scream out OW!

Yet again my dreams are gone,

There's nothing left for me,

I've used up all the hope I had,

No future can I see,

I wish that somewhere there was one,

A person I could love.

I have to leave that up to fate,

Or anyone above.

My angels showed me such a love,

That no one can endure,

They gave me such a memory,

I'd never known before,

It happened when we met again,

I felt the surge inside,

If only I could spread this love,

To everyone worldwide.

My head then shut down completely. I lost my memory. I couldn't walk and talk at the same time. I couldn't work out time, I couldn't even work out how to catch a bus. I still can't work out money, and I can't remember how to get to places that are so familiar to me. I can't even remember what I'm doing, even while I'm doing it. It's scary and it's frustrating.

It was also an opportunity to take up the practice of meditation and living in the moment. Well I had no choice really. Believing that I choose to follow this lifestyle makes it less frustrating and I'd been toying with the idea before I broke my brain.

Memory Shards (part 1) - Steel Ball

Shattered memories

like a mirror broken

make up my brain,

flickering glimpses of

the rememberings that I seek,

seen out the corner of

my third eye,

tantalizing visions

and then black.

.... nothing,

zilch.

I know it is in there,

but it is soooo painful

not thinking.

Stress and tiredness make my head ache,

not a normal ache,

but a solid steel ball,

as if my thoughts and memories

were swallowed and crushed

down to one singularity,

locked,

impenetrable,

blank,

with glimpses

that flicker on the surface,

like an ad for a movie.

NO! Please ....

don't ask about the movie ....

I know the pictures ....

I might remember the words,

odd words ....

very

odd ....

words are what I can't give you,

or a name or a place,

or a date or time ....

time?

What of time?

It means nothing now ....

My head imploded and shut down,

the most beautiful experience

in my world,

an epiphany?

Who knows?

I was carried by the angels,

engulfed by eternity,

dazzled by the iridescent

whiteness

of forever,

I felt pure love,

I felt safe,

their arms holding me tight,

we will look after you ....

as we flew and I began to feel

myself being absorbed into eternity....

NO!

I cannot go!

It was too much for me to bear,

so I fell back down

to earth,

to the bed

where they

had plucked me from,

my dream.

Such beauty,

such love ....

an enlightenment?

Or just another mental shut down!

After that

the steel ball welded

my brain shut,

allowing me only shattered fragments,

glimpses,

leaving my world frozen,

on the edge

of the black abyss,

Again ...

Memory Shards (part 2) - Patience

All the time in the world,

And at the same time,

None.

I can't think for long, counting in seconds, too long!

I sit, I stand, I lay down, No, none of it right,

Computer on,

let's play a game,

I look at the screen,

I have played this so many times ....

I don't recognise it ....?

turn it off.

They've given me leaflets and pieces of paper

about where to find help,

I can't even begin to read it ....

the words just dance

and I can't concentrate long enough.

My head hurts all the time,

ALL of the time!

All thanks to the

Little steel ball that swallowed my mind.

I spend my time asleep.

I have no choice.

Programs on TV wash over me.

Or it's too loud, it's too busy, turn it off!!!

Try the computer ....

Can't remember

Can't work it out

I have no patience for patience ....

Turn it off!!!

Sleep ....

All these years

I thought it was just a joke -

he can't walk and chew gum ....

but here I am ....

Angry,

frustrated ,

in pain,

unable to explain .... it is still in there ....

Inside the steel ball, hidden behind a curtain of pain,

hidden by the loud noises that make me jump,

the people and shapes that rush at me in shops,

the babble of TV or radio and those dancing words on a page,

it is still in there!

I just can't get to it.

For now .... it is a lonely journey

that only I can make,

so .... everyday I'm gonna sit at the computer,

I will put on the game

and I will play it,

for however long I can and

for however long it takes,

it will not beat me ....

Angry, frustrated, and in pain,

I will regain the use of my brain.

They want me to catch three buses to go to an art group,

I can't catch one ....

They want me to arrive on time,

it stresses me so much that

I had to sit for an hour in the rain,

because of my broken brain.

If I need to go to town,

I can do one shop, no other stops,

I've tried, then I cried and we went home.

My worst moment was in class,

yes I am taking a class, to manage my condition,

if I can get there ....

If .... I can leave the house,

if I can .... get out of bed,

If ..... well ....

We were told ....

everybody has hope ....

I sat while others thought

then told about the hope in their life,

all the while searching my steel ball for an answer,

but there was none.

I got up and ran,

there is no hope, no hope for me,

then the teacher came to comfort me,

I was a snivelling mess,

you have issues you need to address.

So, now look at me,

I stand here before you,

you can not know how much patience it takes

to get this far from ....

walking OR talking,

Over 4000 days .... worth of solitaire games,

just to get my brain working again.

Never criticise those games I play,

it's what got me to here, today.

My mum came back into my life eleven years ago, just when my head had imploded after my meeting with my ex. I'd yearned for her for decades, it was such an impossible dream and thirty-four years had passed. I'd sat in a cafe watching mothers and daughters having lunch together thinking I will never have this.

Never say never, we cannot know what is going to happen.

She gave me the courage and the back up to divorce my emotionally abusive husband and, more to the point, of finally ending contact with him.

Now that I belong to someone I have been able to get treatment for my mental health condition. It seems that unless someone has seen you having a bipolar episode then no one believes you. With bipolar I go

from deep depression to euphoria, thankfully not too regularly as some people do, but the last one devastated my memory and processing functions.

Pray for hope

Black

As coal,

Dark

As night,

Rotten

My soul,

Gone is

My fight,

No reason

To try to live,

No person

My love to give,

No dreams

To try to achieve,

No reason

For me to believe,

Black as Thunder,

Dark as Night,

Gone my dreams

And my fight.

All that is left

Is a bag of bones,

No tears are left

Or reasons to moan,

'cos,

No one listens

To what I say,

So I reserve my strength,

And for hope

I pray.

Typing is great. No one knows how long it's taken me to put these few words together. I've put my poems into an anthology and it makes me proud that this book has helped people to get the correct diagnosis and help, because they recognised their experience in my writing. It's also given others permission to talk about their own experiences and courage to tell the world. It's been a bumpy ride. I'm truly grateful for all my experiences and everyone who's had a lesson for me.

Waves of emotion

Waking,

Eyes watering,

Waves of emotion

Crash upon my soul,

The answer apparent.

Tears wash

Uncertainty,

My heart

Finally finds

Reason.

Releasing tensions,

Real-eyes-ing truths,

Re-evaluating parameters,

Resolving questions

Asked for millennia,

Asked again

And again,

Questioning Reason.

Waves wash my soul,

Retreating,

Taking past pains

And permissions,

Washing away misgivings,

Leaving the shore bare

Ready for new footprints.

A new day,

A new awakening,

Real-eyes-ing answers.

I want to touch

Your soul too.

Sharing my elation.

In an awards ceremony backed by Goddesse Education in 2017, I won first place in the category of Warrior Goddess. The judge for my category based her decision on my poetry and my art work. She happened to be a DNA Activator and when she learned of my story, she took me through Light Up. After the honour of receiving this title of warrior goddess, I wrote this. It is my declaration to the world. I am still here.

I am ... 2017

I am a duck billed platypus,

doubted by others that I exist,

exotic in my uniqueness,

made up of different parts

of what others call normal,

from a strange far away land

that no other can imagine.

Just doing my thing.

My normal, my journey.

I am the flower of adversity,

clinging to a barren wall of life,

finding nourishment where I can,

Without roots but with sheer determination

to grow wherever I find myself.

I am a jaffa cake. Biscuit or cake??

I am marmite,

I am survival against the odds,

human spirit,

sheer willpower concentrated,

love and light here to guide others,

to encourage and to help,

a mirror so you can see the good in yourself,

a story old as time to give Hope for a better tomorrow.

I am a Warrior goddess,

not for worship but to stand up and to give a voice

to those who can't be seen,

to give you permission to tell your story.

The underdog gone feral that won't accept other people's rules,

to rebel with peace and love

against the system

for a better tomorrow,

stand up against the bullies and the abusers for a peaceful life,

for ourselves and our children.

I am but one but I speak for many,

I am Trace!!!

TRACY HENHAM

Tracy is an artist and poet who uses her work as therapy and to explore the experiences of childhood trauma which triggered her bipolar condition.

She tries to communicate her experiences so she can understand better what happened. Her last bipolar episode lost many of her processing functions and a large chunk of her memory. Sometimes even a simple task like making a sandwich is too complicated, communication can be difficult and she feels worthless.

She does have an amazing survival instinct and so she has chosen to share her experiences with others, which in turn helps them understand what is happening to themselves or loved ones, and also gives people permission to talk about their trauma, abuse and mental health. They tried to douse her flame but she still shines.

26

BOLLOCKS TO REPRESSED ANGER

I FEEL CONNECTED, CLEANSED AND CENTRED.

M*y marriage breakdown was actually the calm before the REAL storm hit, and this was going to be a much bigger storm to ride.*

Jenny's Story

I'm Jenny, thirty-five years old, single, and I've felt for so long that I'm not playing at my true level. The level where I know I belong. Where my soul has always known we belong but we haven't reached it yet as we've been holding ourselves back for years, keeping ourselves small, not shining too much.

This part of the story starts back in my twenties, when I was in a long term relationship for seven years. Together for over six years, married for nine months.

And then it fell apart.

My partner isn't, and never was, a bad person. We met in our early twenties, thought we knew what we were doing, and carried on doing our thing together. We were best friends with so much in common and, more importantly for me, I loved his family. A family that welcomed me from the start, treated me as their own daughter and loved me for ME.

Nothing else, not for what they wanted me to be, and not for what I could give them. This was the unconditional love from a family that I craved so deeply.

It was a huge draw for me because I'd never really felt that in my own family. My family aren't bad people, they were just unable to love me as I always felt I needed to be loved. It's taken me a long time to understand that I was looking for the security of a loving, accepting family. I was never really seen or heard. With overbearing older siblings, I was living in a family where I was the baby and the youngest girl. If I made any noise or actually spoke up for myself, little notice was taken. So I didn't bother anymore.

This is where my patterns and my 'norm' come from. 'It's not awful, so it's okay'. 'Keep on keeping on'. 'Don't rock the boat or upset anyone'. 'No one listens anyway'. 'We don't talk about feelings here'. 'We can't talk about real stuff, so best just keep it inside'. Just hide it in that little box and it'll go away.

I got so good living with my carefully crafted exterior, my mask in place most of the time, that I had everybody fooled. Including myself to some degree.

August 2012 is when my relationship really started to unravel. Married for nine months, feeling like nothing was getting better, nothing had changed or improved, and I started to realise that I'd made a huge mistake.

The shame I felt was massive. The embarrassment I felt and anticipated was too much on some days. A beautiful wedding, a fortune spent, all the excitement for our families, and then to finally admit to myself and my husband that I was sinking ... was just horrendous. I didn't want what we had, and I had to tell someone.

No one saw it coming, not even me.

When we start to scratch the surface and begin to reveal what's underneath, we know it's not going to be pretty or easy. We just KNOW. Our heart, soul and spirit know when things aren't right and we're not being true to ourselves. We know when we're not being authentic.

I always knew deep down that it wouldn't last, that it was impossible. How could it last? I wasn't being honest with myself.

The shock, the disappointment, the tears, the denial, the upset, the silences, the arguments. That was just the start of it. I had very little support during this time as my family didn't understand my decision at first. So, of course, it's best to just ignore what's going on and not talk about it. This was so difficult for me, but my family didn't know any better way to deal with the situation. Ignorance is bliss I guess.

Thank fuck I am who I am, a woman who has managed to dig deep within, and who has always known who I am. I started to realise that I'd forgotten about myself because I was too busy pretending and putting everyone else's feelings first. I just had to ride the storm and come out the other side.

With all the upset, break up, lack of support, losing my husband's family, most of our mutual friends, separation, moving out, negotiation, debt, remortgaging, and everything else that comes with it, I had so many more emotions, unsettled feelings and questions coming up to the surface.

How had it gone this far?

Why did I go along with something I knew wasn't right?

Why did I struggle so much with open, honest communication?

Why could I not communicate clearly with my husband about my feelings?

What would happen if I spoke up for myself?

Why did I have to keep a brave face on it all?

How had I allowed myself to get so lost and forgotten about?

Well it's easily done. A lifetime of conditioning, of following the suit of the grown ups around us. Living in our 'normal' life, growing up where we just don't talk about things that much.

I'm a huge believer that there's always a reason for everything we go through. So where had all my stuff come from in the first place? I knew there was more, so I had to keep on digging and pulling all the weeds out.

I then started to feel huge anger building up inside me and I didn't understand why. Yes I'd left my husband, but I knew it was for the best. We could be civil with each other and still speak to each other when we needed to, so that situation was manageable, bearable, and we were both moving on.

But it was more than that, more than just a looming divorce. I started to feel such anger and fury inside me that I felt my head was going to explode. Something was trying to escape and I couldn't keep it under control anymore. The final unhealed wounds were coming out, pushed down for too long.

The flashbacks came, confusion, shame, embarrassment, feelings of low self worth. I knew I had to dig even deeper this time. My marriage breakdown was actually the calm before the *real* storm hit, and this was going to be a much bigger storm to ride.

You see, even when we're children, we know what's right and wrong. We are pure, innocent human beings, made of bright, vibrant energy and amazing intuition and sensitivity. So when my flashbacks started about stuff that happened when I was smaller, I knew it had to come out once and for all. The things that I was confused by, didn't understand, had suppressed so much, tried to forget and kept locked in that little box I mentioned earlier: memories that had been locked away for years were starting to seep out.

If my family couldn't handle a divorce, how the hell would they handle this?

The truth is, I just didn't care anymore. All my life I'd been so used to being on my own with my feelings and keeping quiet about what I really thought about things, and I'd had enough of it. I was always so independent. I had to be.

Everyone has a limit, and I'd finally reached mine. Thank God.

I was making myself ill by carrying such toxic energy and bad memories in my body; I had adult acne, migraines and would flare up with hives at least once a year. All of this was a physical manifestation of the internal emotional trauma I was carrying.

I suffered with depression for years too, without even knowing it. I was functioning well, always looked nice and made an effort, kept a nice home, paid bills on time, had a good job, was happy and bubbly most of the time. I'd no idea that depression shows up in many forms.

And so it began. I finally started to use my voice to share what had happened to me. It was also an attempt to understand why I had married someone I knew wasn't the best fit for me. And to understand why I felt such a strong pull to a safe family environment, one which I felt I'd lacked as a child. This part of my story still isn't discussed freely in my family, but I'm more at peace now knowing I don't have to carry my heavy memories anymore.

It was another huge struggle to face alone, and I knew I could do it, with the support of a handful of close friends and my amazing, patient therapist. When I got through the worst of this second storm, I felt absolutely invincible! My strength, courage, resourcefulness and tenacity were so clear, I felt so proud of myself. And I still do to this day, and I will for the rest of my years. I have cured myself of the acne and the migraines, and I'm glowing now more than ever before. It all starts from within.

I'm still learning to manage myself, my feelings and emotions when they come up, and that's great. It never stops, although I would like it to sometimes! We're always learning and EVERYTHING given to us is a lesson. Our job is to figure that lesson out and learn from it.

I'm so grateful to myself everyday for still being here when I felt like giving up so many times. I love myself so much now and, through the charity work that I do, I've turned my experiences into skills to help other women and girls who may have gone through similar situations. I have love, patience, empathy and compassion for those struggling to speak out because I know what it's like to live in that lonely, silent place.

I'd already started to light up before I'd heard of Light Up. My recovery from my own trauma started in 2013, and it wasn't until 2018 that I met my beautiful Activator.

They say what we need to learn the most, we teach. This didn't really occur to me until recently. I've spent thirteen years in law enforcement, and now I know I got into this career to be able to help others, to help victims and to fight for justice. Giving someone a voice is so important to me, and I've been able to make a career out of it, even if it's not exactly in the arena my soul is calling me to. It's merely a stepping stone.

It's through my work that I connected with the Director of a charity that helped victims of trafficking. We'd never actually met in person, but we would most likely have attended the same meetings. I received a group email from her in June last year, informing us that her charity unfortunately couldn't continue to operate. As soon as I read her email I knew I had to meet her. There was no mention of Light Up, but I just knew somehow that we would meet and we would work together. Whatever that would mean in future, I knew it was the start of something bright.

The next week we met for coffee, and straightaway I knew we weren't meeting for the first time. On some level we had met before, and this was just our first meet in person. We shared stories almost immediately, both personal and professional, and she told me about Light Up, what it had done for her, and that she would love to take me through it.

I had my first Light Up session a week later at her beautiful home. I'd experienced something similar before so I thought I knew what to expect. And I was completely wrong.

Going through Light Up allowed me to find ME again. Not just to connect to something else, or imagine a bright white shining light and I'll always be cleansed, centred, and connected to what I think I *should* be.

My activator commented on how quickly and strongly she could see me shift. And I felt that too. I felt different, so light, free and certain of myself. 'I am here now'. A gorgeous feeling.

I did think I would struggle with finding my light, but that was just me overthinking and maybe being a bit fearful that it could actually be this effective and this easy. We spend years clinging on to our old stories, and we can let them go as soon as we're ready to. I was open minded enough to trust my new friend, and I am so glad I did.

My light is a big, shining red love heart called Hope, right in the centre of me, filling my heart and soul, shining so bright and protecting me in gorgeous ruby light.

As I described my light to my Activator, she excused herself, saying she just had to nip upstairs. Minutes later she came back with a present for me. A few days earlier, she'd been having a clear out and had found some earrings she didn't wear them and was going to throw away. The earrings were dangling silver with red hearts made of beautiful glass that the light shone through. They were perfect. We couldn't believe the synchronicity. And at the same time, we could completely believed it was all meant to be! Every time I wear them I feel so blessed.

In the early days after Light Up, I felt such clarity. I'm naturally a woman with high energy and I felt it even more. I read and revisited my workbook, and really started to connect with my big shining red love heart. Hope has always been there, I just forgot to speak to her and love and nurture her.

After a while I began to forget about my light and just carried on as 'normal'. It was at the end of November when I went to the Light Up Christmas get together that I began to feel Hope again.

As we spoke about our lights over dinner, I confessed I'd forgotten about Hope a little, I hadn't really been paying much attention to her. But then I sat and realised what Light Up had given me so far.

I realised that in the six months since my Light Up, I'd connected so much more to my creativity. I love to write but always told myself I wasn't good enough, my writing wasn't neat enough, I didn't know big enough words. Since Light Up I've written everyday, including starting a daily journal and staying consistent with it, and writing poetry and songs.

POETRY! SONGS! ME?! What on earth?!

And I go with it, I'm in love with what comes out when I'm in the flow. I'm not entirely sure yet what I'll write, a poem or a song, it just comes out and I allow it. It will all become clear. As well as my writing, I've noticed something else. I now have the confidence to share my voice. I've started to sing.

I started singing as a little girl in an attempt to escape my trauma. When I did sing, it was loaded with such dark, heavy feelings and I'd get so emotional that it was easier to turn it off than to sing through it. The tears were the tears of Little Jenny trying to get out. Singing was my escapism and would make me feel better, and it also became an anchor to the bad times.

And, as with writing, I'd not given myself permission to sing. I was scared to be heard. I felt I couldn't cope if people thought I was rubbish or told me to be quiet. I didn't want criticism of the one thing that I loved the most. It goes back to Little Me being stuck in silence. I felt like 'who will listen anyway?'

Now I sing for me, for how light it makes me, how emotional I get, and the sense of absolute freedom it gives me. If I feel connection to a song and its lyrics, I can get lost for hours singing and feeling every bit of it. It's one of the few things that makes my whole being feel completely alive. And this year I'm ready to do something about it: to give myself absolute permission to follow my passion and work with musicians who can help me bring my own words to life.

I know I'm a healer, and I help people heal through my words and shared experiences. Light Up has given me the connection to myself that I was lacking, and the extra push I needed to fulfil my desires and greatest loves: Myself and Music.

Music is so powerful, and I choose to give myself and others that powerful connection through music. Music bonds us all, we relate to it in our own individual ways. I love how we can connect so strongly to how we're feeling without having to speak at all. A song can do that to us. That's why I fell in love with music in the first place: a song could explain whatever it was Little Jenny was feeling but didn't know how to say.

I've gone full circle, and I'm still only just getting started. I feel that now is my time to shine. Truly shine. Unapologetically. As bright as I can. As bright as I choose. To shine bright no matter what. To never dim to make anyone else feel comfortable. To listen to myself and choose what is best for me and for Hope.

I'm ready. It's time. I choose to shine.

I'm so grateful for all that I have been through and experienced in my life.

I wrote this poem last year, 2018, and I now feel ready to share my journey so far.

OUR STRUGGLES ARE OUR SAVIOUR

Our struggles are our saviour, they are so so hard to say,

To think out loud makes them real, so inside they shall stay.

Our struggles are our saviour, they cause such pain to us,

We can't see why we're having them, but Trust the Universe.

Our struggles are our saviour, wrapped in shame and deceit,

When they build up tall inside your soul you just can't take the heat.

As the heat builds up and the anger grows you hold your head in pain,

To feel your head explode in shame you fall upon the ground.

The bedroom floor became my friend, I was down there all the time,

Keeping curtains closed avoiding light, I'm here on borrowed time.

Our struggles are our saviour, I can see it now so clear,

For the woman I have fought to be, I love her, she is here.

The curtains are wide open now and all the windows too,

Shame no longer lives here but for a while it did, it's true.

I have come to this place of honesty, of truth,

I am here, happy, I am whole, no longer living outside of my walls.

Our struggles are our saviour I am grateful to them all,

My colours are shining brightly now as I live my life stood tall.

JENNY SHEPHERD

Jenny is 35 years old, from Leeds, and has a BA in Criminal Justice from Liverpool John Moores University. Since graduating in 2005, Jenny has worked in law enforcement. Jenny is passionate about helping others to find their voice, to be seen and feel heard, and wants to help women and young girls know they don't have to confront their past alone. Jenny also volunteers for a helpline supporting women and girls affected by rape and sexual violence.

Jenny is using her passion for helping and empowering women by making a career transition from law enforcement to life coaching and is a certified NLP Practitioner focusing on Health and Happiness. In 2018 Jenny started her own business, and is CEO and Founder of GLOW-Goddess.co.uk. Jenny's dream is to create a tribe of GLOWGoddesses, where women Grow, Live, Overcome and WIN: helping women to see their worth, get back to themselves and live a life they love.

Jenny writes poetry, is a singer-songwriter, and is looking forward to the next part of her journey, wherever that may lead her.

27

BOLLOCKS TO FEELING LOST DESPITE MY PROFESSIONAL SUCCESSES

NOW I LIVE MY OWN LIFE AND FOLLOW MY TRUEST PASSIONS, WHILST ALSO SUPPORTING OTHERS

I spent years with my eyes blinkered, half-open, letting life unfurl around me, looking externally for confirmation and affirmation rather than owning my experience.

Derek's Story

I recently had a problem with my hearing.

Over the festive period, whilst in Athens with my partner, I developed an infection in my right ear. My other ear had been fuzzy for some time and, by January, it had reached a stage where I couldn't hear out of my right ear at all and my hearing was getting so poor in my left ear that I was almost deaf.

What made this so difficult for me was that I'm a professional classical musician. Attending orchestra rehearsal became such an ordeal that I chose to leave halfway through - and believe me, it's difficult for me to leave something I feel so passionate about.

Rather than continue to suffer in silence, I grabbed the bull by the horns, took full ownership of my problem and booked myself an appointment for the following day. I was given micro-suction, which I can best describe as having a tiny Dyson vacuum cleaner in both ears which, over the course of the short fifteen minute procedure, removed any offensive materials. And then the 'pop' happened. I could hear perfectly again - better than I'd been able to for years.

Why do I start my chapter with a story about ears, you ask? Well, prior to Light Up, in the olden days, I would have done what I'd always done. I'd have just sat and waited for it to get better on its own, hoping that I might still be able to hear just about well enough. I'd have continued to participate in an agonising rehearsal because I'd have felt I'd be letting people down if I left early. I'd have been worried that there might be something seriously wrong with my hearing so I'd have been too scared to get it looked at. I'd have felt that other people had it much worse than I do. And I'd have continued to annoy my friends by being barely able to hear conversations, and I'd have felt guilty about that too. All BOLLOCKS. All my headspace anxiously overworking, like a pet dog playing the alpha dog and making a dog's mess of it.

This story serves as a brilliant metaphor for, and is also the perfect reminder to me of my Light Up experience. I can hear perfectly now, with the deepest clarity. I can see everything. I can feel everything. I can enjoy being. And it is my choice to live my life this way, to be in control of my being.

I spent years with my eyes blinkered, half-open, letting life unfurl around me, looking externally for confirmation and affirmation rather than owning my experience. Feeling I wasn't good enough, that I wasn't part of the 'in crowd', that I wasn't attractive enough, that I was a failure.

All BOLLOCKS.

Now, thanks to Light Up, I've chosen to hoover the years of doubt away, to rid myself of the bollocks I was spoon-fed from an early age, to live my life each day to its fullest, and to remember who I am, who I've always been - my beautiful authentic self in all its glory.

My life has been filled with experiences that have formed the stepping stones and I'm grateful for every last one of them; every single moment of pain, pleasure, excitement, disappointment, happiness and sadness. Every moment has brought me to where I am today.

The day I was born my mother almost died. I was an en caul birth (some call this condition 'born with a veil') which means I emerged fully inside the amniotic sac, which looks like a thin and filmy membrane. The doctor had to break my mother's waters after I was born. In fact I was in such a rush to emerge into the world that my mother gave birth to me alone in the hospital before Nurse Joanie, who looked after me during my first moments, came in to check.

My mother had a big bleed after giving birth and had to be taken for an emergency hysterectomy. During the operation she suffered a cardiac arrest, which they found out was caused by an allergy to the anaesthetic. She was dead for fifteen minutes before she came back to life again after vigorous CPR.

She's talked often about this experience. She could see herself and the doctors below her. She felt peaceful. She could see a bright light, inside which was a gentle outstretched hand inviting her to go into the light. It was her choice, and her choice alone, to come back.

You see it's always about choice. Not anyone else's choice – that's bollocks. It's *my own* choice always. And with that comes full responsibility and ownership for my whole being and everything I choose to do.

I offer my first thank you to my beautiful mother who brought me into the world. My second thank you goes to my wonderful, kind father for sharing his DNA. My third is to beautiful Nurse Joanie, who looked after me in the precious first hours of this life.

Some say that being an en caul birth means I'm special, that I'm blessed. Well I am special - and no more special than any other person in this world. We are all special. We're all limitless in what we can achieve. There are countless examples in history of what we can accomplish when we *choose* to believe it and no matter what bollocks anyone else says, that's a fact. We all have the capacity to be great, to be successful, to be brilliant, when we choose to be our authentic selves, to truly love ourselves.

My mother told me many times that I was a beautiful child, always smiling, only ever crying if I hurt myself. Perhaps I had the knowledge (intuition!) that my mother would feed me, so I had no reason to cry for food. I was happy being, smiling and laughing as I grew. I could talk before I could walk (which explains a lot to those who know me well). I acknowledge now that I was born fully lit up, as most of us are, and it's only as we get spoon fed all the bollocks about the 'rules of life' according to everyone else, that we begin to dim and to forget.

I was lucky as a child. My father was in the forces so we moved around a lot, and I saw more of the world than some of my classmates. I was academically brilliant, maybe a little precocious at times. My parents loved me, deeply, and I felt it. I'm extremely grateful for this experience.

After my father finished his time in the army in 1984, we moved to Yorkshire and it was there, aged eleven, that I found my passion. I began studying the flute, and boy, was I good at that! We all have our own unique passions in life, and this was one that I chose.

My teenage years were spent sociably at school, even though at the time I was still tightly hidden away in the closet regarding my sexual orientation. I was filled with insecurities and worries about being different to other children. I worried that I was a freak, that it was wrong to be gay, all the bollocks that I'd been told. So I hid behind the mask of being straight for many years.

I decided to follow my passion and study music at university. My fourth thank you goes to my music teacher at school, Lesley Wood, who encouraged me every step of the way.

My father died suddenly in 1991, aged only forty-seven, from a massive cardiac arrest whilst playing cricket (one of his favourite sports). It was a month before I (the youngest of three boys – the baby) went to university, leaving my mother alone and widowed at age forty-five. I took over the mantle of holding the family unit together, without question. I found my own solace for my father's death by helping others at university who'd also lost parents.

After so many years of hiding away and leading a sometimes duplicitous lifestyle, I finally came out. My fifth thank you is to my mother, my family and my friends old and new, who all chose to love me for who I am and allowed me to be myself.

Because I felt so insecure about being a 'good enough' musician, I started a 'proper' job and began my career a couple of years after university. Had I realised then that my insecurities were mere bollocks, I'd probably have jumped straight into the music profession, as I have done in recent years.

In 1998 I found out that I was HIV positive. My partner at the time, Andy, was dying, although we didn't realise it until he was admitted to hospital, suffocating with pneumonia. Thanks to the wonders of medicine he survived, and thanks to medication, I've been wonderfully well ever since my diagnosis.

I sought solace by focusing on my partner and working with charities to support others who weren't able to cope with their HIV status in the way that I was. As comforting as it may have appeared, I know now that choosing to live my life looking for others to help, rather than facing my own demons, only served to focus me away from myself. My sixth thank you goes to all the medical professionals out there who have provided, and continue to provide, their support to me and many others with HIV.

Andy and I broke up in 2002 and I moved to London three years later, having met a new partner, Graeme. By this time my career was surging forwards and I was working in major roles at IBM, running multi-million pound projects with more and more responsibility, travel and benefits. Despite this success, I still felt lost at times, as if I'd done myself a disservice by not choosing a career in music. More bollocks, right? I'd been playing with orchestras and other groups since finishing university, so I figured I had the best of both worlds, but it never quelled that feeling of 'what if'. Regret can be a powerful way to sabotage ourselves and it can cause endless hours of procrastination.

Feeling somewhat lost I decided, in 2007, to invest in myself and study in the evenings and weekends to become a barrister. I'd looked at the legal profession as an option when I was younger (although top of the list had always been owning a sweet shop ... and there are still many years ahead for me to do that!) I also shuffled across IBM into Human Resources to look after Diversity and Inclusion which, in a nutshell, is about businesses embracing difference and authenticity in their workforce.

Graeme and I had our civil partnership in 2009 and I moved jobs in 2010, halfway through my legal training, to work at BCG as Human Resources manager. I was admitted to the Bar of England and Wales (that's not a drinking establishment!) in 2011. I am grateful for all of the training and experience it gave me, but by that time I'd decided, without regret, that I didn't choose to be a barrister after all.

In 2013 Graeme and I broke up, two weeks before we completed on buying a new property together. We decided to continue with the purchase, and I know now that this was more because Graeme wished to, I believe because he hoped we might get back together again. My continuous habit of looking to others to live my own life was like a stuck record.

I started a new job at KPMG, leaving two years later. It wasn't an enjoyable experience and yet I worked with some truly wonderful people from whom I learned a lot. There were also some proper tossers there who made my life hell. So my seventh thank you is to all the tossers I've met in my life and the insight they've given me into what I will never choose as my path - so I could find my own perfect path.

I set up my own consulting business with a colleague from KPMG. I was doing my best to get my business up and running and at the same time was feeling stressed about letting my business partners down. I was demotivated. Financial issues were taking their toll and I'd begun to feel less and less self-worth. Old bollocks of the largest variety were beginning to infiltrate my life and I was looking everywhere else for the answers.

After my Light Up, I realised that I'd spent my whole life in this endless cycle of helping others rather than living my own life and following my own passions. It took time for me to truly listen to myself. My head had often been a major contributor to my moments of self-disbelief. Knowing that I have a super computer inside there that is my loyal servant rather than my boss has proved invaluable.

I love words and I'm analytical, so focusing on the power of the words we use I've found great fun to play with. It has (as has Light Up overall) literally changed my life. I now feel I'm living my own life and enjoying myself, and others around me can see the change.

The beautiful thing is that it didn't tell me anything I didn't already know, it provided me with the simple tools to remember what all the BOLLOCKS had encouraged me to forget.

In August 2017 I met the most beautiful man ever, my soulmate Panos, who inspires me every day. I broke my mould at last as he isn't someone who requires fixing and he doesn't judge me for anything I choose to do. I haven't met anyone with a bad word to say about him. He allows me to shine. In the past I'd have run a mile from someone as lovely as Panos and this time I embraced it.

I met him just before I started my Activator training. No coincidence – I don't believe in coincidences any more. I knew I would choose to become an Activator from the moment I first spoke about Light Up, and I feel blessed to have the opportunity to share this wonderful work with others and be some part of their journey. Because it is their journey in the end, not mine.

In 2018 I left my business. I was no longer feeling passionate about where it was headed and I put my friendship with my business partner above my pride. In the past I'd have carried on regardless. I was shifting those old habits and choosing for me, trusting myself at every step, with the knowledge that this was part of a journey.

I continued to shine and to peel off more layers of old skin that were getting in the way of my spiritual growth throughout 2018. In November my house, which I still shared with my ex, was finally sold.

Yes I had foggy patches in the middle, where old habits reared their ugly head and I've had many challenges, especially from Panos. He gave me the best advice ever in December 2018. I'd been meandering around trying (I use this word deliberately) to get on with my Light Up work, without as much success as I'd hoped. I was feeling doubtful and pressured to find other work. It's understandable - money is a useful form of energy in the world. I was stuck in my head all the way. Total bollocks!

Panos said to me, 'how can you teach Light Up if you're not *being* it?' Profound and useful words which continue to impact me now, and a big fat kick up the ass. I was trying rather than doing. I was in familiar territory, observing rather than being. I was desperately searching for myself when I was here all the time. Panos's challenge shifted me into a new gear. I love him, from my depths, and to him goes my eighth thank you.

Since then, since I've started to be and stay truly lit, so much has happened. Work is coming in, I'm delivering Light Ups, I'm doing amazing stuff with my music, and I'm living every day right here, right now. I am the glorious beautiful lit up person I was when I was born, with the same childish inquisitiveness again and the same fascination with this world which we're so fortunate to be given an opportunity to spend time in. I've made my choice now and I choose to follow my passion. Not anyone else's, mine. And it's happening. Right here, right now. Life is beautiful.

If we spend too much time looking backwards at our lives, we'll bang into or fall over something as we move forwards. There could be opportunities missed or obstacles we could have avoided. If we spend too much time looking forwards in our lives, we may step over an opportunity or trip over something. I choose to live now in this very moment. There is only now.

The ninth thank you goes to my Activator Sharon, my tenth to Melanie Pledger and my eleventh to my fellow Light Up activators. I have nothing except love for you all, you beauties. You've allowed me to strip myself bare and stand proudly in the darkest, stormiest weather, without fear.

My twelfth thank you is to everyone who has taken the brave step to go through Light Up, to re-find and re-member, to re-connect with their authentic selves.

And my final thank you is to Phoenix. Phoenix is my light, my instant connection to everything and everyone. I love you. I love me. We are amazing. I am amazing.

DEREK BENTON

Derek Benton Professional Activator

Being what could be labelled a high achiever, I am an accomplished, adaptable HR professional. I went on to study law, qualifying as a Barrister. I am also a professional classical musician, having studied flute in Manchester under the tuition of Alan Lockwood from the BBC Philharmonic. I am the principal flute player of the London Gay Symphony Orchestra and am co-founder of Chamber Made, a new exciting ensemble approach introducing chamber music in an inclusive, creative and informative way.

As a Professional Activator, I focus on life-changing personal development with others, guiding them to reconnect with their true authentic selves, to develop a recognition of their power and ability to do what they choose, to listen to and trust their intuition, and to remember their purpose.

If I were to look back at my career and my life so far, I feel my greatest achievement is very simple. I've been able to make choices where I have had a positive impact on those around me, on society and the world as a whole. I've brought warmth and comfort into people's lives through my music, I've guided people through to reconnect with their humanity through my work and, importantly, I've found peace, understanding and happiness with myself.

I dedicate my chapter to Panos.

BOLLOCKS TO BEING AFRAID OF WHAT OTHERS WOULD THINK

I'VE CONNECTED WITH THE TRUE INNER ME THAT WAS THERE ALL ALONG.

I knew that there was this life that I'd dreamt of as a little girl and something inside kept niggling away at me, like a wasp at a barbecue. Happy as I was ... was this it for me?

Charlotte's story

When I was a little girl, I dreamed of being a singer and an actress. I loved West End musicals and films, and often practised my Oscar acceptance speech in the mirror at home. I felt confident and knew that I was destined to make a difference in the world in some way. My light shone brightly.

I'm from a mining town in the East Midlands where this kind of career path was seen as a 'pipe dream'. Not by my parents - they always said I could do anything I put my mind to - and I believed that. In theory. But by the time I got to secondary school, although I appeared very confident, I was so scared of what people would say that I very rarely put myself forward for school plays. I had a bit of a 'too cool for school' attitude. It was almost like I felt I had to hide the creative side of me to fit in with everybody else and be liked. My light started to shine a little less brightly.

From the age of ten I sang in a choir. We rehearsed every Friday night without fail and I had many concert dates throughout the year. That choir was, and still is, an institution. The discipline was very strict, and that discipline made us the best. During my nine years with them, we won Sainsburys' Choir of the Year twice, and Choir of the World in a competition in Japan during a month-long tour. We travelled the globe and I had some amazing times.

Singing was, and still is, a passion of mine. But my need to fit in and be liked caused me problems. I tried too hard, and this led to me being bullied for a while. It was at its worst while we were in Japan. I felt isolated and alone, not knowing what to do for the best.

It wasn't the type of choir where we could volunteer for solos. There were some incredible singers there who've gone on to have professional careers. Although I knew I wasn't as good as them, at times I felt ignored. Other girls with a similar talent level to me were given the parts I really wanted and I was overlooked. True or not I'll never know, but that's how it felt.

To me it meant that I wasn't good enough. My formative years were spent feeling I was worthy of more but being too scared to ask. 'I'm obviously not good enough' became a core belief.

I knew there was a way out of the 'norm'. My brother left home when I was eleven, moving to London to pursue his career in television. I too wanted an exciting life full of experiences and it was the driving force behind my decision to go to college to study Drama and Theatre in Nottingham, rather than to the local college that all my friends went to.

I had to get up at 5.30 (my hair took a long time!) every morning and take the hour and a half bus ride to college. And I loved it. I did well on my one-year course, passed with distinction, then went on to the two-year course with a view to finishing this and going to drama school or university.

About six weeks into the two-year course I panicked. What if I don't get a job? What if I'm shit? I switched courses to do media, much to the dismay of my drama teacher. I enjoyed it ... and I knew deep down that I'd made a mistake and bottled on my dream.

I finished college, left choir and moved to London. My brother's boyfriend ran a recruitment agency and told me I'd be great at selling. I had an interview on the Thursday, got the job on the Friday, and started on the Monday at a huge international publishing house.

My ten years in London were a mix of really great jobs, some not so good ones, some bad decisions, some great friends, lots of clubbing, travelling and very little self-care. I worked in the music department of the BBC and was a runner on the Saturday Show for over a year. My job was to look after the celebrities and basically run around for everyone else. Then I went to ITV and worked on 'Popstars: The Rivals', the programme that launched Girls Aloud. It was bloody hard work and long hours, and I loved it.

I look back at that time and I almost can't believe some of the things I did. At the time it was fun and 'living in the moment' but it now seems so reckless - and at times dangerous! I met a man and we very quickly moved in together. My weeks were spent at work and my weekends with my huge group of friends. It was a great time of my life ... and underneath it all, I still wasn't happy. Was this it? My dream life seemed like a distant memory.

When I found out I was pregnant, aged twenty-four, I felt like the first person in the world to be expecting. I felt so special. And then I had a miscarriage. I remember like it was yesterday the feeling of being told my baby's heart wasn't beating at my twelve-week scan. I was heartbroken.

After losing the baby, I threw myself back into my social life and just got on with work and life and everything went back to 'fine'. The light got dimmer.

Another five years passed. I was working as a sales manager in a posh health club, we'd bought a house together and I got pregnant again. However the relationship wasn't what it had been. We'd stopped socialising together and were basically just sharing a home, neither of us particularly happy but neither of us with the balls to say anything.

I had our son and six months later I left. I knew if I was going to be happy, then I had to be out of this relationship. I knew he wouldn't leave as we'd just had our baby, so I did. I left my house, my job, my friends, my entire life and moved back home to my parents. I was now almost thirty, a single mum, with no job, and back where I started. The light was almost out!

I know my story so far is not unique. On the whole life had been great, I'd had a good time, made some amazing friends and I loved being a mum. But over the years the light inside me had dimmed. I'd boxed away the version of me I knew I could be and settled with my lot.

I decided to retrain as a hairdresser. I'd been around salons most of my life as my mum was one, so I was good at it. I got a job in a salon and worked there for the next five years. I met my now husband and got married. Life was good - good in the sense that I was in a loving happy relationship and we had a nice house. But we were living hand to mouth and never had any spare money for the finer things in life. It wasn't enough.

I knew that there was this life that I'd dreamt of as a little girl and something inside kept niggling away at me, like a wasp at a barbecue. Happy as I was ... was this *it* for me?

Now, if that *was* it for me, I could have been happy: I'd got a great family, my health, great friends. But I didn't feel fulfilled in my work, I wasn't growing in any way and this mark that I knew I wanted to leave on the world was nowhere to be seen.

One day a bunch of mail dropped onto the mat: takeaway menus, flyers, bills etc, and a card with a piece of paper stapled to it which said 'Would you like to earn an extra £2000 flexibly around what you already do?' Well the answer was obviously 'YES PLEASE'.

I had no idea what it was about, other than something to do with weight loss. It was a local number so I decided to call. A lovely lady answered the phone and I arranged to meet her. She took me through the business and I walked out feeling very excited about the possibility of earning a six figure income, travelling and building a business. I didn't really understand how it all worked but I liked the sound of it.

By the time I got home, I'd talked myself out of it. 'I can't do that, no one will buy anything, no one will want to join my team.' I came up with all the excuses as to why it wouldn't work. 'You're not good enough,' whispered away in my ear.

Three weeks later the lady called me back. We chatted, and something inside kept telling me to go for it. I spoke to my mum, borrowed the £199 for my startup box and away I went. My light had been switched on! It felt good!

For the first year I just dipped in and out, thanks to my old negative self-belief. I went from feeling like I could take over the world to not believing for a minute I'd ever achieve all the things they were telling me were possible.

This new business opened my world to the power of personal development. I'd always been interested in it but looking back, though I understood it in theory, I'd never really actioned the things I learnt. I spent most of my twenties passionately putting the world to rights, I was the person everyone came to for advice and I always encouraged people to 'go for it' and believe in themselves. Shame I didn't take my own advice back then.

Now I realised that If my life was going to change, I had to change. A defining moment for me was at a company event. I was a year into my business and doing okay. A girl was recognised on stage who was a similar age to me and who was earning £5000 a month. At that time, I was earning about £600! £5000 a month, and she was no different to me. She didn't have wings or a magic wand; she was just making it happen. I took myself off to the loo, cried a few tears, and had a very stern word with myself. It was time to stop faffing about and get on with it.

I did. Within the next eighteen months I grew my business to over £6000 a month, with a business turnover of £1.5 million. I achieved all the big company incentives and life was sweet. I was on fire! We moved house, I bought my first new car and I fully expected my journey to continue on that path.

The part of the business I *loved* was developing people, showing them what was possible. I was good at it and became even more obsessed with personal and professional development. I'd experienced such change myself that I was eager to help others. I'd stopped watching TV; instead I watched YouTube videos, read books and took courses. I just loved the feeling of growth. It lit me up. I looked at motivational speakers and teachers and wished I could do what they did.

Then my business started to plateau and I just couldn't seem to make myself engage. My light was starting to dim and I didn't know how to get it back. I'd been growing my business for almost six years, and that old lack of fulfilment was back. I realised that even when the money came, I didn't feel satisfied and would catch myself saying 'I'll be happy when I'm earning *this* much ... I'll be happy when I've achieved *this* position'. It was never enough. Why did I still have this feeling?

What started the massive shift in me was the death of my friend Michelle. We'd only known each other for five years but I loved her. So much so that three months after meeting her, she was a guest at my wedding - I had family members that weren't invited! She was just the most incredible person: funny, outrageous, kind, thoughtful and supportive. She had light oozing out of her, from the crazy curly hair on her head right down to her toes.

When she told me she'd found a lump in her breast, I brushed it off as a cyst. How could she have cancer? She was the healthiest person I knew; she drank green tea and put mango in salads!!!! She was my personal trainer for god's sake. She went to get it checked out. She got the news on her fortieth birthday: it was grade four triple negative breast cancer.

One day when we were having lunch together, she started talking about gratitude. She told me that although the cancer was the worst thing she'd ever been through, in some ways it was also the best. She had never felt more loved and more grateful for every breath. As she said this, she took three long breaths in and out and tears ran down our faces. I will never forget that moment.

Two years later she was gone. I was in South Africa at the time with the business. I don't think I have every felt that sad. I texted her to tell her how much I loved her, knowing she would never see it.

The experience of knowing and loving her, and then losing her, was the biggest lesson I hope I ever get in not sitting around waiting for life to happen. It's happening right now!! This is it! And I say this with all the love in the world. If we don't like it or we long for more - then do something about it! This is our one life and we haven't got time to spend worrying about what other people think. We have to do what makes US happy!

I realised that I still hadn't found it … whatever *it* was. I love my business and will be forever grateful to it. It gave and taught me so much. And now I know it was the stepping stone to what I was truly meant to do.

'You should coach, you'd be really good at it.'

'I didn't know I could do that, I thought you needed a degree. Could I?' was my excited response.

I'd been coaching and mentoring my team for years, but could I make a career out of it? My heroes were people like Brendon Burchard, Marie Forleo and Tony Robbins. I created a fantasy personal development family that had Oprah as my mum and Brene Brown, Marie, Brendon and Simon Sinek as my siblings. I was a total personal growth geek!

Having been asked to speak on many occasions on stage at company events and trainings, I knew I wanted more of that. I loved knowing that something I said had a positive impact on somebody listening. I know how much my life has been transformed by all the books I've read, the seminars and trainings I've been to, and the YouTube videos I've watched, so to be the person that did that for others ticked every box there was going!

I enrolled in a programme to show me how to build an on online coaching business. It was money I didn't have but I was so excited I jumped in feet first. Six weeks in I realised that I wasn't ready to learn how to market myself as a great coach; I needed to *become* a great coach first.

It just so happened that a friend of mine was about to do an Ultimate Coaching qualification in London with a respected international coaching school. I left the programme and enrolled on the course. It was seven days of intense training with an examination at the end. A week later I emerged as an NLP and Timeline Therapy practitioner and qualified coach. I've never felt more excited and happy. I had the practical tools to help people change on a subconscious level.

In my first business, it had always fascinated me that everyone started the same way, with the same box, the same training and the same opportunity. Some went on to become millionaires yet others never got past the first promotion. Why?

It wasn't just about hard work - I've never bought into the 'just work hard and it will happen' theory. It's so much more than that. It's also not just about mindset either. I've always been very intuitively led and always believed there is a universal power, bigger than we are, that we can tap into. But if I'm honest, over the years my head had been making the decision more often than not.

Throughout my training I'd shifted many of my subconscious limiting beliefs using NLP and timeline therapy. It was life changing. I felt and thought in a different way than I had before. I became so much clearer about what I wanted out of this life and I was determined to make it

284 | B.O.L.L.O.C.K.S TO THAT

happen more than ever before, and also to enjoy the journey and put how I feel first.

I reached out to a friend who's a DNA Activator for some support with someone I was helping at the time. I knew about DNA Light Up and thought it would be ideal for this person. She agreed and also suggested that I go through the process too, so that I understood it. It was a very easy yes.

Having been around personal development for some years, the process seemed simple. Yet it was so powerful. The impact it had on me was profound and since that day I now trust my intuition one hundred percent. Light Up re-connects us with our light, the inner us that has always been there, the light that was there when I was a little girl. As we get older, we're all in danger of losing sight of our light and settling for a life more ordinary than extraordinary.

The process was fundamental in my acceptance of my calling to do the work I love. Before Light Up I was constantly in my head, thinking 'what if (insert negative) this' or 'what if (insert negative) that'. It taught me to just feel my way through and if I did, I couldn't go far wrong. And the results have been amazing! When I put my signature programme together, I had my experience with light up as the cherry on the cake.

I developed my Truly.Madly.Deeply framework. Truly sort your shit out! Fall madly in love with yourself. And then attract and manifest the big bold beautiful life you deeply desire and bloody deserve, by connecting with the light that shines so brightly inside you; the inner you, the part of you that just knows best. Trust that and you can be, do and have anything you want.

I turned forty last year, and I have never felt so excited about my future, more fulfilled in my work and in love with my big bold beautiful life!

CHARLOTTE PRIDMORE

I'm a transformation coach, an NLP and Timeline Therapy practitioner and I love to work with female entrepreneurs to show them how to fully step into there BIG BOLD BEAUTIFUL LIFE! I have a unique framework and my signature programme is called TRULY.MAD-LY.DEEPLY which in a nutshell means Truly sort your shit out once and for all, fall MADLY in love with yourself, then attract and manifest the life, relationship, business you DEEPLY desire and bloody well deserve!

I am ridiculously passionate about my family, my friends, personal and professional development, music and singing.

Three things I wish I'd known sooner in life are:

1) Everything is a choice.

2) What the laws of the universe are and how essential they are to happiness and success

3) The only validation necessary is the validation we give to ourselves.

Sharing my story in this book has meant the world to me because I see so many women settling, too scared to ask for more. My mission in life is to help as many women as possible say "Bollocks to settling, I am going to be unapologetically myself, ask for what I want and expect it to happen because I deserve to live my big, bold, beautiful life however I choose to define it!"

This chapter is dedicated to Michelle, my darling friend. Her passing gave me my mission. We are given one amazing life and it is our responsibility to not waste a second of it being anyone else but our beautiful selves.

29

BOLLOCKS TO PRETENDING TO BE STRONG, PROFESSIONAL AND ALWAYS IN CONTROL

I'VE GAINED COURAGE AND SPEAK MY TRUTH WITH CONFIDENCE.

This is when I realised that I didn't have a business problem - I had personal problems reflecting in my business. I was done hiding. I was done fighting. I was done chasing love or acceptance. I was done looking outside of me for solutions. I was done pretending.

Claudia's Story

It was an evening in September 2002. I'd just said good-bye to my freshly divorced ex-husband after a coffee in the shopping centre next to the court where the judge had just declared our marriage null and void.

With the greatest courage I could muster at this stage, I'd told him 'I will take care of the children now,' even though I'd lost my 120K job the week before.

Let me take a step back and explain. I met the father of my children in October 1991. At the time he was a client of the company I was working for and we met at an exhibition. One thing led to another and three months later we were married and I was pregnant. My inner voice was violently shouting at me, on the day of the wedding, that this was a really bad idea. I did it anyway. After all, parents and friends had travelled to attend, everything was organised and I'd bought my new outfit.

Yes, an outfit, not a dress. My husband D had been married before and just didn't fancy another white wedding. I went along with it, even though deep inside I so wished this to be MY special day with a white dress, really romantic.

It wasn't. I learned in the registry that D hadn't told his parents that we would use my name as the family name. I could literally see his mum's face falling and his dad's face turning to stone when the registrar announced that we were now Mr. and Mrs. Hesse.

Too late to listen to my inner voice, so I pretended that it wasn't there and that it was only a last-minute panic. After all, I hardly knew the man that I just married.

And yes, it turned out to be one of my biggest mistakes in my life in one way. And one of my biggest learning experiences in another.

Re-start with hurdles

Back to the moment after the divorce. I was in good spirits. After all I'd been given the chance to restart my life, to be alone with my children.

I was escaping from an exhausting and soul-destroying marriage with someone whose strategy was to keep me as small as possible - so that he could appear larger; someone who shamelessly pushed any button he found to make me feel shame - a feeling, I'd learn years later, that's one of the most destructive for our sanity and well-being.

At least I'd received a nice severance package that I knew would keep me afloat for a while.

I could now, finally, spend more time with my children, after having worked my butt off for the previous nine years as sole breadwinner for the family, and then taking over all duties at the weekend, so that my husband could recover from his exhausting week with the kids.

All great, right?

Well not really. Under the surface, deep inside of me, there were doubts and fears doing their destructive work.

"I got fired – that means I'm not good enough, I'm unwanted, I don't belong, I'm out."

"What happens if I don't find a job anymore?"

"How the heck can I go back into a leading position with two young children?"

"What if my money runs out and I have nothing lined up for the future?"

"What if I lose my house?"

These were just a few of the questions running up and down inside my head. Little did I know that this would only be the start of another fifteen year-long challenging and exhausting roller-coaster ride. Until I finally came to a point where I took the plunge to go all-in after having circled the topic – myself – for decades.

Before this step in my life happened, I started a business with one partner and gave it up again after a year. I started a second business with three other partners – back in my previous industry (IT) - and we had a blast. Together we built up a successful publishing company which became the number one go to magazine in its niche. On top of which, we all made a decent amount of money.

I then moved to a new country and helped my sister in building up a Montessori school in Switzerland, as well as continuing to manage my work at the publisher.

I was able to send my daughter to an expensive International School and pay for her studies abroad, including her master's degree.

I met a man with whom I had a long-distance relationship over many years and who introduced me to parts of life I'd never experienced before.

Oh, did I mention that I still kept my house in Germany, and I had two horses?

Great life, hey?

At least, that's how it looked from the outside. And I did my best to keep this picture up.

I did not talk about …

- my sister firing me, officially because money was tight, unofficially because there were old sibling conflicts still brewing under the surface.
- the feeling of having to fight and struggle every day to keep things together.
- the sleepless nights when I worried about big bills coming in and how to pay them.
- how the responsibility for two kids with a no-show-no-pay father weighed heavily on my shoulders.
- how I struggled to make things right between the new partner and my kids, an area where I realised that I was failing.
- how I was so tired every day that I fell asleep on the sofa with the book falling on my face.

And so, I kept fighting - to keep the brave face on and the money coming in.

After all I wasn't just a tough business woman, I was also supposed to be a good mother, successful and STRONG. Which made me feel tons of shame just thinking about the struggles I was going through internally.

How could anyone still love and accept me if I admitted that I had weak and desperate moments in my life?

Self-fulfilling prophecy is a bitch

Because that's exactly what happened. The enormous amount of energy and discipline it took to hold myself and this great picture up had a tendency to collapse suddenly at regular intervals. It was simply unsustainable.

I remember one scene at Munich airport so clearly it feels like yesterday. I had to go on a business trip and my partner at the time took me to the airport.

He'd come to see me from the UK and we'd just spent a week together at my place. It turned out to be the usual juggling act: how the heck could I satisfy all those different parts of my life - keeping the business up, looking after the children, spending time with my partner?

He showed up when *his* agenda allowed it. Not that he was bound to something mundane like a job. Nope, he simply had to manage all the functions and events happening at the various boarding schools of his sons.

So, he'd 'announce' that he was coming and staying – for how long I had no idea as he never booked a return flight. On the rare occasions when he did, he'd change it depending on how things went.

This time it was really not great as I knew I had to travel for business while he was there, which increased the pressure on me by miles!

We had a great relationship. But only when I went to the UK with zero plans and no kids with me, so I could completely and utterly adapt to his schedule and go along with whatever he had planned (and admittedly he was very good at creating a good time). And I did just that, always with a little fear attached. The classic 'what if' questions came up again. What if he doesn't really love me? Am I good enough? After all, he was from the upper middle class with a trust fund in the background and I was, well, what was I?

The result was that I was often watching him like a hawk, trying to figure out what's the 'right' behaviour for me and to read his wishes from his eyes, always terrified I would make mistakes which could lead to a break-up.

Pretty exhausting. Just writing this now makes me almost breathless.

And yet I was still caught up in it. I didn't really speak up when he did things I disliked. At least not in any kind of constructive conversation. I bottled up whatever bugged me, tried to suppress my sadness, frustration or worry – which ultimately resulted in situations like the one at the Munich airport.

Back to the story. He was saying goodbye to me before I went through security control, and suddenly I started sobbing and crying uncontrollably for no apparent reason.

Completely and utterly gobsmacked, he looked at me and asked: 'What the hell is wrong with you?' Suffice to say that in his circles showing such kinds of emotion in public is more than frowned upon and he hated it with a passion. It embarrassed him.

I couldn't even explain what had just happened. There I stood, in business attire with my little laptop bag, sobbing like a child that had just lost its favourite toy. I couldn't even give a reason for it, except: 'I'm so exhausted, I have no idea how to deal with all this anymore.' To which he replied: 'I have no idea why you act like that. This is not the strong woman I know. Pull yourself together.'

Wow.

So, I wasn't right because I was weak. Contrary to the picture I'd projected of being always strong.

And on top of it there was no helping hand. *None at all.*

My biggest fears and beliefs were confirmed: I *have to be* strong. All the time. *And* I've got to get through all of the shit life throws at me *on my own.*

So, I pulled myself together, put my chin up, pushed back the tears as soon as I could, and got myself on the plane. I am strong. I can do this alone.

Until it happened again. And again. And again. Always with a few months in between. And I realised that there was a clear pattern of sucking stuff up, fighting through and getting back on my feet again – normally on my own.

Intuitively I knew that this was not healthy or good – and still I didn't have the slightest idea how to change it and didn't even give a thought to the fact that I could shift it. I simply accepted that I had to be strong, that life's a struggle and I have to fight it all alone.

After years and years (in total almost ten), I finally realised that this man was not good for me. My overdeveloped loyalty faltered, and after a number of on-and-off years I finally left him. Interestingly, as soon as I put my requirements at the same level as his and stopped pleasing him, he started chasing me and would not let go. For many years I still felt flattered on the one side and tempted by habitual behaviour on the other – hence the on-and-off situation. In a nutshell, I let someone else make decisions about my life.

It would take me a long time to recognise it though - this pattern of opportunistically going through the motions. It only became crystal clear about two years ago – in 2017. I'll tell you about that in a moment.

The journey of finding

I've always been a self-development junkie. I can't even count the number of books I've read on topics like how to have a great relationship, loving myself, overcoming struggles, communicating in the right way ... you name it. Spiced up with some inspirational reads from authors like Paulo Coelho and the like.

I learned A LOT.

And I changed.

For one, I realised that I would no longer be a people-pleaser. Particularly with men. Yes, that was exactly what I found I did. Funnily enough I was always known for speaking my mind, even as a child. Which sometimes embarrassed my mum or my sister, as I was just not holding back. Speaking the truth, they would frantically look where they could hide, hoping not to be associated with me. Even my kids experienced that later when I made it very clear in shops what I did not agree with.

Strangely enough though, there were clearly situations where I'd not only lost this way of behaving but completely gone over to the opposite side. In romantic relationships, and to some degree, in the business environment - anywhere close relationships were involved.

When I looked closely, I realised that what lay behind this was my fear of not belonging, not being loved or accepted. What happens if I speak up and say what I *really* think and feel? Will I be left? Will I be fired? Will I lose my credibility and be looked at differently? That was a risk that I couldn't control.

So, I swallowed what was deep inside of me. I was unhappy. Torn. Upset. In the worst case, I developed resentment, a poison for every relationship.

Hey, all those books had to pay off, right? I was getting better and better at analysing my own behaviour and seeing repeated patterns. I even knew how to change it: I basically had to master the courage to stand up for myself and say what was on my mind. I did it when I was really young, so why wouldn't it work now?

What was missing was simply that I had no idea how to develop this courage. Every time I faced such a situation, my heart throbbed in my throat, I felt extremely nervous, anxious and fearful. Even knowing where this came from, I found it hard to overcome.

I knew the theory. Eventually there came the opportunity to test it out.

The love-story

Some time ago my best girlfriend asked me why I didn't try online dating. To which I said: 'Are you crazy? That's not for me!' (Without really knowing why I said that.) 'You´ve got nothing to lose, right? Why don't you just give it a try?' she said.

And so I did.

Jeez, it was worse than I thought!! A bit like online shopping. Swipe. Ehhmm, no. Swipe. No. Swipe. Hmm, not bad. Swipe. Oh he looks nice. Swipe. Cringe.

We're not even talking about the messages that came in telling me the (sad) stories of their lives or asking for sex right away. I met with one man. No spark whatsoever.

Can't do this - that's what I thought after a couple of weeks.

Then I came across a profile pic that looked really interesting. Black and white. And so I checked him out. British. Exactly what I liked. Funny, at least in the text he wrote (claiming that he could iron a shirt quicker than any woman. Really?).

I send a message saying: 'Finally something different, very refreshing to see.'

That was all. I didn't hear back from him for three weeks and had almost forgotten about it. Then suddenly a message out of the blue: 'I was on holiday, didn't check anything. So sorry.'

We started mailing each other, asking questions, some playful, some serious. I'd decided not to take any sh** nor to make things looks different from what they were. 'Brutal' honesty. No compromises.

It was surprisingly easy in the beginning - it was in writing and I didn't really know the man yet. I even asked him if he was one of those boring bankers, as I loathe them. Bang. Had he said yes, that would have probably been it. I was willing to risk that. Huh! In a fascinating way I surprised myself.

Over a period of some weeks we exchanged information and ... gulp ... it still all sounded rather good. Despite - or maybe because - I was so honest and direct. It seemed to work. I found the courage to stay with and acknowledge what was important to me!

Finally, he asked if we could meet and we arranged to get together in between where he and I lived (which was 300 km apart from each other, thankfully still in the same country). We met for lunch. After all I didn't want to risk meeting someone for dinner and not getting out, in case it was horrible. Hey, mails are one thing, meeting up another, right?

So, we met for lunch at noon. And I went home at one ... am.

We'd spent lunch, several coffees, a walk and a dinner together in the city where we met. And could not stop talking. That's when he already knew that this was for him. I took the liberty of checking out another area of a relationship which is important for me when we met the second time.

That's almost five years ago. Four years ago, we moved in with each other. We still talk. A lot. We've been through various family crises and other tough stuff. This was when I realised that applying this honesty was getting more complicated – when things go wrong, when arguments come up, when I realised that sometimes we're not on the same page. When suddenly far more is at risk – not the start of a relationship, but the full-blown life together.

Phew. Almost there, but not quite.

Things happen for a reason

I knew that there was something missing, so I kept on searching. Not every day. Not even weekly or monthly. I basically got on with my life, dealt with all the stuff that comes along with a family which is distributed across four different countries, adolescent kids and a business to run. In other words: plain madness. At least a lot of the time. Also, of course there were moments of fun. Still rather exhausting at times.

Life was good.

So good, that in the midst of all of this I decided to be brave and change the direction of my business. I'd realised quite some time ago that my publishing business bored me and that it had served its purpose – it was time to move on to something new. Everything around me pointed in a single direction: it was time to focus more on what my passion really is

- the human condition and how we can get out of fear and into courage. From caged to being free.

Looking at it from where I stand now, it's almost funny how the individual puzzle pieces fell into place. The puzzle was so big that I couldn't see it at first.

Let me take a step back and give you some context. I live in Switzerland and for many years most of my business income came from Germany. No problem generally, until in 2011 the Euro crashed against the Swiss Franc and I lost about twenty-five percent of my income and cash assets within a single day.

I can still remember it as if it was yesterday: I was sitting in the car, driving to have my little luxury session of reflexology massage. I heard the news on the radio and my heart almost stopped. The headline was the collapse of the Euro. That could not be! I must have misheard it. Immediately I double checked the news on my phone and my heart sank even further. I felt ice-cold inside. One of my deepest fears was triggered - not having enough money, having no money, being ruined.

Thankfully I'm a very pragmatic person and within days I'd secured myself another income source within the country, filing contracts in the caves of a local company, which saved me short-term, and a few days later, a good friend of mine emailed me about a consultant in Zurich who was looking for someone to help with his marketing and sales.

'Perfect', I thought, 'that's for me. Let's meet this guy and see what happens.'

M. was a lovely guy. We got on well and decided to give it a go. What followed was a fascinating learning and growing experience professionally and personally. We built a training business together which worked really well. I learned about a completely different way to run a business and deal with projects, all about people and processes, which confirmed what I'd believed for many years already. I even went through a couple of certifications myself.

This gave me the spark to pivot my business. Without M. this would not have happened. This, however, was not the end of it.

With my usual enthusiasm I threw myself into developing a model around Personal Leadership which became very clear very quickly. All the parts and necessary areas simply poured out of me without effort. Except one.

I got stuck, had sleepless nights with thoughts bouncing around in my head endlessly without any progress. I'd gone through countless courses, watched learning and expert videos until they came out of my ears and worked like a horse. Without finding the missing piece.

Unlearning in process

Again, it was M. who pointed me in the right direction and a single call changed everything.

He had the (questionable) privilege of listening to me ranting about going round in circles. He's really good at listening. He gave me the name of someone to speak to. Someone who could offer me the chance to get out of what was incredibly exhausting, frustrating and confusing.

Know that feeling when we're really desperate and we grab every straw? Yep, that was me back then.

Interestingly enough this was the second time he'd talked about this 'someone'. The first time I simply heard, but the information didn't fall on any kind of fertile ground. This time it did. Still I hesitated to take the leap and go through another 'course'. I'd learned enough.

It was my wonderful partner who gave me the nudge. 'When are you going?' he asked after I told him about the chat I'd had with Melanie (Pledger).

'Huh? I haven't decided yet', was my answer. 'Of course, you have,' he replied.

And sure enough I had – without even knowing it.

Two weeks after the call I got on a plane to see Mel and go through an intensive weekend of what I hoped would bring movement and clarification to my new business.

I learned a lot that weekend.

- how to tap into my power, which gives me stability and calmness
- how to speak my truth in a simple way
- how to quieten the voices in my head and listen to the voice of my heart and soul

I had epiphanies (love this word!) and real-eye-sations. (Ha! Playing with words is another thing I love). I probably unlearned even more.

The belief that life is hard and requires me to fight every day.

The belief that I have to earn the love of others whilst pleasing them.

The belief that I can only be strong *or* weak, pragmatic *or* spiritual, professional *or* playful.

The belief that anything on the inside can be fixed or healed from the outside.

I felt ridiculous. And sad. Agitated and angry. I laughed and cried. I was tired. Professional. Honest. And serene. With moments of exquisite quietness in my head.

And this is when I realised that I did not have a business problem - I had personal problems reflecting in my business. And more than a year later, having worked with many people, I know that this is true FOR ALL OF US!!

I walked out a different person. I just didn't know it ... *yet* (in fact I had moments where I asked myself what this was all about).

I was done hiding. I was done fighting. I was done chasing love or acceptance. I was done looking outside of me for solutions. And I was done pretending.

On top of that I'd found the missing puzzle piece for my concept, which would turn out to be a method which produces results *every* coach has been dreaming of.

Don't believe for a minute that this all went perfectly well from one minute to the next. Sometimes it does and sometimes it doesn't. I'm still practising and will continue to do so for the rest of my years. With far more ease than I ever thought possible. And with the clear knowledge that I can.

Life will throw challenges at us. Sometimes more and sometimes less often, depending on where we are in our journey (not that I assume it's getting less ... maybe different). We might be affected by the crises of people around us, by political systems in our countries, by economic changes.

What makes all the difference though is how *we* deal with it and react to it. And that is probably the most important lesson I've learned in all of my life.

Next to the fact that I have the power to choose. If I decide to, I can tap into *my* power source burning brightly inside of me.

More powerful than any tool or trick could ever be.

The power that provides me with a fountain of love and appreciation for myself and others. With knowledge that I didn't even know I had.

With the kindness to forgive myself. And others.

With the wisdom that I'm a part of something much bigger than myself.

With the serenity to accept my life and where I am.

With the grace to surrender to the path without giving up.

With the trust that whatever the path might be, it will be the right one for me.

With the strength to create *my* vision and shape *my* reality in a way that serves me and others.

With the curiosity to find out what I don't know and to understand myself and others.

With the courage and confidence to speak my truth and to unapologetically be ME.

Finally, my honesty and my meanwhile incredibly well developed sense of seeing, sensing and knowing the truth - not just inside of me, often also with other people around me – lead to a breaking point. I don't regret a single moment of honesty and pushing for the truth. Despite the fact that it triggered a situation which is painful. This though is a story for ano

CLAUDIA HESSE

I'm a Personal Leadership Activator. After thirty years in leading positions in international IT organisations, I've finally found my true passion – or more to the point – allowed it to come through and take the place it deserves. I've been what you can call a "self-development junkie", basically all my life since my teenage years, always searching. What began as a "let's look up how to heal a broken heart" interest quickly turned into the desire to work out how humans tick – and why communication and relationships seemed to be so darn complicated. In my professional and in my private life.

This quickly became a lifelong addiction, until I turned it into my business to help (mainly) business executives to get out of being stuck and into clarity, confidence, congruence and courage. In short – owning their life and career.

I'm fifty-four now. I have raised two children on my own and managed to have a good, if exhausting, life with them. Not knowing earlier how much more relaxed and empowered I could have walked through my life, might be one of the very few regrets I have. It would have also prevented me from believing that my worth depends on "stuff" outside of me: money, status, possessions, achievements. A dangerous place to be.

I might be a slow learner – or it was all along "the plan" that I would only come to this point in my life when I did and could write up this story: to encourage you, dear reader, to believe and to look into the most powerful gift that we all have and that cost me decades of exploring and learning and finding. Your personal light, the source for magnificent resilience and courage and the key to a wholehearted life full of love.

I am German and live in Switzerland with my partner and a pug. My two children are in their twenties now and I have been running my own business since 2004. I am crazy about horses and love gardening, reading, learning and singing. This chapter is dedicated to my beautiful children Sina and David, who were (and sometimes still are) my best teachers.

30

BOLLOCKS TO IMPOSTOR SYNDROME

I KNOW WHO I AM AND I'VE FALLEN IN LOVE WITH ALL MY MESSY HUMAN-NESS.

I *was always waiting - expecting - to be found out. I lived in fear and expectation of being judged harshly and found wanting myself.*

Sharon's Story

A damp, overcast winter's afternoon. Husband, dog and I are tramping round a field, chatting away and catching up with where each other is at. We do it most days.

I say something … can't remember what … and Husband responds unexpectedly.

'That's the old you talking', he says. 'That's not who you are anymore. Not since you did that Light Up thing.'

'What? Sorry? What on earth do you mean?!'

He stands still abruptly, staring at me in surprise. Even the dog looks taken aback.

'Surely you're aware of it? You're not the same woman any more.'

'What ARE you talking about?' I am, quite genuinely, baffled. 'Explain!'

So he does. I am, he informs me, more confident, calmer, clearer, less stressed, I make decisions in a heartbeat, I don't faff as much, I'm sleeping better, I'm happier and just ... nicer to be with.

It's like an adult telling a child how much they've grown. It's obvious to the adult. And the child hasn't noticed. Until, of course, she realises she's able to reach something that was previously beyond her.

I refrain from demanding where and when I've ever faffed and if I'm nicer now does that mean I was horrid in the past, and instead concede that yes, I *have* been sleeping better in recent weeks.

'And it's all started shifting since you did that Light Up thing,' he says.

Husband is generally pretty wise and observant and I've learned, over the years, to pay attention when he makes announcements like this. I ponder. And yes ... perhaps there is something in what he says. I *am* feeling happier.

The 'Light Up thing' was a two part, thoroughly enjoyable but 'hardly life changing' (as I remember saying at the time), personal development journey that I'd been through a couple of months previously. I'd done it out of curiosity, not because anything was wrong with my life or required fixing. Simply because, as a coach and trainer myself, I was always open to exploring what else was out there, and this particular 'thing' had intrigued me. My head kept telling me I didn't need to do 'yet another course', but some irresistible inner nudge wouldn't let me pass this one by.

And it was great. It was playful, simple and experiential. Aspects of it were not unfamiliar. It reminded me of some stuff I'd forgotten and gave me back some forgotten tools in a new guise. No lightning bolts of self-realisation, no chandelier moments, no major epiphanies. I didn't regret the investment of time and money I'd made in doing it. And I honestly did *not* believe that it would change the course of my life.

That life had been remarkably happy and blessed. Fortune smiled on me, giving me loving supportive parents and an uneventful childhood, untouched by major trauma or tragedy. I loved school, both the academic and the social side, had a brilliant time at university and The Best Time Ever at drama school.

Being an actress in the seventies and early eighties (we weren't called actors till a couple of decades later!) was enormous fun as well as hard work. The lucky breaks outweighed the crushing disappointments and I enjoyed moderate success, while somehow avoiding the worst excesses of the sexism that dogged the profession. I had a pretty wild time, with a variety of experiments and a few close shaves, yet somehow remained protected by innocence, positivity and simple good luck.

Then I met and married my soulmate (aka Husband), still my best friend after three and a half decades, two amazing children and a ton of bonkers adventures together. We've neither of us ever had a 'proper job' and yet somehow managed to keep a roof over our heads and food on the table while pursuing our various passions ... acting, film making, writing, coaching; joint ventures and independent projects; always committed to being a stand for each other's greatness, not our smallness.

Because we're human ... and there's plenty of smallness. Shedloads of the BOLLOCKS that few of us escape: the conditioning, the social pressures, the limiting beliefs, the insecurities, the lazy unhelpful habits, the comparing self to others, the mental (in both senses of the word) limits that we humans put on ourselves.

Being a full-time mum while the children were tiny, living in a little country cottage with two dogs, two gerbils and a rabbit, was (mostly) pure joy, and sometimes lonely and str e ssful. Husband was busy being an actor, sometimes away all week and only back on Sundays, sometimes around twenty-four seven. Money was often tight and we (mostly) didn't care. Life was (mostly) very good indeed.

Once the kids were at school I was able to work again and explored new career paths. I qualified as a counsellor, toyed with the idea of training as a psychotherapist ... and ended up unexpectedly writing and producing corporate videos. I started coaching people in presentation skills, helping them to relax, be themselves and enjoy themselves in front of a camera or audience. This morphed into more regular 'life coaching'.

As a coach I knew I didn't have the answers for anyone (because I certainly didn't have them for myself), but I was a good listener and I got better at asking the questions that helped people to access their own answers. I worked with private clients, in the corporate world and in the public sector, and some clients stayed with me for years. Yet after pretty much every session, I wondered if I'd actually made a difference. Had I really helped? Was I worth what these people were paying me?

Because all the time that I was so good at seeking out the best in other people, I was not so hot at doing it for myself. I judged no-one (well, I did my best not to judge), and I lived in fear and expectation of being judged harshly and found wanting myself. I was generally confident, and frequently felt insecure. I was loving and generous, and at times could behave with the most unbelievable small mindedness and pettiness. I was mostly happy and content, and there were periods of bleak depression. I could take on the world and triumph, and the same night I'd be curled in a ball with a panic attack, hitting my head on the wall to distract from the inner torment. I was ambitious, and fear of failure often paralysed me. I was an optimist who suffered with anxiety and could worry for England. I was easy going, with a control freak side that sometimes bordered on the obsessive. I was a rebel, and I cared terribly about what people thought of me.

And I never felt like I was enough. Not good enough, not clever enough, not pretty enough, not old enough (eventually that one got replaced by not young enough), not kind enough, not funny enough, not thoughtful enough, not wise enough ...

Never, ever ever ever enough.

Impostor syndrome, in all its malevolent glory, dogged my every step. I was always waiting - expecting - to be found out, unmasked, exposed.

And what was my crime? Not matching the impossible standards that I set for myself and that I assumed other people also set for me (despite all the evidence to the contrary telling me that they were all too concerned about themselves to even notice me).

And back then we didn't even have to contend with the absurd pressures created by social media!

It wasn't that anything bad had ever happened to me. It was simply that life had got to me and slowly worn me down. Life, and some of those insidious ingrained habits, beliefs and ways of thinking that I'd never consciously adopted and yet now seemed to have taken control and become part of me. And they were slowly robbing me of joy.

Habits like: People pleasing. Worrying about the opinions of others. Stressing about outcomes that I had no control over. Overthinking. Neglecting self-care. Doubting myself. Feeling guilty for I didn't even know what. Taking things personally. Saying 'yes' when everything inside was screaming 'no'. Trying to look good. (I say trying because I rarely succeeded.)

I was adept at covering up all this inner angst and showing a happy smiling face to the world. I'm pretty sure that nobody, except perhaps Husband, ever guessed. I knew though. And I didn't like it.

I was an actor accustomed to wearing masks and playing different roles. I wore so many masks that I'd lost touch with who I actually was beneath them all. The advice to 'just be yourself' confused me, because - who the heck was I? There were far too many 'me's to choose from. I hadn't yet real-eyes-ed that the times we're at our best are generally the times when we're strong enough, authentic enough, courageous enough, to let our mask slip and reveal our ugly, raw, broken, vulnerable, beautiful human side.

The mask didn't feel great. It felt dishonest, out of integrity, confusing - for me and for others. And sometimes it was also agonisingly painful.

I was very very open to discovering what was 'missing'. Cue years and years of 'personal development': courses, trainings, qualifications, seminars, workshops. Books - so many books, so many hours spent in the Mind Body Spirit section of bookshops. Counselling, therapy, psychoanalysis, coaching, self-realisation, human potential exploration - from the conventional and accredited, to the alternative and complementary, to the woo woo and wacky, I was a sucker for it all. A self-help junkie.

There were breakthroughs aplenty. Moments when I felt I'd found the answer, the magic remedy, the solution that could heal me, heal humanity, heal the world. Moments when this whole bonkers beautiful agonising messy thing called life actually made some kind of weird sense.

That's all they ever were though - moments. Nothing ever seemed to make a real and lasting difference. Much of it turned out to be simply just more wafty bollocks.

The greatest clarity I got was when I was sharing stuff with others, in one on one coaching, in workshops, trainings and seminars. It was spooky how often I found that whatever issue a client was struggling with weirdly mirrored exactly what was going on for me too.

And ... talking about it was not *being* it. Sometimes the gap between the two felt disgusting, dishonest and devoid of integrity. Was I really making a difference to anyone? Or was it all so much hot air, signifying ... nothing much at all really. Was I really just a big fat fake?

Fat? Oh yes, there were body issues too! I'm still astonished when people describe me as tiny or petite. That hasn't been my own body image, regardless of what was in the mirror. Inside I felt lumbering, clumsy, plump. It didn't matter what the scales - or anybody else - said. Cue endless fad diets and weight loss regimes.

Menopause hit me hard, and early. Cue a decade of slowly losing the plot. Hot flushes weren't just a physical inconvenience, they were an emotional wrecking ball. The hormonal tsunami robbed me of sleep, eroded my confidence, chipped away at my mental health, and left me in a permanent low level state of guilt, tension and panic.

I responded by setting myself bigger goals in my business and career. Smart move - not.

Whatever I was doing I felt I should be doing something else. I was spinning more and more plates, terrified of dropping one, afraid of letting people down, feeling I was failing miserably at life. The habit of 'I can do this by myself', that started as childhood independence, intensified into an inability to accept support. And so I didn't seek help.

Even as the hormones settled, the ways of thinking and being that I'd gotten into left me feeling washed up, beached, exhausted. The joy had slowly leached out of my life. I fear I wasn't a lot of fun to live with.

Of course, you'd never have guessed. Like ninety-five percent who struggle with their mental health, I covered it up. I kept the mask in place. I appeared to be fully functioning, even happy and successful. And I was struggling.

And then, out of the blue, along came this 'Light Up thing'.

I so very nearly passed it by. I believe the universe sometimes sprinkles bread crumbs to show us the way, and sometimes it hits us round the head with a stale baguette. Either way, how grateful am I that something inside nudged me to pause and pay attention.

What I experienced were two enjoyable, playful sessions that at the time I vastly underestimated. And yet, notwithstanding, seeds were planted, shifts were activated, memories were awakened and something in me was reconnected at a very profound level.

And apparently those two sessions were still making a difference to me, my mood and my mindset, months later, as Husband gently pointed out to me.

I now know, several years later, that those two sessions shifted *everything*.

I have a different relationship with myself now. I've fallen in love (forgive the cliche - and I promise you, it doesn't feel like a cliche when it actually happens!) with myself and all my messy human-ness.

I've stopped listening to what everyone else thinks (or what I think they think!) and started listening to my own inner voice. Not the mean, nasty, carping critic in my head (who may have my best interests at heart yet sometimes has a very funny way of showing it). No. To that quiet, intuitive, inner knowing that never has and never will let me down. The mean voice hasn't gone - I just no longer honour it with my attention.

I respond to life in the present moment instead of from past condition-ing. I have way more fun, and I laugh more often and more heartily. Fear no longer stops me or holds me back. *I know who I am.*

All those plates that I used to spin? I've laid some gently down so that I can focus on the ones that matter, the ones I feel passionate about. And instead of thinking of them as plates that are in danger of falling and smashing, I've replaced them all with a 'portfolio career'. I imagine it as a beautiful squashy soft leather briefcase that lives somewhere around my solar plexus (it's a wonderful thing, the imagination). It keeps everything safe and I can pull out whatever it is that I'm engaged with at the moment so I can focus just on that. My boundaries are strong and clear.

I've become more compassionate, with myself and with others. I get over upsets in a heartbeat. I get fascinated far more than I get frustrated. I feel no need to paste over my cracks. Instead I embrace them, because it's through the cracks that the light shines out. The light that's in all of us.

It was inevitable that I'd go on and train to deliver this work to others. It was partly gratitude, because I feel in service to this work, this thing that has slowly, invisibly, transformed me and my life, giving me back my joy, my connection to the wellspring. It was partly that I was curious to delve deeper and understand how Light Up works its magic despite its apparent simplicity. And partly I was curious about how it would work with others.

What I can tell you is that every single Light Up is unique. Every single one is surprising, unexpected, beautiful. And every single time an extraordinary magic occurs, whether it's in a few tiny shifts or in a massive upheaval.

What truly astonishes me is that the long term effects are often more powerful and profound than the short term. That was certainly the case for me.

Catching up with clients months, years sometimes, after their initial Light Up, I've come to expect two general responses. Either people say: 'It changed everything. I don't recognise myself. My life is not the same. I'm not the same' Or they say: 'I loved it and - honestly - I can't remember much about it.' So I ask them what's been happening in the intervening period. 'Well!' they say. 'Loads has shifted, big changes, major decisions ... I deal with stuff very differently now ...' and they start to grin as they begin to make the connections.

Charles Bukowski asked the question (seen sometimes as a FaceBook meme): '*Can you remember who you were before the world taught you who you should be?*' Sometimes the words '*and dimmed your f***ing shine?*' are added.

Well now I do remember! And I remember at the cellular level.

I believe every newborn soul is like at shining diamond at birth. Over time we get grubby, dimmed down, covered in horse manure and general detritus as we do our best to fit in and get by. The bollocks gets to us. We're aware - because we can never completely forget - that we were born to shine. So we do our best - we paint ourselves with varnish in an attempt to reflect and sparkle again. And it never really works. It's only when we release our grip on the externals, when we stop looking for the answer 'out there', that we discover that our light has never gone away. It's still in there, waiting for us to notice, to listen, to re-ignite.

Husband was right. I'm not the same woman. And I'm the woman I always was. Except now ... now I shine.

SHARON BOTT

Sharon Bott Professional Activator

I've been variously an actor and voice-over artist, a writer and producer, a coach, mentor and trainer, a business owner, and I'm now Head of Training at DNA Light Up.

For me passion is the pepper and salt of life - it brings out the flavour. Within Light Up, my passion is helping people reconnect with their own core power, so no matter what life chucks at them (it will - that's what life does), they can shine. Imagine a world where everyone is lit up? Imagine being a part of making that happen?

I wish I'd known earlier in life that I was enough, just as I was, just as we all are. Enough - and with huge potential for growth and transformation, from the inside out. Imagine a world where every child, every young person, everyone, trusts their intuition and feels empowered to make a positive difference?

The next generation is growing up in a world where so much - education, finance, politics, the environment - is broken or off kilter. And yet there also are some amazing shifts happening that offer hope for our future. Imagine the message of Light Up rippling round the world, encouraging people to reclaim their power? BRING IT ON!

EPILOGUE

By Sharon Bott, Head of Training, DNA Light Up

A bunch of very different stories, from a bunch of very different people - different in background, circumstances, age, gender, nationality. What do they all have in common?

Each narrator has been through Light up. And it appears to have made a difference.

So what *is* Light Up? How does it work?

And what makes it unlike any other form of therapy, coaching, counselling or therapeutic intervention?

A few years ago I ran into someone I knew who looked - well, different. I was curious. 'What have you been up to?' I asked. 'You look all lit up!'

She grinned and asked if I'd ever heard of DNA Light Up, or Mel Pledger. Nope (and having been around the personal development world, working as a coach and trainer for some twenty years, I reckoned I'd come across most everything). 'It's important I put you two in touch!' she said.

She did. One thing led to another and very soon, nudged by curiosity and trusting the instant connection I'd felt with Mel, I went through Light Up with one of her newly trained Activators. Several years on, I'm now delivering Light Up myself (best job in the world!) and I'm Head of Training for DNA Light Up.

Why do I choose to share this work?

Because in all my years of coaching and mentoring, I have never come across anything that so gently, so profoundly and so *permanently* makes such a difference. I've not found anything that gets results like this so quickly, so powerfully, and without any requirement for people to talk about what's happened in their past.

The absolute simplicity of the golden thread of this work puts people back in touch with their own wisdom and answers, their own power and inner tools - often after decades of feeling disconnected, disempowered and damaged. They feel whole again. They can ditch whatever baggage they've been dragging around. Whatever life chucks at them, they now *know* they can handle it. And they do. I've seen it again and again and again with clients. You've read the stories here. And there are countless more where these came from.

Light Up is for everyone.

Individuals, groups, families, businesses, children, people who've experienced trauma or abuse, people at the height of their success. Everyone. And our personalised pricing means it's also affordable - for everyone.

Light Up happens either face to face, or via an online video connection platform. It happens one to one, or in groups. Whatever is appropriate for you. It happens in just two or three sessions, with an online follow up programme and lifetime membership of an online community included. We also offer talks and workshops so that people can find out more.

Light Up works. Every time.

And it *keeps on* working. Because it's more about un-learning than learning. It's about remembering who we are - and always were, before life 'got to us' and we learnt to squash ourselves down. It's about reconnecting with our inner power and reclaiming what is already rightfully ours.

The process is fast and playful. The results are instant - sometimes subtle, occasionally radical, always life-changing and long lasting. It will complement and support any existing personal development you may have done or be doing, and it won't disrupt any spiritual or religious beliefs you may hold.

We often refer to the work as IN-tuition - because this is groundbreaking human development *from the inside out*.

The D (of DNA) stands for Discover - experientially reconnecting us with the four pillars of our inborn power. The N stands for Ngage - identifying the surprising and commonly misunderstood obstacles to true connection, both externally (ENgage) and internally (INgage). The A stands for Activate - reconnecting us with our intuition and learning how to use it in every aspect of our life.

We've long been aware of the importance of brainpower, of IQ, of mindset. Increasingly we're also recognising the value of EQ, our emotional intelligence, our heart space. Light Up connects these up with our lesser known superpower, SQ - intuition, inner knowing, our sixth sense, the seat of our human genius. It's a bit like going from one or two bars of reception on our mobile phone, to all five bars. Imagine having access to full bandwidth at all times!

And the results we can expect from Light Up?

Improved confidence.

Quicker and more reliable decision making.

Clearer discernment.

Greater resilience in the face of pretty much anything.

Less anxiety and overwhelm.

Sharper focus.

Deeper relaxation.

Increased performance.

Readier access to happiness, contentment and joy.

And people we haven't seen in a while telling us that we look 'all lit up!'

Please take a look at our website www.dnalightup.net. Contact details for all of the Activators can be found there. Choose who you'd like to chat to and get in touch to find out more and get all your questions answered.

AFTERWORD

It's a tough being human in the 21st century!

A collection of real-life stories that shine a light on the diverse and often debilitating pressure we all face today – and how it feels to break free from limitations

So here we all are... living in the modern age. We've got everything at our fingertips. Internet. Computers. Smart phones. Alexa to answer our questions and respond to our every whim. We can regulate light and heat in our homes even when we're away. Home surveillance cameras mean we can keep intruders away and maintain contact with our pets. We can video-connect with friends and family across the world. There is always somewhere open for us to buy food and groceries, and we have the means to connect and share in all manner of ways at any time of the day or night.

So how come we feel so dissatisfied? Why is it that mental health issues such as depression, anxiety, bipolar, PTSD, addictions, eating-disorders, self-esteem, isolation, addiction, codependency, abuse, self-esteem and other modern-day sufferings remain such an on-going and growing problem in a sophisticated society that allegedly has it all?

This is a book written by everyday people for everyday people. People like you and like me. People who've done their utmost to navigate the world and live their lives in the best way they know how. Who've followed advice (or not) from parents, teachers, friends and colleagues, who've perhaps sought help from therapists, counsellors, coaches and mentors. And yet real and lasting fulfilment (or happiness, peace, freedom, relief or anything else) has somehow remained that elusive prize that's always just out of reach – whether that's by a whisker or by a country mile.

I'm certain you'll be able to identify with at least one of these heartfelt accounts, because each one is real and like all of us, each is unique. And there's a shared thread linking them all together. The troubles are different, the circumstances are personal. And there's a collective recognition that at some point in their life, each of these people believed themselves to be different. Wrong. Not enough. Or too much. In fact, I challenge you not to be inspired and uplifted as you get to know them and celebrate their personal victories as they overcome their suffering and create a new life for themselves!

There is another common thread running through these stories. Because this is also the story of DNA Light Up. All proceeds from the sale of this book go directly to fund groups and individuals who don't have the resources to access this work themselves.

Thank you for buying this book. Thank you for identifying with our authors. Thank you for making a difference.

www.dnalightup.net

Printed in Poland
by Amazon Fulfillment
Poland Sp. z o.o., Wrocław